The World's
Best Poetry

Volume X

Poetical Quotations;
General Indexes

Poetry Anthology Press

The World's Best Poetry

Survey of American Poetry

The World's Best Poetry

Volume X

Poetical Quotations; General Indexes

Edited by Bliss Carman

Prepared by
The Editorial Board, Granger Book Co., Inc.

 Poetry Anthology Press
Great Neck, New York

TABLE OF CONTENTS

PREFACE TO VOLUME X

This volume contains 2,700 memorable passages from poems not included elsewhere in this anthology. While the sources of these fragments could not find a proper place in the work as a whole, these selections are included for the benefit of the general reader and for seekers of specific expressions and thoughts.

The passages are alphabetically arranged under more than 300 subject headings; these are listed in the Index of Topics on pages ix-xxiii with appropriate cross-references to other themes. The 400 poets quoted are listed in the section beginning on page xxv.

In addition, this volume contains a General Index of Authors and Titles and a General Index of First Lines and Titles for the entire work.

Preface

The publications of **Poetry Anthology Press** constitute a comprehensive conspectus of international verse in English designed to form the core of a library's poetry collection. Covering the entire range of poetic literature, these anthologies encompass all topics and national literatures.

Each collection, published in a multivolume continuing series format, is devoted to a major area of the whole undertaking and contains complete author, title, and first line indexes. Biographical data is also provided.

The World's Best Poetry, with coverage through the 19th century, is topically classified and arranged by subject matter. Supplements keep the 10 volume foundation collection current and complete.

Survey of American Poetry is an anthology of American verse arranged chronologically in 10 volumes. Each volume presents a significant period of American poetic history, from 1607 to date.

INDEX OF TOPICS.

WITH CROSS-REFERENCES.

AUTHORS QUOTED.

THAXTER, CELIA LAIGHTON .... America, 1835–1894
THOMAS, FREDERICK WILLIAM .... America, 1808–1866
THOMPSON, FRANCIS .... England, about 1861–
THOMSON, JAMES .... England, 1700–1748
TICKELL, THOMAS .... England, 1686–1740
TIGHE, MRS. MARY .... Ireland, 1773–1810
TOBIN, JOHN .... England, 1770–1804
TOURNEUR, CYRIL .... England, about 1600
TRUMBULL, JOHN .... America, 1750–1831
TUCKERMAN, HENRY THEODORE .... America, 1813–1871
TURNER, CHARLES TENNYSON .... England, 1808–1879
TUPPER, MARTIN FARQUHAR .... England, 1810–1889
TUSSER, THOMAS .... England, about 1515–1580

VAUGHAN, HENRY, M.D............ Wales,   1621–1695

WADE, J. A...................... England, 1800–1875
WALLACE, JOHN AIKMAN.
WALLACE, WILLIAM ROSS .... America, 1819–1881
WALLER, EDMUND .... England, 1605–1687
WARNER, ANNA B............... America, XIX. Century
WARTON, THOMAS .... England, 1728–1790
WATSON, WILLIAM .... England, 1858–
WATTS, ALARIC ATTILA .... England, 1797–1864
WATTS, ISAAC, D.D................ England, 1674–1748
WEBB, CHARLES HENRY .... America, 1834–
WEBSTER, DANIEL .... America, 1782–1852
WEBSTER, JOHN .... England, about 1580–1662
WELSH, CHARLES .... England, 1850–
WESLEY, REV. CHARLES ....˙..... England, 1708–1788
WESTMACOTT, CHARLES M........... England, 1788–1868
WHITE, HENRY KIRKE .... England, 1785–1806
WHITEHEAD, PAUL .... England, 1710–1774
WHITMAN, SARAH HELEN POWER..... America, 1803–1878
WHITMAN, WALT .... America, 1819–1892
WHITTIER, JOHN GREENLEAF .... America, 1807–1892
WILDE, RICHARD HENRY .... Ireland, 1789–1847
WILLIS, NATHANIEL PARKER .... America, 1806–1867
WINTER, WILLIAM .... America, 1836–
WITHER, GEORGE .... England, 1588–1667
WOLCOTT, DR. JOHN (*Peter Pindar*).. England, 1738–1819
WOLFE, REV. CHARLES .... Ireland, 1791–1823
WOOLSEY, SARAH CHAUNCEY (*Susan
   Coolidge*) .... America, about 1845–
WOOLSON, CONSTANCE FENIMORE...... America, 1848–1894
WORDSWORTH, WILLIAM .... England, 1770–1850
WOTTON, SIR HENRY .... England, 1568–1639
WROTHER, MISS .... England,

YALDEN, REV. THOMAS .... England, 1671–1736
YOUNG. DR. EDWARD .... England, 1684–1765
YOUNG, SIR JOHN .... England,

POETICAL QUOTATIONS.

" Next to the originator of a good sentence is the first quoter of it. . . . We are as much informed of a writer's genius by what he selects as by what he originates."—R. W. EMERSON.

From " QUOTATION AND ORIGINALITY."

ABSENCE.

'T is said that absence conquers love;
  But oh ! believe it not.
I 've tried, alas ! its power to prove,
  But thou art not forgot.
Absence Conquers Love.   F. W. THOMAS.

Absence makes the heart grow fonder ;
  Isle of Beauty, fare thee well !
Isle of Beauty.   T. H. BAYLY.

Though absent, present in desires they be ;
  Our souls much further than our eyes can see.
Sonnet.   M. DRAYTON.

There 's not a wind but whispers of thy name.
Mirandola.   B. W. PROCTER.

Short absence hurt him more,
And made his wound far greater than before ;
Absence not long enough to root out quite
All love, increases love at second sight.
Henry II.   T. MAY.

How like a winter hath my absence been
  From thee, the pleasure of the fleeting year !
What freezings have I felt, what dark days seen !
  What old December's bareness everywhere.
Sonnet XCVII.   SHAKESPEARE.

1

Days of absence, sad and dreary,
 Clothed in sorrow's dark array,—
Days of absence, I am weary ;
 She I love is far away.
Days of Absence.   J. J. ROUSSEAU.

Love reckons hours for months, and days for years ;
And every little absence is an age.
 Amphictrion.   J. DRYDEN.

What ! keep a week away ? Seven days and nights ?
Eightscore eight hours? And lovers' absent hours
More tedious than the dial eightscore times?
O, weary reckoning !
 Othello, Act iii. *Sc.* 4.   SHAKESPEARE.

                   Long did his wife,
 Suckling her babe, her only one, look out
 The way he went at parting,—but he came not !
Italy.   S. ROGERS.

 With what a deep devotedness of woe
 I wept thy absence—o'er and o'er again
 Thinking of thee, still thee, till thought grew pain,
 And memory, like a drop that, night and day
 Falls cold and ceaseless, wore my heart away !
Lalla Rookh : Veiled Prophet of Khorassan.   T. MOORE.

 Condemned whole years in absence to deplore,
 And image charms he must behold no more.
Eloise to Abélard.   A. POPE.

ACTION.

 The flighty purpose never is o'ertook,
  Unless the deed go with it.
Macbeth, Act. iv. *Sc.* 1.   SHAKESPEARE.

                   If our virtues
Did not go forth of us, 't were all alike
As if we had them not. Spirits are not finely touched,
But to fine issues ; nor Nature never lends
The smallest scruple of her excellence,
But, like a thrifty goddess, she determines
Herself the glory of a creditor—
Both thanks and use.
 Measure for Measure, Act i. *Sc.* 1.   SHAKESPEARE.

         We must not stint
 Our necessary actions, in the fear
  To cope malicious censurers.
King Henry VIII., Act i. *Sc.* 2.   SHAKESPEARE.

That light we see is burning in my hall.
How far that little candle throws his beams !
So shines a good deed in a naughty world.
Merchant of Venice, Act v. *Sc.* 1.　　　SHAKESPEARE.

Our acts our angels are, or good or ill,
Our fatal shadows that walk by us still.
An Honest Man's Fortune.　　　J. FLETCHER.

ADMIRATION.

She is pretty to walk with,
And witty to talk with,
And pleasant, too, to think on.
Brennoralt, Act ii.　　　SIR J. SUCKLING.

But from the hoop's bewitching round,
Her very shoe has power to wound.
Fables : The Spider and the Bee.　　　E. MOORE.

That eagle's fate and mine are one,
　Which, on the shaft that made him die,
Espied a feather of his own,
　Wherewith he wont to soar so high.
To a Lady singing a Song of his Composing. E. WALLER.

See, how she leans her cheek upon her hand !
O, that I were a glove upon that hand,
That I might touch that cheek !
Romeo and Juliet, Act ii. *Sc.* 2.　　　SHAKESPEARE.

The light that lies
In woman's eyes.
The time I 've lost in Wooing.　　　T. MOORE.

Is she not more than painting can express,
Or youthful poets fancy when they love ?
The Fair Penitent, Act iii. *Sc.* 1.　　　N. ROWE.

O, thou art fairer than the evening·air
Clad in the beauty of a thousand stars.
Faustus.　　　C. MARLOWE.

The dimple that thy chin contains has beauty in its round
That never has been fathomed yet by myriad thoughts
　profound.
Odes, CXLIII.　　　HAFIZ.

Beauty stands
In the admiration only of weak minds
Led captive.　Cease to admire, and all her plumes
Fall flat and shrink into a trivial toy,
　At every sudden slighting quite abashed.
Paradise Regained, Bk. II.　　　MILTON.

ADORNMENT.

The ornament of beauty is suspect,
A crow that flies in heaven's sweetest air.
Sonnet LXX.   SHAKESPEARE.

A native grace
Sat fair-proportioned in her polished limbs,
Veiled in a simple robe their best attire,
Beyond the pomp of dress ; for loveliness
Needs not the foreign aid of ornament,
But is, when unadorned, adorned the most.
The Seasons : Autumn.   J. THOMSON.

She 's adorned
Amply that in her husband's eye looks lovely,—
The truest mirror that an honest wife
Can see her beauty in.
The Honeymoon, Act iii. *Sc.* 4.   J. TOBIN.

Terrible he rode alone,
With his Yemen sword for aid ;
Ornament it carried none,
But the notches on the blade.
The Death Feud.   An Arab War Song.
Anonymous Translation.

ADVENTURE.

Naught venture, naught have.
Five Hundred Points of Good Husbandry.   October's
Abstract.   T. TUSSER.

We must take the current when it serves,
Or lose our ventures.
Julius Cæsar, Act iv. *Sc.* 3.   SHAKESPEARE.

Fierce warres, and faithful loves shall moralize my song.
Faërie Queene, Bk. I. Proem.   E. SPENSER.

Send danger from the east unto the west,
So honor cross it from the north to south,
And let them grapple : O ! the blood more stirs
To rouse a lion than to start a hare !

.   .   .   .   .   .

By Heaven, methinks, it were an easy leap,
To pluck bright honor from the pale-faced moon,
Or dive into the bottom of the deep,
Where fathom-line could never touch the ground,
And pluck up drownèd honor by the locks.
K. Henry IV., Pt. I. Act i. *Sc.* 3.   SHAKESPEARE.

A wild dedication of yourselves
To unpathed waters, undreamed shores.
Winter's Tale, Act iv. *Sc.* 3.   SHAKESPEARE.

ADVERSITY.

Sweet are the uses of adversity,
Which, like the toad, ugly and venomous,
Wears yet a precious jewel in his head.
As You Like It, Act i. *Sc.* 3.   SHAKESPEARE.

Calamity is man's true touchstone.
Four Plays in One : The Triumph of Honor, Sc. 1.
          BEAUMONT AND FLETCHER.

More safe I sing with mortal voice, unchanged
To hoarse or mute, though fallen on evil days,
On evil days though fallen, and evil tongues.
Paradise Lost, Bk. VII.   MILTON.

Tho' losses and crosses
Be lessons right severe,
There 's wit there, ye 'll get there,
Ye 'll find nae otherwhere.
Epistle to Davie.   R. BURNS.

By adversity are wrought
The greatest work of admiration,
And all the fair examples of renown
Out of distress and misery are grown.
On the Earl of Southampton.   S. DANIEL.

Aromatic plants bestow
No spicy fragrance while they grow ;
But crushed or trodden to the ground,
Diffuse their balmy sweets around.
The Captivity, Act i.   O. GOLDSMITH.

The Good are better made by Ill,
As odors crushed are sweeter still.
Jacqueline.   S. ROGERS.

Daughter of Jove, relentless power,
Thou tamer of the human breast,
Whose iron scourge and torturing hour
The bad affright, afflict the best !
Hymn to Adversity.   T. GRAY.

'T is better to be lowly born,
And range with humble livers in content,
Than to be perked up in a glistering grief,
And wear a golden sorrow.
King Henry VIII., Act ii. *Sc.* 3.   SHAKESPEARE.

As if Misfortune made the throne her seat,
And none could be unhappy but the great.
The Fair Penitent : Prologue.   N. ROWE.

None think the great unhappy, but the great.
Love of Fame, Satire I.   DR. E. YOUNG.

My pride fell with my fortunes.
As You Like It, Act i. *Sc.* 2.   SHAKESPEARE.

We have seen better days.
Timon of Athens, Act iv. *Sc.* 2.   SHAKESPEARE.

If ever you have looked on better days ;
If ever been where bells have knolled to church.
As You Like It, Act ii. *Sc.* 7.   SHAKESPEARE.

O, who can hold a fire in his hand
By thinking on the frosty Caucasus?
Or cloy the hungry edge of appetite
By bare imagination of a feast?
Or wallow naked in December snow,
By thinking on fantastic Summer's heat ?
O, no ! the apprehension of the good
Gives but the greater feeling to the worse.
King Richard II., Act i. *Sc.* 2.   SHAKESPEARE.

A poor, infirm, weak, and despised old man.
King Lear, Act iii. *Sc.* 2.   SHAKESPEARE.

Eating the bitter bread of banishment.
King Richard II., Act iii. *Sc.* 1.   SHAKESPEARE.

For sufferance is the badge of all our tribe.
Merchant of Venice, Act i. *Sc.* 3.   SHAKESPEARE.

Lord of himself,—that heritage of woe !
Lara, Canto I.   LORD BYRON.

Lord of thy presence, and no land beside.
King John, Act i. *Sc.* 1.   SHAKESPEARE.

Heaven is not always angry when he strikes,
But most chastises those whom most he likes.
Verses to his Friend under Affliction.   J. POMFRET.

As sunshine, broken in the rill,
Though turned astray, is sunshine still.
Fire Worshippers.   T. MOORE.

On Fortune's cap we are not the very button.
Hamlet, Act ii. *Sc.* 2.   SHAKESPEARE.

Cheered up himself with ends of verse,
And sayings of philosophers.
Hudibras, Pt. I. Canto III.   S. BUTLER.

O life ! thou art a galling load,
Along a rough, a weary road,
To wretches such as I !
Despondency.   R. BURNS.

A wretched soul, bruised with adversity.
Comedy of Errors, Act ii. *Sc.* 1.   SHAKESPEARE.

Affliction's sons are brothers in distress ;
A brother to relieve, how exquisite the bliss !
A Winter Night.   R. BURNS.

Henceforth I 'll bear
Affliction till it do cry out itself,
Enough, enough, and die.
King Lear, Act iv. *Sc.* 6.   SHAKESPEARE.

On me, on me
Time and change can heap no more !
The painful past with blighting grief
Hath left my heart a withered leaf.
Time and change can do no more.
Dirge.   R. H. HORNE.

I wish thy lot, now bad, still worse, my friend,
For when at worst,they say, things always mend.
To a Friend in Distress.   DR. J. OWEN.

The wine of life is drawn, and the mere lees
Is left this vault to brag of.
Macbeth, Act ii. *Sc.* 3.   SHAKESPEARE.

Things at the worst will cease, or else climb upward
To what they were before.
Macbeth, Act iv. *Sc.* 2.   SHAKESPEARE.

I am not now in fortune's power ;
He that is down can fall no lower.
Hudibras, Pt. I. Canto III.   S. BUTLER.

The worst is not
So long as we can say, *This is the worst.*
King Lear, Act iv. *Sc.* 1.   SHAKESPEARE.

ADVICE.

The worst men often give the best advice.
Our deeds are sometimes better than our thoughts.
Festus : Sc. A Village Feast.   P. J. BAILEY.

I pray thee cease thy counsel,
Which falls into mine ears as profitless
As water in a sieve.
Much Ado About Nothing, Act v. *Sc.* 1.   SHAKESPEARE.

O Life ! how pleasant in thy morning,
Young Fancy's rays the hills adorning !
Cold-pausing Caution's lesson scorning,
        We frisk away,
Like schoolboys at th' expected warning,
        To joy and play.
Epistle to James Smith.   R. BURNS.

Know when to speake ; for many times it brings
Danger to give the best advice to kings.
Hesperides' Caution in Councell.   R. HERRICK.

AGE.

I 'm growing fonder of my staff ;
I 'm growing dimmer in the eyes ;
I 'm growing fainter in my laugh ;
I 'm growing deeper in my sighs ;
I 'm growing careless of my dress ;
I 'm growing frugal of my gold ;
I 'm growing wise ; I 'm growing,—yes,—
I 'm growing old.
I 'm Growing Old.   J. G. SAXE.

And his big manly voice,
Turning again toward childish treble, pipes
And whistles in his sound.
As You Like It, Act ii. *Sc.* 7.   SHAKESPEARE.

Time has laid his hand
Upon my heart, gently, not smiting it,
But as a harper lays his open palm
Upon his harp, to deaden its vibrations.
The Golden Legend, IV.   H. W. LONGFELLOW.

Years steal
Fire from the mind, as vigor from the limb ;
And life's enchanted cup but sparkles near the brim.
Childe Harold, Canto III.   LORD BYRON.

For we are old, and on our quick'st decrees
The inaudible and noiseless foot of Time
Steals ere we can effect them.
All's Well that Ends Well, Act v. *Sc.* 3.   SHAKESPEARE.

Strange! that a harp of thousand strings
Should keep in tune so long.
Hymns and Spiritual Songs, Bk. II.   DR. I. WATTS.

Thus aged men, full loth and slow,
The vanities of life forego,
And count their youthful follies o'er,
Till Memory lends her light no more.
Rokeby, Canto V.   SIR W. SCOTT.

Though I look old, yet I am strong and lusty ;
For in my youth I never did apply
Hot and rebellious liquors in my blood ;
Nor did not with unbashful forehead woo
The means of weakness and debility ;
Therefore my age is as a lusty winter,
Frosty, but kindly.
As You Like It, Act ii. Sc. 3.   SHAKESPEARE.

But grant, the virtues of a temp'rate prime
Bless with an age exempt from scorn or crime ;
An age that melts with unperceived decay,
And glides in modest innocence away.
Vanity of Human Wishes.   DR. S. JOHNSON.

Who soweth good seed shall surely reap ;
The year grows rich as it groweth old,
And life's latest sands are its sands of gold !
To the " Bouquet Club."   J. C. R. DORR.

The spring, like youth, fresh blossoms doth produce,
But autumn makes them ripe and fit for use :
So Age a mature mellowness doth set
On the green promises of youthful heat.
Cato Major, Pt. IV.   SIR J. DENHAM.

My May of life
Is fallen into the sear, the yellow leaf :
And that which should accompany old age,
As honor, love, obedience, troops of friends,
I must not look to have ; but, in their stead,
Curses, not loud, but deep. mouth-honor, breath,
Which the poor heart would fain deny, and dare not.
Macbeth, Act v. Sc. 3.   SHAKESPEARE.

What is the worst of woes that wait on age ?
What stamps the wrinkle deeper on the brow ?
To view each loved one blotted from life's page,
And be alone on earth as I am now.
Childe Harold, Canto II.   LORD BYRON.

His silver hairs
Will purchase us a good opinion,
And buy men's voices to commend our deeds :
It shall be said—his judgment ruled our hands.
Julius Cæsar, Act ii. Sc. 1.   SHAKESPEARE.

As you are old and reverend, you should be wise.
King Lear, Act i. *Sc.* 4.   SHAKESPEARE.

So may'st thou live, till like ripe fruit thou drop
Into thy mother's lap, or be with ease
Gathered, not harshly plucked for death mature.
Paradise Lost, Bk. XI.   MILTON.

AIR.

DUNCAN.   This castle hath a pleasant seat : the air
Nimbly and sweetly recommends itself
Unto our gentle senses.
    BANQUO. . . . The heaven's breath
Smells wooingly here : no jutty, frieze,
Buttress, nor coigne of vantage, but this bird
Hath made his pendent bed and procreant cradle :
Where they most breed and haunt, I have observed,
The air is delicate.
Macbeth, Act i. *Sc.* 6.   SHAKESPEARE.

Joyous the birds ; fresh gales and gentle airs
Whispered it to the woods, and from their wings
Flung rose, flung odors from the spicy shrub.
Paradise Lost, Bk. VIII.   MILTON.

HAMLET.   The air bites shrewdly ; it is very cold.
HORATIO.   It is a nipping and an eager air.
Hamlet, Act i. *Sc.* 4.   SHAKESPEARE.

                    The parching air
Burns frore, and cold performs the effect of fire.
Paradise Lost, Bk. II.   MILTON.

Drew audience and attention still as night
Or summer's noontide air.
Paradise Lost, Bk. II.   MILTON.

As one who long in populous city pent,
Where houses thick and sewers annoy the air.
Paradise Lost, Bk. IX.   MILTON.

Nor waste their sweetness in the desert air.
Gotham, Bk. II.   C. CHURCHILL.

AMBITION.

Ambition is our idol, on whose wings
Great minds are carried only to extreme ;
To be sublimely great, or to be nothing.
The Loyal Brother, Act i. *Sc.* 1.   T. SOUTHERNE.

To reign is worth ambition, though in hell :
Better to reign in hell, than serve in heaven.
Paradise Lost, Bk. I.   MILTON.

Rather than be less
Cared not to be at all.
Paradise Lost, Bk. II.   MILTON.

Lowliness is young ambition's ladder,
Whereto the climber-upward turns his face ;
But when he once attains the upmost round,
He then unto the ladder turns his back,
Looks in the clouds, scorning the base degrees
By which he did ascend.
Julius Cæsar, Act ii. *Sc.* 1.   SHAKESPEARE.

I have no spur
To prick the sides of my intent ; but only
Vaulting ambition. which o'erleaps itself,
And falls on the other.
Macbeth, Act i. *Sc.* 7.   SHAKESPEARE.

But wild ambition loves to slide, not stand,
And Fortune's ice prefers to Virtue's land.
Absalom and Achitophel, Pt. I.   J. DRYDEN.

Ambition's monstrous stomach does increase
By eating, and it fears to starve unless
It still may feed, and all it sees devour.
Playhouse to Let.   SIR W. DAVENANT.

But see how oft ambition's aims are crossed,
And chiefs contend 'til all the prize is lost !
Rape of the Lock, Canto V.   A. POPE.

O, sons of earth ! attempt ye still to rise,
By mountains piled on mountains to the skies ?
Heaven still with laughter the vain toil surveys,
And buries madmen in the heaps they raise.
Essay on Man, Epistle IV.   A. POPE.

The very substance of the ambitious is merely the shadow
of a dream.
Hamlet, Act ii. *Sc.* 2.   SHAKESPEARE.

Why then doth flesh, a bubble-glass of breath,
Hunt after honour and advancement vain,
And rear a trophy for devouring death ?
Ruins of Time.   E. SPENSER.

Oh, sons of earth ! attempt ye still to rise
By mountains piled on mountains to the skies ?
Heaven still with laughter the vain toil surveys,
And buries madmen in the heaps they raise.
Essay on Man.   A. POPE.

ANGEL.

In this dim world of clouding cares,
We rarely know. till 'wildered eyes
See white wings lessening up the skies,
The Angels with us unawares.
Ballad of Babe Christabel.   G. MASSEY.

Around our pillows golden ladders rise,
And up and down the skies,
With wingèd sandals shod,
The angels come, and go, the Messengers of God !
Nor, though they fade from us, do they depart—
It is the childly heart :
We walk as heretofore,
Adown their shining ranks, but see them nevermore.
Hymn to the Beautiful.   R. H. STODDARD.

For God will deign
To visit oft the dwellings of just men
Delighted, and with frequent intercourse
Thither will send his wingèd messengers
On errands of supernal grace.
Paradise Lost, Bk. VII.   MILTON.

But sad as angels for the good man's sin,
Weep to record, and blush to give it in.
The Pleasures of Hope, Pt. II.   T. CAMPBELL.

What though my wingèd hours of bliss have been,
Like angel-visits, few and far between.
The Pleasures of Hope, Pt. II.   T. CAMPBELL.

ANGER.

Anger is like
A full-hot horse ; who being allowed his way,
Self-mettle tires him.
King Henry VIII., Act i. Sc. 1.   SHAKESPEARE.

Being once chafed, he cannot
Be reined again to temperance ; then he speaks
What 's in his heart.
Coriolanus, Act iii. Sc. 3.   SHAKESPEARE.

I am very sorry, good Horatio,
That to Laertes I forgot myself,

.   .   .   .   .   .

But, sure. the bravery of his grief did put me
Into a towering passion.
Hamlet, Act v. Sc. 2.   SHAKESPEARE.

Senseless, and deformed,
Convulsive Anger storms at large ; or, pale
And silent, settles into fell revenge.
The Seasons : Spring.   J. THOMSON.

Be advised ;
Heat not a furnace for your foe so hot
That it do singe yourself : we may outrun.
By violent swiftness, that which we run at,
And lose by over-running.
King Henry VIII., Act i. *Sc.* 1.   SHAKESPEARE.

Never anger made good guard for itself.
Antony and Cleopatra, Act iv. *Sc.* 1.   SHAKESPEARE.

ANGLING.

All 's fish they get
That cometh to net.
Five Hundred Points of Good Husbandry.   T. TUSSER.

In genial spring, beneath the quivering shade,
Where cooling vapors breathe along the mead,
The patient fisher takes his silent stand,
Intent, his angle trembling in his hand ;
With looks unmoved, he hopes the scaly breed,
And eyes the dancing cork, and bending reed.
Windsor Forest.   A. POPE.

Now is the time,
While yet the dark-brown water aids the guile,
To tempt the trout. The well-dissembled fly,
The rod fine tapering with elastic spring,
Snatched from the hoary steed the floating line,
And all thy slender wat'ry stores prepare.
The Seasons : Spring.   J. THOMSON.

Just in the dubious point, where with the pool
Is mixed the trembling stream, or where it boils
Around the stone, or from the hollowed bank
Reverted plays in undulating flow,
There throw, nice judging, the delusive fly ;
And as you lead it round in artful curve,
With eye attentive mark the springing game.
Straight as above the surface of the flood
They wanton rise, or urged by hunger leap,
Then fix, with gentle twitch, the barbèd hook :
Some lightly tossing to the grassy bank,
And to the shelving shore slow-dragging some,
With various hand proportioned to their force.
The Seasons : Spring.   J. THOMSON.

Give me mine angle, we 'll to the river ; there,
My music playing far off, I will betray
Tawny-finned fishes ; my bended hook shall pierce
Their shiny jaws.
Antony and Cleopatra, Act ii. *Sc.* 5.   SHAKESPEARE.

His angle-rod made of a sturdy oak ;
His line a cable which in storms ne'er broke ;
His hook he baited with a dragon's tail,
  And sat upon a rock, and bobbed for whale.
Upon a Giant's Angling.   W. KING.

ANIMALS.

A harmless necessary cat.
Merchant of Venice, Act iv. *Sc.* 1.   SHAKESPEARE.

Confound the cats ! All cats—alway–
Cats of all colors, black, white, gray ;
By night a nuisance and by day—
          Confound the cats !
A Dithyramb on Cats.   O. T. DOBBIN.

I am his Highness' dog at Kew ;
  Pray tell me, sir, whose dog are you ?
On the Collar of a Dog.   A. POPE.

The little dogs and all,
Tray, Blanche, and Sweetheart, see, they bark at me.
King Lear, Act iii. *Sc.* 6.   SHAKESPEARE.

How, in his mid-career, the spaniel struck,
Stiff, by the tainted gale, with open nose,
Outstretched and finely sensible, draws full,
  Fearful and cautious, on the latent prey.
The Seasons : Autumn.   J. THOMSON.

A horse ! a horse ! My kingdom for a horse !
King Richard III., Act v. *Sc.* 4.   SHAKESPEARE.

The courser pawed the ground with restless feet,
  And snorting foamed, and champed the golden bit.
Palamon and Arcite, Pt. III.   J. DRYDEN.

Round-hoofed, short-jointed, fetlocks shag and long,
Broad breast, full eye, small head and nostril wide,
High crest, short ears, straight legs and passing strong,
Thin mane, thick tail, broad buttock, tender hide :
Look, what a horse should have he did not lack,
Save a proud rider on so proud a back.
  Venus and Adonis.   SHAKESPEARE.

Oft in this season too the horse, provoked
  While his big sinews full of spirits swell,
Trembling with vigor, in the heat of blood,
  Springs the high fence. . . . his nervous chest,
  Luxuriant and erect, the seat of strength!
The Seasons : Summer.   J. THOMSON.

Champing his foam, and bounding o'er the plain,
Arch his high neck, and graceful spread his mane.
The Courser.   SIR R. BLACKMORE.

Is it the wind those branches stirs?
No, no! from out the forest prance
  A trampling troop; I see them come!
In one vast squadron they advance!
  I strove to cry,—my lips were dumb.
The steeds rush on in plunging pride;
But where are they the reins to guide!
A thousand horse,—and none to ride!
With flowing tail, and flying mane,
  Wide nostrils, never stretched by pain,
Mouths bloodless to the bit or rein,
  And feet that iron never shod,
  And flanks unscarred by spur or rod,
A thousand horse, the wild, the free,
Like waves that follow o'er the sea,
  Came thickly thundering on.
Mazeppa.   LORD BYRON.

I holde a mouses herte nat worth a leek.
That hath but oon hole for to sterte to.
Preamble, Wyves Tale of Bath.   CHAUCER.

When now, unsparing as the scourge of war,
Blast follow blasts and groves dismantled roar ;
Around their home the storm-pinched cattle lows,
No nourishment in frozen pasture grows.
The Farmer's Boy : Winter.   R. BLOOMFIELD.

Rural confusion! on the grassy bank
Some ruminating lie ; while others stand
Half in the flood, and, often bending, sip
The circling surface. In the middle droops
The strong laborious ox, of honest front,
Which incomposed he shakes ; and from his sides
The troublous insects lashes with his tail,
Returning still.
The Seasons : Summer.   J. THOMSON.

Tossed from rock to rock,
Incessant bleatings run around the hills.
At last, of snowy white, the gathered flocks
Are in the wattled pen innumerous pressed,
Head above head : and ranged in lusty rows,
The shepherds sit, and whet the sounding shears.
The Seasons: Summer.   J. THOMSON.

The lamb thy riot dooms to bleed to-day,
Had he thy reason, would he skip and play?
Pleased to the last, he crops the flowery food,
And licks the hand just raised to shed his blood.
Essay on Man, Epistle I.   A. POPE.

Welcome, ye shades! ye bowery thickets, hail! . . .
Delicious is your shelter to the soul,
As to the hunted hart the sallying spring,
Or stream full-flowing, that his swelling sides
Laves, as he floats along the herbaged brink.
The Seasons: Autumn.   J. THOMSON.

A poor sequestered stag,
That from the hunter's aim had ta'en a hurt,
Did come to languish ;   .   .   .
.   .   .   .   and the big round tears
Coursed one another down his innocent nose
In piteous chase.
As You Like It, Act ii. *Sc.* 1.   SHAKESPEARE.

Cruel as Death, and hungry as the Grave!
Burning for blood! bony, and gaunt, and grim!
Assembling wolves in raging troops descend ;
And, pouring o'er the country, bear along,
Keen as the north wind sweeps the glossy snows.
All is their prize.
The Seasons: Winter.   J. THOMSON.

ANTHOLOGY.

Infinite riches in a little room.
The Jew of Malta, Act i.   C. MARLOWE.

APPARITION.

Thin, airy shoals of visionary ghosts.
Odyssey.   HOMER.   *Trans. of* POPE.

My people too were scared with eerie sounds,
A footstep, a low throbbing in the walls,
A noise of falling weights that never fell,
Weird whispers, bells that rang without a hand,
Door-handles turned when none was at the door,
And bolted doors that opened of themselves ;

And one betwixt the dark and light had seen
Her, bending by the cradle of her babe.
The Ring.   A. TENNYSON.

Great Pompey's shade complains that we are slow,
And Scipio's ghost walks unavenged amongst us !
Cato, Act ii. *Sc.* 1.   J. ADDISON.

> Now it is the time of night,
> That the graves, all gaping wide,
> Every one lets forth his sprite,
> In the church-way paths to glide.

Midsummer Night's Dream, Act v. *Sc.* 1.
                SHAKESPEARE.

For night's swift dragons cut the clouds full fast,
And yonder shines Aurora's harbinger ;
At whose approach, ghosts, wandering here and there,
Troop home to churchyards.
Midsummer Night's Dream, iii. 2.   SHAKESPEARE.

APPEARANCE.

Such was Zuleika ! such around her shone
The nameless charms unmarked by her alone ;
The light of love, the purity of grace,
The mind, the music breathing from her face,
The heart whose softness harmonized the whole,
And oh ! that eye was in itself a Soul.
Bride of Abydos, Canto I.   LORD BYRON.

There's nothing ill can dwell in such a temple ;
If the ill spirit have so fair a house,
Good things will strive to dwell with 't.
The Tempest, Act i. *Sc.* 2.   SHAKESPEARE.

Exceeding fair she was not ; and yet fair
In that she never studied to be fairer
Than Nature made her ; beauty cost her nothing,
Her virtues were so rare.
All Fools, Act i. *Sc.* 1.   G. CHAPMAN.

Her glossy hair was clustered o'er a brow
Bright with intelligence, and fair and smooth ;
Her eyebrow's shape was like the aërial bow,
Her cheek all purple with the beam of youth,
Mounting, at times, to a transparent glow,
As if her veins ran lightning.
Don Juan, Canto I.   LORD BYRON.

The glass of fashion, and the mould of form,
The observed of all observers !
Hamlet, Act iii. *Sc.* 1.   SHAKESPEARE.
2

They brought one Pinch, a hungry lean-faced villain,
A mere anatomy, a mountebank,
A threadbare juggler, and a fortune-teller,
A needy, hollow-eyed, sharp-looking wretch,
A living-dead man.
Comedy of Errors, Act v. *Sc.* 1.   SHAKESPEARE.

Falstaff sweats to death,
And lards the lean earth as he walks along ;
Were,'t not for laughing, I should pity him.
K. Henry IV., Pt. I. Act ii. *Sc.* 2.   SHAKESPEARE.

Yond' Cassius has a lean and hungry look ;
He thinks too much : such men are dangerous.
Julius Cæsar, Act i. *Sc.* 2.   SHAKESPEARE.

Seemed washing his hands with invisible soap
In imperceptible water.
Miss Kilmansegg.   T. HOOD.

Her pretty feet
Like snailes did creep
A little out, and then,
As if they playèd at bo-peep,
Did soon draw in agen.
Upon her Feet.   R. HERRICK.

Who the silent man can prize,
If a fool he be or wise ?
Yet, though lonely seem the wood,
Therein may lurk the beast of blood ;
Often bashful looks conceal
Tongue of fire and heart of steel ;
And deem not thou in forest gray,
Every dappled skin thy prey,
Lest thou rouse, with luckless spear,
The tiger for the fallow-deer !
The Gulistan.   BISHOP HEBER.

HORATIO.   I saw him once : he was a goodly king.
HAMLET.   He was a man, take him for all in all,
I shall not look upon his like again.
Hamlet, Act i. *Sc.* 2.   SHAKESPEARE.

On his bold visage middle age
Had slightly pressed his signet sage,
Yet had not quenched the open truth,
And fiery vehemence of youth ;
Forward and frolic glee was there,
The will to do, the soul to dare,
The sparkling glance, soon blown to fire
Of hasty love or headlong ire.
The Lady of the Lake, Canto I.   SIR W. SCOTT.

Mislike me not for my complexion,
The shadowed livery of the burnished sun,
To whom I am a neighbor, and near bred.
Bring me the fairest creature northward born,
Where Phœbus' fire scarce thaws the icicles,
And let us make incision for your love,
To prove whose blood is reddest, his or mine.
Merchant of Venice, Act ii. *Sc.* 1.   SHAKESPEARE.

Incensed with indignation Satan stood
Unterrified, and like a comet burned,
That fires the length of Ophiucus huge
In th' arctic sky, and from his horrid hair
Shakes pestilence and war.
Paradise Lost, Bk. II.   MILTON.

Look here, upon this picture, and on this ;
The counterfeit presentment of two brothers.
See, what a grace was seated on this brow :
Hyperion's curls ; the front of Jove himself ;
An eye like Mars, to threaten and command ;
A station like the herald Mercury,
New lighted on a heaven-kissing hill ;
A combination, and a form, indeed,
Where every god did seem to set his seal,
To give the world assurance of a man.
Hamlet, Act iii. *Sc.* 4.   SHAKESPEARE.

Ay, every inch a king.
King Lear, Act iv. *Sc.* 6.   SHAKESPEARE.

ARCHITECTURE.

When we mean to build,
We first survey the plot, then draw the model ;
And when we see the figure of the house,
Then must we rate the cost of the erection.
Henry IV., Pt. II. Act i. *Sc.* 3.   SHAKESPEARE.

The hasty multitude
Admiring entered, and the work some praise,
And some the architect : his hand was known
In heaven by many a towered structure high,
Where sceptred angels held their residence,
And sat as princes.
Paradise Lost, Bk. I.   MILTON.

Old houses mended,
Cost little less than new, before they 're ended.
Prologue to the Double Gallant.   C. CIBBER.

The architect
Built his great heart into these sculptured stones,

And with him toiled his children, and their lives
Were builded, with his own, into the walls,
As offerings unto God.
The Golden Legend, Pt. III.   In the Cathedral.
                                    H. W. LONGFELLOW.

ARGUMENT.

He 'd undertake to prove, by force
Of argument, a man 's no horse.
He 'd prove a buzzard is no fowl,
And that a Lord may be an owl,
A calf an Alderman, a goose a Justice,
And rooks, Committee-men or Trustees.
Hudibras, Pt. I. Canto I.   S. BUTLER.

Reproachful speech from either side
The want of argument supplied ;
They rail, reviled ; as often ends
The contests of disputing friends.
Fables : Sexton and Earth Worm.   J. GAY.

Be calm in arguing ; for fierceness makes
Error a fault, and truth discourtesy.
The Temple : The Church Porch.   G. HERBERT.

In argument
Similes are like songs in love ;
They must describe ; they nothing prove.
Alma, Canto III.   M. PRIOR.

One single positive weighs more,
You know, than negatives a score.
Epistle to Fleetwood Shepherd.   M. PRIOR.

Who shall decide, when doctors disagree,
And soundest casuists doubt, like you and me ?
Moral Essays, Epistle III.   A. POPE.

ARISTOCRACY.

How vain are all hereditary honors,
Those poor possessions from another's deeds.
Parricide.   J. SHIRLEY.

He lives to build, not boast, a generous race ;
No tenth transmitter of a foolish face.
The Bastard.   R. SAVAGE.

Let wealth and commerce, laws and learning die,
But leave us still our old nobility.
England's Trust, Pt. III.   LORD J. MANNERS.

Whoe'er amidst the sons
Of reason, valor, liberty, and virtue,
Displays distinguished merit, is a noble
Of Nature's own creating.
Coriolanus, Act iii. Sc. 3.   J. THOMSON.

Fond man ! though all the heroes of your line
Bedeck your halls, and round your galleries shine
In proud display ; yet take this truth from me—
Virtue alone is true nobility !
Satire VIII.   JUVENAL.   *Trans. of* GIFFORD.

Boast not the titles of your ancestors, brave youth !
They're their possessions, none of yours.
Catiline.   B. JONSON.

Nobler is a limited command
Given by the love of all your native land,
Than a successive title, long and dark,
Drawn from the mouldy rolls of Noah's ark.
Absalom and Achitophel, I.   J. DRYDEN.

As though there were a tie,
And obligation to posterity !
We get them, bear them, breed and nurse.
What has posterity done for us,
That we, lest they their rights should lose,
Should trust our necks to gripe of noose ?
McFingal, Canto II.   J. TRUMBULL.

They that on glorious ancestors enlarge,
Produce their debt, instead of their discharge.
Love of Fame, Satire I.   DR. E. YOUNG.

Few sons attain the praise of their great sires, and most
their sires disgrace.
Odyssey, Bk. II.   HOMER.   *Trans. of* POPE.

He stands for fame on his forefather's feet,
By heraldry, proved valiant or discreet !
Love of Fame, Satire I.   DR. E. YOUNG.

Great families of yesterday we show,
And lords whose parents were the Lord knows who.
The True-Born Englishman, Pt. I.   D. DEFOE.

ART.

For Art is Nature made by Man
To Man the interpreter of God.
The Artist.   LORD LYTTON (*Owen Meredith*).

In the elder days of Art,
Builders wrought with greatest care
Each minute and unseen part ;
For the gods see everywhere.
The Builders.   H. W. LONGFELLOW.

It is not strength, but art, obtains the prize,
And to be swift is less than to be wise.
'T is more by art, than force of numerous strokes.
Iliad, Bk. XXIII.   HOMER.   *Trans.* of POPE.

His pencil was striking, resistless, and grand ;
His manners were gentle, complying, and bland ;
Still born to improve us in every part,
His pencil our faces, his manners our heart.
Retaliation (Sir Joshua Reynolds).   O. GOLDSMITH.

Around the mighty master came
The marvels which his pencil wrought,
Those miracles of power whose fame
Is wide as human thought.
Raphael.   J. G. WHITTIER.

ASPIRATION.

Oh ! could I throw aside these earthly bands
That tie me down where wretched mortals sigh—
To join blest spirits in celestial lands !
To Laura in Death.   PETRARCH.

Happy the heart that keeps its twilight hour,
And, in the depths of heavenly peace reclined,
Loves to commune with thoughts of tender power,—
Thoughts that ascend, like angels beautiful,
A shining Jacob's ladder of the mind !
Sonnet IX.   P. H. HAYNE.

The desire of the moth for the star,
Of the night for the morrow,
The devotion to something afar
From the sphere of our sorrow.
To —— : One word is too often profaned.
                            P. B. SHELLEY.

I held it truth, with him who sings
To one clear harp in divers tones,
That men may rise on stepping-stones
Of their dead selves to higher things.
In Memoriam, I.   A. TENNYSON.

AUTHORITY.

The rule
Of the many is not well.   One must be chief
In war and one the king.
Iliad, Bk. II.   HOMER.   *Trans. of* BRYANT.

Authority intoxicates,
And makes mere sots of magistrates ;
The fumes of it invade the brain,
And make men giddy, proud, and vain.
Miscellaneous Thoughts.   S. BUTLER.

Thou hast seen a farmer's dog bark at a beggar,
And the creature run from the cur : There,
There, thou might'st behold the great image of authority ;
A dog 's obeyed in office.
King Lear, Act iv. *Sc.* 6.   SHAKESPEARE.

O, what authority and show of truth
Can cunning sin cover itself withal !
Much Ado about Nothing, Act iv. *Sc.* 1.   SHAKESPEARE.

AUTHORSHIP.

But words are things, and a small drop of ink,
Falling, like dew, upon a thought, produces
That which makes thousands, perhaps millions, think.
Don Juan, Canto III.   LORD BYRON.

Habits of close attention, thinking heads,
Become more rare as dissipation spreads,
Till authors hear at length one general cry
Tickle and entertain us, or we die !
Retirement.   W. COWPER.

The unhappy man, who once has trailed a pen,
Lives not to please himself, but other men ;
Is always drudging, wastes his life and blood,
Yet only eats and drinks what you think good.
Prologue to Lee's Cæsar Borgia.   J. DRYDEN.

Lest men suspect your tale untrue
Keep probability in view.
The traveller leaping o'er those bounds,
The credit of his book confounds.
The Painter who pleased Nobody and Everybody.
J. GAY.

Immodest words admit of no defence.
For want of decency is want of sense.

.   .   .   .   .   .
But foul descriptions are offensive still,
Either for being like or being ill.
Essay on Translated Verse.   EARL OF ROSCOMMON.

Shut, shut the door, good John ! fatigued I said,
Tie up the knocker, say I'm sick, I'm dead.
The Dog-star rages ! nay, 't is past a doubt,
All Bedlam, or Parnassus, is let out :
Fire in each eye, and papers in each hand,
They rave, recite, and madden round the land.
Epistle to Dr. Arbuthnot : Prologue to the Satires.
                                                        A. POPE.

Why did I write ? what sin to me unknown
Dipped me in ink,—my parents', or my own !
Epistle to Dr. Arbuthnot : Prologue to the Satires.
                                                        A. POPE.

                        And so I penned   ʟ
It down, until at last it came to be,
For length and breadth, the bigness which you see.
Pilgrim's Progress : Apology for his Book.
                                                        J. BUNYAN.

None but an author knows an author's cares,
Or Fancy's fondness for the child she bears.
The Progress of Error.   W. COWPER.

Whether the charmer sinner it, or saint it,
If folly grow romantic, I must paint it.
Moral Essays, Epistle II.   A. POPE.

" You write with ease, to show your breeding,
But easy writing 's curst hard reading."
Clio's Protest.   R. B. SHERIDAN.

True ease in writing comes from art, not chance,
As those move easiest who have learned to dance.
'T is not enough no harshness gives offence ;
The sound must seem an echo to the sense.
Soft is the strain when zephyr gently blows,
And the smooth stream in smoother numbers flows ;
But when loud surges lash the sounding shore,
The hoarse rough verse should like the torrent roar.
When Ajax strives some rock's vast weight to throw
The line too labors, and the words move slow ;
Not so when swift Camilla scours the plain,
Flies o'er th' unbending corn, and skims along the main.
        .   .   ◦   .   .   .

Then, at the last and only couplet fraught
With some unmeaning thing they call a thought,
A needless Alexandrine ends the song,
That, like a wounded snake, drags its slow length along.
Essay on Criticism, Part II.　　　　A. POPE.

Abstruse and mystic thought you must express
With painful care, but seeming easiness ;
For truth shines brightest thro' the plainest dress.
Essay on Translated Verse.　　　　W. DILLON.

It may be glorious to write
Thoughts that shall glad the two or three
High souls, like those far stars that come in sight
Once in a century.
Incident in a Railroad Car.　　　　J. R. LOWELL.

E'en copious Dryden wanted, or forgot,
The last and greatest art—the art to blot.
Horace, Bk. II. Epistle I.　　　　A. POPE.

Whatever hath been written shall remain,
Nor be erased nor written o'er again ;
The unwritten only still belongs to thee :
Take heed, and ponder well, what that shall be.
Morituri Salutamus.　　　　H. W. LONGFELLOW.

BABY.

A sweet, new blossom of Humanity,
Fresh fallen from God's own home to flower on earth.
Wooed and Won.　　　　G. MASSEY.

The hair she means to have is gold,
Her eyes are blue, she 's twelve weeks old,
　　Plump are her fists and pinky.
She fluttered down in lucky hour
From some blue deep in yon sky bower—
　　I call her " Little Dinky."
Little Dinky.　　　　F. LOCKER-LAMPSON.

As living jewels dropped unstained from heaven.
Course of Time, Bk. V.　　　　R. POLLOK.

God mark thee to his grace !
Thou wast the prettiest babe that e'er I nursed :
An I might live to see thee married once,
I have my wish.
Romeo and Juliet, Act i. Sc. 3.　　　　SHAKESPEARE.

Suck, baby ! suck ! mother's love grows by giving :
Drain the sweet founts that only thrive by wasting !
The Gypsy's Malison.　　　　C. LAMB.

BATTLE.

Now the storm begins to lower,
  (Haste, the loom of hell prepare,)
Iron sleet of arrowy shower
  Hurtles in the darkened air.

Glittering lances are the loom,
  Where the dusky warp we strain,
Weaving many a soldier's doom,
  Orkney's woe, and Randoer's bane.
The Fatal Sisters.   T. GRAY.

            Wheel the wild dance,
            While lightnings glance,
            And thunders rattle loud ;
            And call the brave
            To bloody grave,
            To sleep without a shroud.
The Dance of Death.   SIR W. SCOTT.

            He made me mad
To see him shine so brisk, and smell so sweet,
And talk so like a waiting gentlewoman,

    .   .   .   .   .
And that it was great pity, so it was,
That villanous saltpetre should be digged
Out of the bowels of the harmless earth,
Which many a good tall fellow had destroyed.
K. Henry IV., Pt. I. Act i. *Sc.* 3.   SHAKESPEARE.

By Heaven ! it is a splendid sight to see
(For one who hath no friend, no brother there)
Their rival scarfs of mixed embroidery,
Their various arms that glitter in the air !
What gallant war-hounds rouse them from their lair,
And gnash their fangs, loud yelling for the prey !
All join the chase, but few the triumph share ;
The grave shall bear the chiefest prize away,
And havoc scarce for joy can number their array.
Childe Harold, Canto I.   LORD BYRON.

            From the glittering staff unfurled
Th' imperial ensign, which, full high advanced,
Shone like a meteor, streaming to the wind,
With gems and golden lustre rich imblazed,
Seraphic arms and trophies ; all the while
Sonorous metal blowing martial sounds :
At which the universal host upsent
A shout that tore hell's concave, and beyond
Frighted the reign of Chaos and old Night.
Paradise Lost, Bk. I.   MILTON.

When Greeks joined Greeks, then was the tug of war.
Alexander the Great, Act iv. *Sc.* 2.   N. LEE.

> That voice . . . heard so oft
> In worst extremes, and on the perilous edge
> Of battle when it raged.
Paradise Lost, Bk. I.   MILTON.

Fight, gentlemen of England ! fight, bold yeomen !
Draw, archers, draw your arrows to the head !
Spur your proud horses hard, and ride in blood ;
Amaze the welkin with your broken staves !
King Richard III., Act v. *Sc.* 3.   SHAKESPEARE.

We must have bloody noses and cracked crowns,
And pass them current too.   God 's me, my horse !
King Henry IV., Pt. I. Act ii. *Sc.* 3.   SHAKESPEARE.

> Never be it said
That Fate itself could awe the soul of Richard.
Hence, babbling dreams ; you threaten here in vain ;
Conscience, avaunt, Richard 's himself again !
Hark ! the shrill trumpet sounds.   To horse ! away !
My soul 's in arms, and eager for the fray.
Shakespeare's Richard III. (Altered), Act. v. *Sc.* 3.
                    C. CIBBER.

BEAUTY.

> Is she not passing fair ?
Two Gentlemen of Verona, Act iv. *Sc.* 4.   SHAKESPEARE.

And she is fair, and fairer than that word.
Merchant of Venice, Act i. *Sc.* 1.   SHAKESPEARE.

Beauty provoketh thieves sooner than gold.
As You Like It, Act i. *Sc.* 3.   SHAKESPEARE.

> Old as I am, for ladies' love unfit,
> The power of beauty I remember yet.
Cymon and Iphigenia.   J. DRYDEN.

> Her beauty hangs upon the cheek of night
> Like a rich jewel in an Ethiop's ear.
Romeo and Juliet, Act i. *Sc.* 5.   SHAKESPEARE.

A rosebud set with little wilful thorns,
And sweet as English air could make her, she.
The Princess.   A. TENNYSON.

> Thou who hast
> The fatal gift of beauty.
Childe Harold, Canto IV.   LORD BYRON.

Yet I 'll not shed her blood ;
Nor scar that whiter skin of hers than snow,
And smooth as monumental alabaster.
Othello, Act v. *Sc.* 2.   SHAKESPEARE.

No longer shall thy bodice, aptly laced,
From thy full bosom to thy slender waist,
That air and harmony of shape express,
Fine by degrees, and beautifully less.
Henry and Emma.   M. PRIOR.

The beautiful are never desolate ;
But some one always loves them—God or man.
If man abandons, God himself takes them.
Festus: Sc.Water and Wood.   P. J. BAILEY.

There 's nothing that allays an angry mind
So soon as a sweet beauty.
The Elder Brother, Act iii. *Sc.* 5.
          BEAUMONT AND FLETCHER.

          The beautiful seems right
By force of beauty, and the feeble wrong
Because of weakness.
Aurora Leigh.   E. B. BROWNING.

How near to good is what is fair,
    Which we no sooner see,
But with the lines and outward air
    Our senses taken be.
We wish to see it still, and prove
    What ways we may deserve ;
We court, we praise, we more than love,
    We are not grieved to serve.
Love Freed from Ignorance and Folly.   B. JONSON.

There 's nothing ill can dwell in such a temple :
If the ill spirit have so fair a house,
Good things will strive to dwell with't.
Tempest, Act i. *Sc.* 2.   SHAKESPEARE.

A daughter of the gods, divinely tall,
    And most divinely fair.
A Dream of Fair Women.   A. TENNYSON.

Beauty is Nature's coin, must not be hoarded,
But must be current, and the good thereof
Consists in mutual and partaken bliss,
Unsavory in th' enjoyment of itself :
If you let slip time, like a neglected rose,
It withers on the stalk with languished head.
Comus.   MILTON.

Thoughtless of beauty, she was Beauty's self.
The Seasons : Autumn. J. THOMSON.

In beauty, faults conspicuous grow ;
The smallest speck is seen on snow.
Fables: Peacock, Turkey, and Goose. J. GAY.

The maid who modestly conceals
Her beauties, while she hides, reveals :
Gives but a glimpse, and fancy draws
Whate'er the Grecian Venus was.
The Spider and the Bee. E. MOORE.

Beauty is but a vain and doubtful good ;
A shining gloss that vadeth suddenly ;
A flower that dies when first it 'gins to bud ;
A brittle glass that 's broken presently ;
A doubtful good, a gloss, a glass, a flower,
Lost, vaded, broken, dead within an hour.
The Passionate Pilgrim. SHAKESPEARE.

BELL.

Tuned be its metal mouth alone
To things eternal and sublime.
And as the swift-winged hours speed on
May it record the flight of time !
Song of the Bell. F. SCHILLER. *Trans.* E. A. BOWRING.

The bells themselves are the best of preachers,
Their brazen lips are learnèd teachers,
From their pulpits of stone, in the upper air,
Sounding aloft, without crack or flaw,
Shriller than trumpets under the Law,
Now a sermon and now a prayer.
Christus: The Golden Legend, Pt. III.
H. W. LONGFELLOW.

And the Sabbath bell,
That over wood and wild and mountain dell
Wanders so far, chasing all thoughts unholy
With sounds most musical, most melancholy.
Human Life. S. ROGERS.

Sweet Sunday bells ! your measured sound
Enhances the repose profound
Of all these golden fields around,
And range of mountain, sunshine-drowned.
Sunday Bells. W. ALLINGHAM.

Like sweet bells jangled, out of tune and harsh.
Hamlet, Act iii. *Sc.* 1. SHAKESPEARE.

Seize the loud, vociferous bells, and
Clashing, clanging to the pavement
Hurl them from their windy tower !
Christus : The Golden Legend. Prologue.

H. W. LONGFELLOW.

Yet the first bringer of unwelcome news
Hath but a losing office, and his tongue
Sounds ever after as a sullen bell,
Remembered tolling a departing friend.
K. Henry IV., Pt. II. Act i. *Sc.* 1.   SHAKESPEARE.

BIBLE.

My Book and Heart
Must never part.
New England Primer.

Within that awful volume lies
The mystery of mysteries !
.   .   .   .
And better had they ne'er been born,
Who read to doubt, or read to scorn.
The Monastery.   SIR W. SCOTT.

God, in the gospel of his Son,
Makes his eternal counsels known ;
'T is here his richest mercy shines,
And truth is drawn in fairest lines.
The Glory of the Scriptures.   B. BEDDOME.

Holy Bible, book divine,
Precious treasure, thou art mine ;
Mine to tell me whence I came,
Mine to teach me what I am.

Mine to chide me when I rove,
Mine to show a Saviour's love ;
Mine art thou to guide my feet,
Mine to judge, condemn, acquit.
Holy Bible, Book Divine.   J. BURTON.

The heavens declare thy glory, Lord ;
In every star thy wisdom shines ;
But when our eyes behold thy word,
We read thy name in fairer lines.
God's Word and Works.   DR. I. WATTS.

Just knows, and knows no more, her Bible true.
Truth.   W. COWPER.

A glory gilds the sacred page,
  Majestic like the sun,
It gives a light to every age,
  It gives, but borrows none.
Olney Hymns.   W. COWPER.

Starres are poore books, and oftentimes do misse ;
  This book starres lights to eternal blisse.
The Church : The Holy Scriptures, Pt. II.
                         G. HERBERT.

BIRDS.

Do you ne'er think what wondrous beings these ?
Do you ne'er think who made them, and who taught
The dialect they speak, where melodies
  Alone are the interpreters of thought ?
Whose household words are songs in many keys,
  Sweeter than instrument of man e'er caught !
Tales of a Wayside Inn : The Poet's Tale.
                H. W. LONGFELLOW.

I shall not ask Jean Jaques Rousseau
If birds confabulate or no.
'T is clear that they were always able
To hold discourse—at least in fable.
Pairing Time Anticipated.   W. COWPER.

The black-bird whistles from the thorny brake ;
The mellow bullfinch answers from the grove :
Nor are the linnets, o'er the flowering furze
Poured out profusely, silent. Joined to these,
Innumerous songsters, in the freshening shade
Of new-sprung leaves, their modulations mix
Mellifluous. The jay, the rook, the daw,
And each harsh pipe, discordant heard alone,
Aid the full concert : while the stock-dove breathes
A melancholy murmur through the whole.
The Seasons : Spring.   J. THOMSON.

Whither away, Bluebird,
    Whither away ?
The blast is chill, yet in the upper sky
  Thou still canst find the color of thy wing,
    The hue of·May.
Warbler, why speed thy southern flight ? ah, why,
Thou too, whose song first told us of the Spring ?
    Whither away ?
Flight of Birds.   E. C. STEDMAN.

The crack-brained bobolink courts his crazy mate,
  Poised on a bulrush tipsy with his weight.
Spring.   C. W. HOLMES.

One day in the bluest of summer weather,
Sketching under a whispering oak,
I heard five bobolinks laughing together,
Over some ornithological joke.
Bird Language.   C. P. CRANCH.

Sing away, ay, sing away,
Merry little bird,
Always gayest of the gay,
Though a woodland roundelay
You ne'er sung nor heard ;
Though your life from youth to age
Passes in a narrow cage.
The Canary in his Cage.   D. M. MULOCK CRAIK.

The cock, that is the trumpet to the morn,
Doth with his lofty and shrill-sounding throat
Awake the god of day.
Hamlet, Act i. *Sc.* 1.   SHAKESPEARE.

Bird of the broad and sweeping wing,
Thy home is high in heaven,
Where wide the storms their banners fling,
And the tempest clouds are driven.
To the Eagle.   J. G. PERCIVAL.

Where the hawk,
High in the beetling cliff, his aëry builds.
The Seasons : Spring.   J. THOMSON.

And the humming-bird that hung
Like a jewel up among
The tilted honeysuckle horns
They mesmerized and swung
In the palpitating air,
Drowsed with odors strange and rare,
And, with whispered laughter, slipped away
And left him hanging there.
The South Wind and the Sun.   J. W. RILEY.

"Most musical, most melancholy " bird !
A melancholy bird !   Oh ! idle thought !
In nature there is nothing melancholy.
The Nightingale.   S. T. COLERIDGE.

Then from the neighboring thicket the mocking-bird, wildest of singers,
Swinging aloft on a willow spray that hung o'er the water,
Shook from his little throat such floods of delirious music,
That the whole air and the woods and the waves seemed silent to listen.
Evangeline, Pt. II.   H. W. LONGFELLOW.

Rise with the lark, and with the lark to bed.
The Village Curate.   J. HURDIS.

> The merry lark he soars on high,
>   No worldly thought o'ertakes him.
> He sings aloud to the clear blue sky,
>   And the daylight that awakes him.
Song.   H. COLERIDGE.

> What bird so sings, yet so does wail?
> O, 't is the ravished nightingale—
> Jug, jug, jug, jug—tereu—she cries,
> And still her woes at midnight rise.
> Brave prick-song! who is 't now we hear?
> None but the lark so shrill and clear,
> Now at heaven's gate she claps her wings,
> The morn not waking till she sings.
> Hark, hark! but what a pretty note,
> Poor Robin-redbreast tunes his throat;
> Hark, how the jolly cuckoos sing
> "Cuckoo!" to welcome in the spring.
Alexander and Campaspe, Act v. *Sc.* 1.   JOHN LYLY.

> O nightingale, that on yon bloomy spray
>   Warblest at eve, when all the woods are still;
>   Thou with fresh hope the lover's heart dost fill
> While the jolly Hours lead on propitious May.
> Thy liquid notes, that close the eye of day,
>
> .   .   .   .
>
> Portend success in love.
To the Nightingale.   MILTON.

> O honey-throated warbler of the grove!
> That in the glooming woodland art so proud
> Of answering thy sweet mates in soft or loud,
> Thou dost not own a note we do not love.
To the Nightingale.   C. T. TURNER.

> Lend me your song, ye Nightingales! O, pour
> The mazy-running soul of melody
>   Into my varied verse.
The Seasons : Spring.   J. THOMSON.

> The crow doth sing as sweetly as the lark
> When neither is attended; and I think
> The nightingale, if she should sing by day,
> When every goose is cackling, would be thought
> No better a musician than the wren.
> How many things by season seasoned are
> To their right praise and true perfection.
Merchant of Venice, Act v. *Sc.* 1.   SHAKESPEARE.
3

A falcon, towering in her pride of place,
Was by a mousing owl hawked at and killed.
Macbeth, Act ii. *Sc.* 4.   SHAKESPEARE.

Call for the robin-redbreast and the wren,
Since o'er shady groves they hover,
And with leaves and flowers do cover
The friendless bodies of unburied men.
The White Devil, Act v. *Sc.* 2.   J. WEBSTER.

Now when the primrose makes a splendid show,
And lilies face the March-winds in full blow,
And humbler growths as moved with one desire
Put on, to welcome spring, their best attire,
Poor Robin is yet flowerless; but how gay
With his red stalks upon this sunny day !
Poor Robin.   W. WORDSWORTH.

The swallow twitters about the eaves ;
    Blithely she sings, and sweet and clear ;
Around her climb the woodbine leaves
    In a golden atmosphere.
The Swallow.   C. THAXTER.

                    The stately-sailing swan
Gives out his snowy plumage to the gale ;
And, arching proud his neck, with oary feet
Bears forward fierce, and guards his osier isle,
Protective of his young.
The Seasons : Spring.   J. THOMSON.

BLESSING.

Blessings star forth forever ; but a curse
Is like a cloud—it passes.
Festus : Sc. Hades.   P. J. BAILEY.

To heal divisions, to relieve the oppressed,
In virtue rich ; in blessing others, blessed.
Odyssey, Bk. VII.   HOMER. *Trans. of* POPE.

Like birds, whose beauties languish half concealed,
Till, mounted on the wing, their glossy plumes
Expanded, shine with azure, green, and gold ;
How blessings brighten as they take their flight !
Night Thoughts, Night II.   DR. E. YOUNG.

In the nine heavens are eight Paradises ;
Where is the ninth one ? In the human breast.
Only the blessèd dwell in the Paradises,
But blessedness dwells in the human breast.
Oriental Poetry : The Ninth Paradise.   W. R. ALGER.

BLUSH.

Who has not seen that feeling born of flame
Crimson the cheek at mention of a name?
The rapturous touch of some divine surprise
Flash deep suffusion of celestial dyes:
When hands clasped hands, and lips to lips were pressed
And the heart's secret was at once confessed?
The Microcosm: Man.   A. COLES.

By noting of the lady I have marked
A thousand blushing apparitions start
Into her face; a thousand innocent shames
In angel whiteness bear away those blushes.
Much Ado About Nothing, Act iv. *Sc.* 1.   SHAKESPEARE.

From every blush that kindles in thy cheeks,
Ten thousand little loves and graces spring
To revel in the roses.
Tamerlane, Act i. *Sc.* 1.   N. ROWE.

While mantling on the maiden's cheek,
Young roses kindled into thought.
Evenings in Greece: Evening II. Song.   T. MOORE.

The rising blushes, which her cheek o'erspread,
Are opening roses in the lily's bed.
Dione, Act ii. *Sc.* 3.   J. GAY.

Girls blush, sometimes, because they are alive,
Half wishing they were dead to save the shame.
The sudden blush devours them, neck and brow;
They have drawn too near the fire of life, like gnats,
And flare up bodily, wings and all.
Aurora Leigh.   E. B. BROWNING.

The man that blushes is not quite a brute.
Night Thoughts, Night VII.   DR. E. YOUNG.

BOATING.

Faintly as tolls the evening chime,
Our voices keep tune and our oars keep time,
Soon as the woods on shore look dim,
We 'll sing at Saint Ann's our parting hymn;
Row, brothers, row, the stream runs fast,
The rapids are near and the daylight 's past!
A Canadian Boat Song.   T. MOORE.

And all the way, to guide their chime,
With falling oars they kept the time.
Bermudas.   A. MARVELL.

Oh, swiftly glides the bonnie boat,
Just parted from the shore,
And to the fisher's chorus-note,
Soft moves the dipping oar!
Oh, Swiftly glides the Bonnie Boat.   J. BAILLIE.

Learn of the little nautilus to sail,
Spread the thin oar, and catch the driving gale.
Essay on Man, Epistle III.   A. POPE.

On the great streams the ships may go
About men's business to and fro.
But I, the egg-shell pinnace, sleep
On crystal waters ankle-deep :
I, whose diminutive design,
Of sweeter cedar, pithier pine,
Is fashioned on so frail a mould,
A hand may launch, a hand withhold :
I, rather, with the leaping trout
Wind, among lilies, in and out ;
I, the unnamed, inviolate,
Green, rustic rivers navigate.
The Canoe Speaks.   R. L. STEVENSON.

Row us forth ! Unfurl thy sail !
What care we for tempest blowing ?
Let us kiss the blustering gale !
Let us breast the waters flowing !
Though the North rush cold and loud,
Love shall warm and make us merry ;
Though the waves all weave a shroud,
We will dare the Humber ferry !
The Humber Ferry.   B. W. PROCTER (*Barry Cornwall*).

BOOKS.

Dreams, books, are each a world ; and books, we know,
Are a substantial world, both pure and good ;
Round these, with tendrils strong as flesh and blood,
Our pastime and our happiness will grow.
Personal Talk.   W. WORDSWORTH.

Silent companions of the lonely hour,
Friends, who can alter or forsake,
Who for inconstant roving have no power,
And all neglect, perforce, must calmly take.
To My Books.   MRS. C. NORTON.

Some books are drenchèd sands,
On which a great soul's wealth lies all in heaps,
Like a wrecked argosy.
A Life Drama.   ALEX. SMITH.

Worthy books
Are not companions—they are solitudes:
We lose ourselves in them and all our cares.
Festus: Sc. A Village Feast. Evening.　　P. J. BAILEY.

'T is pleasant, sure, to see one's name in print;
A book 's a book, although there 's nothing in 't.
English Bards and Scotch Reviewers.　　LORD BYRON.

Golden volumes! richest treasures,
Objects of delicious pleasures!
You my eyes rejoicing please,
You my hands in rapture seize!
Brilliant wits and musing sages,
Lights who beamed through many ages!
Left to your conscious leaves their story,
And dared to trust you with their glory;
And now their hope of fame achieved,
Dear volumes! you have not deceived!
Curiosities of Literature. Libraries.　　I. DISRAELI.

That place that does contain
My books, the best companions, is to me
A glorious court, where hourly I converse
With the old sages and philosophers.
The Elder Brother, Act i. Sc. 2.
BEAUMONT AND FLETCHER.

BORROWING.

Who goeth a-borrowing,
Goeth a-sorrowing.
Five Hundred Points of Good Husbandry. June's Abstract.　　T. TUSSER.

Neither a borrower nor a lender be :
For loan oft loses both itself and friend,
And borrowing dulls the edge of husbandry.
Hamlet, Act i. Sc. 3.　　SHAKESPEARE.

It is a very good world to live in,
To lend, or to spend, or to give in ;
But to beg or to borrow, or to get a man's own,
It is the very worst world that ever was known.
Attributed to EARL OF ROCHESTER.

BOY.

O lord ! my boy, my Arthur, my fair son !
My life, my joy, my food, my all the world !
My widow-comfort, and my sorrow's cure !
King John, Act iii. Sc. 4.　　SHAKESPEARE.

A little curly-headed, good-for-nothing,
And mischief-making monkey from his birth.
Don Juan, Canto I.   LORD BYRON.

A little bench of heedless bishops here,
And there a chancellor in embryo.
The Schoolmistress.   W. SHENSTONE.

Look here upon thy brother Geffrey's face ;
These eyes, these brows, were moulded out of his :
This little abstract doth contain that large
Which died in Geffrey : and the hand of time
Shall draw this brief unto as large a volume.
King John, Act ii. *Sc.* 1.   SHAKESPEARE.

O, 't is a parlous boy ;
Bold, quick, ingenious, forward, capable ;
He is all the mother's from the top to toe.
Richard III., Act iii. *Sc.* 1.   SHAKESPEARE.

Thou wilt scarce be a man before thy mother.
Love's Cure, Act ii. *Sc.* 2.   BEAUMONT AND FLETCHER.

But strive still to be a man before your mother.
Motto of No. III. Connoisseur.   W. COWPER.

CARE.

When one is past, another care we have ;
Thus woe succeeds a woe, as wave a wave.
Sorrows Succeed.   R. HERRICK.

Old Care has a mortgage on every estate,
And that 's what you pay for the wealth that you get.
Gifts of the Gods.   J. G. SAXE.

O polished perturbation ! golden care !
That keepest the ports of slumber open wide
To many a watchful night !
K. Henry IV., Pt. II. Act iv. *Sc.* 5.   SHAKESPEARE.

Let one unceasing, earnest prayer
Be, too, for light,—for strength to bear
Our portion of the weight of care,
That crushes into dumb despair
One half the human race.
The Goblet of Life.   H. W. LONGFELLOW.

Let the world slide, let the world go :
A fig for care, and a fig for woe !
If I can't pay, why I can owe,
And death makes equal the high and low.
Be Merry Friends.   J. HEYWOOD.

Begone, dull Care, I prithee begone from me ;
Begone, dull Care, thou and I shall never agree.
Begone, Old Care.   PLAYFORD'S *Musical Companion.*

CHANCE.

That power
Which erring men call Chance.
Comus.   MILTON.

Chance will not do the work—Chance sends the breeze ;
But if the pilot slumber at the helm,
The very wind that wafts us towards the port
May dash us on the shelves.—The steersman's part is vigilance,
Blow it or rough or smooth.
Fortunes of Nigel.   SIR W. SCOTT.

I shall show the cinders of my spirits
Through the ashes of my chance.
Antony and Cleopatra, Act v. *Sc.* 2.   SHAKESPEARE.

And grasps the skirts of happy chance.
And breasts the blows of circumstance.
In Memoriam, LXIII.   A. TENNYSON.

You 'll see that, since our fate is ruled by chance,
    Each man, unknowing, great,
Should frame life so that at some future hour
    Fact and his dreamings meet.
To His Orphan Grandchildren.   V. HUGO.

CHANGE.

Weep not that the world changes—did it keep
A stable, changeless state, it were cause indeed to weep.
Mutation.   W. C. BRYANT.

Manners with fortunes, humors turn with climes,
Tenets with books, and principles with times.
Moral Essays, Epistle I. Pt. II.   A. POPE.

As hope and fear alternate chase
Our course through life's uncertain race.
Rokeby, Canto VI.   SIR W. SCOTT.

This world is not for aye, nor 't is not strange
That even our loves should with our fortunes change.
Hamlet, Act iii. *Sc.* 2.   SHAKESPEARE.

Man's wretched state,
That floures so fresh at morne, and fades at evening late.
Faërie Queene, Bk. III. Canto IX.   E. SPENSER.

Imperious Cæsar, dead and turned to clay,
Might stop a hole to keep the wind away :
O, that that earth, which kept the world in awe,
Should patch a wall to expel the winter's flaw !
Hamlet, Act v. Sc. 1.   SHAKESPEARE.

The seed ye sow, another reaps ;
The wealth ye find, another keeps ;
The robes ye weave, another wears ;
The arms ye forge, another bears.
To Men of England.   P. B. SHELLEY.

The flower that smiles to-day
To-morrow dies ;
All that we wish to stay
Tempts and then flies :
What is this world's delight ?
Lightning that mocks the night,
Brief even as bright.
Mutability.   P. B. SHELLEY.

Sometimes an hour of Fate's serenest weather
Strikes through our changeful sky its coming beams ;
Somewhere above us, in elusive ether,
Waits the fulfilment of our dearest dreams.
Ad Amicos.   B. TAYLOR.

CHARITY.

The primal duties shine aloft, like stars ;
The charities that soothe, and heal, and bless,
Are scattered at the feet of man, like flowers.
The Excursion, Bk. IX.   W. WORDSWORTH.

'T is hers to pluck the amaranthine flower
Of Faith, and round the sufferer's temples bind
Wreaths that endure affliction's heaviest shower,
And do not shrink from sorrow's keenest wind.
Sonnet XXXV.   W. WORDSWORTH.

Who will not mercie unto others show,
How can he mercie ever hope to have ?
Faërie Queene, Bk. VI.   E. SPENSER.

Whene'er I take my walks abroad,
How many poor I see !
What shall I render to my God
For all his gifts to me ?
Divine Songs.   DR. I. WATTS.

In Faith and Hope the world will disagree,
But all mankind's concern is charity.
Essays on Man, Epistle III.   A. POPE.

Do good by stealth, and blush to find it fame.
Epilogue to Satires, Dial. I.   A. POPE.

True charity makes others' wants their own.
Poor Man's Comfort.   R. DABORNE.

He hath a tear for pity, and a hand
Open as day for melting charity.
King Henry IV., Pt. II. Act iv. Sc. 4.   SHAKESPEARE.

O chime of sweet Saint Charity,
   Peal soon that Easter morn
When Christ for all shall risen be,
   And in all hearts new-born !
That Pentecost when utterance clear
   To all men shall be given,
When all shall say *My Brother* here,
   And hear *My Son* in heaven !
Godminster Chimes.   J. R. LOWELL.

Charity itself fulfils the law,
And who can sever love from charity ?
Love's Labor 's Lost.   SHAKESPEARE.

That man may last, but never lives,
Who much receives but nothing gives ;
Whom none can love, whom none can thank,
Creation's blot, creation's blank.
When Jesus Dwelt.   T. GIBBONS.

CHILDHOOD.

A babe in a house is a well-spring of pleasure.
Of Education.   M. F. TUPPER.

Behold the child, by Nature's kindly law,
Pleased with a rattle, tickled with a straw.
Essay on Man, Epistle II.   A. POPE.

In winter I get up at night
And dress by yellow candlelight,
In summer, quite the other way,
I have to go to bed by day.
Bed in Summer.   R. L. STEVENSON.

Sweet childish days, that were as long
As twenty days are now.
To a Butterfly.   W. WORDSWORTH.

When they are young, they
Are like bells rung backwards, nothing but noise
And giddiness.
Wit without Money.   BEAUMONT AND FLETCHER.

A truthful page is childhood's lovely face,
  Whereon sweet Innocence has record made,—
An outward semblance of the young heart's grace,
  Where truth, and love, and trust are all portrayed.
  On a Picture of Lillie.   B. P. SHILLABER.

      And the King with his golden sceptre,
        The Pope with Saint Peter's key,
      Can never unlock the one little heart
        That is opened only to me.
      For I am the Lord of a Realm,
        And I am Pope of a See ;
      Indeed I 'm supreme in the kingdom
        That is sitting. just now, on my knee.
  The King and The Pope.   C. H. WEBB.

      Now I lay me down to take my sleep,
      I pray the Lord my soul to keep :
      If I should die before I wake,
      I pray the Lord my soul to take.
                      New England Primer.

            And children know,
      Instinctive taught. the friend and foe.
  Lady of the Lake, Canto II.   SIR W. SCOTT.

      Sweet childish days, that were as long
        As twenty days are now.
  To a Butterfly.   W. WORDSWORTH.

  Oh, Mirth and Innocence ! Oh, Milk and Water !
  Ye happy mixtures of more happy days !
  Beppo.   LORD BYRON.

            They are as gentle
        As zephyrs blowing below the violet.
  Cymbeline, Act iv. *Sc.* 2.   SHAKESPEARE.

  Men are but children of a larger growth.
  All for Love, Act iv. *Sc.* 1.   J. DRYDEN.

        The childhood shows the man
      As morning shows the day.
  Paradise Regained, Bk. IV.   MILTON.

CHRISTMAS.

  O most illustrious of the days of time !
  Day full of joy and benison to earth
  When Thou wast born, sweet Babe of Bethlehem !
  With dazzling pomp descending angels sung
  Good-will and peace to men, to God due praise.
  The Microcosm and Other Poems.   A. COLES.

Blow, bugles of battle, the marches of peace ;
East, west, north, and south let the long quarrel cease ;
Sing the song of great joy that the angels began,
Sing of glory to God and of good-will to man !
A Christmas Carmen.   J. G. WHITTIER.

Oh, come, all ye faithful !
Triumphantly sing !
Come, see in the manger
The angels' dread King !
To Bethlehem hasten
With joyful accord ;
Oh, hasten, oh, hasten,
To worship the Lord !
Christmas Day.   Unknown Latin Author.
Trans. of E. CASWELL.

God rest ye, merry gentlemen ; let nothing you dis-
may,
For Jesus Christ, our Saviour, was born on Christmas-
day.
The dawn rose red o'er Bethlehem, the stars shone through
the gray,
When Jesus Christ, our Saviour, was born on Christmas-
day.
A Christmas Carol.   D. M. MULOCK CRAIK.

Now thrice-welcome Christmas, which brings us good
cheer,
Minced pies and plum porridge, good ale and strong beer,
With pig, goose, and capon, the best that may be,—
So well doth the weather and our stomachs agree. . . .
But those on whose tables no victuals appear,
O, may they keep Lent all the rest of the year !
Poor Robin's Almanack, 1695.

CHURCH.

Lord of the worlds above,
How pleasant and how fair
The dwellings of thy love,
Thine earthly temples, are !
To thine abode
My heart aspires,
With warm desires
To see my God.
The House of God.   W. COWPER.

" What is a church ? " Let Truth and Reason speak,
They would reply, " The faithful, pure and meek,
From Christian folds, the one selected race,
Of all professions, and in every place."
The Borough, Letter II.   G. CRABBE.

Spires whose "silent fingers point to heaven."
The Excursion, Bk. VI.   W. WORDSWORTH.

I love thy church, O God:
    Her walls before thee stand,
Dear as the apple of thine eye,
    And graven on thy hand.

. . . . .

For her my tears shall fall,
    For her my prayers ascend ;
To her my cares and toils be given,
    Till toils and cares shall end.
Love to the Church.   T. DWIGHT.

As some to Church repair,
Not for the doctrine, but the music there.
Essay on Criticism.   A. POPE.

Who builds a church to God, and not to fame,
Will never mark the marble with his name.
Moral Essays, Epistle III.   A. POPE.

CITY.

God the first garden made, and the first city Cain.
The Garden, Essay V.   A. COWLEY.

I live not in myself, but I become
Portion of that around me ; and to me
High mountains are a feeling, but the hum
Of human cities torture.
Childe Harold, Canto III.   LORD BYRON.

The people are the city.
Coriolanus, Act iii. Sc. 1.   SHAKESPEARE.

Ah, what can ever be more stately and admirable to me
    than mast-hemmed Manhattan ?
River and sunset and scallop-edged waves of flood-
    tide ?
The sea-gulls oscillating their bodies, the hay-boat in the
    twilight, and the belated lighter ?
Crossing Brooklyn Ferry.   W. WHITMAN.

A mighty mass of brick, and smoke, and shipping,
    Dirty and dusty, but as wide as eye
Could reach, with here and there a sail just skipping
    In sight, then lost amidst the forestry
Of masts ; a wilderness of steeples peeping
    On tiptoe through their sea-coal canopy ;
A huge, dun cupola, like a foolscap crown
On a fool's head—and there is London Town,
Don Juan, Canto X.   LORD BYRON.

On the Ægean shore a city stands,
Built nobly, pure the air, and light the soil,
Athens, the eye of Greece, mother of arts
And eloquence, native to famous wits,
Or hospitable, in her sweet recess,
City or suburban, studious walks and shades ;
See there the olive grove of Academe,
Plato's retirement, where the Attic bird
Trills her thick-warbled notes the summer long.
Paradise Regained, Bk. IV.   MILTON.

I stood in Venice, on the Bridge of Sighs ;
A palace and a prison on each hand :
I saw from out the wave her structures rise
As from the stroke of the enchanter's wand ;
A thousand years their cloudy wings expand
Around me, and a dying glory smiles
O'er the far times, when many a subject land
Looked to the wingèd Lion's marble piles,
Where Venice sate in state, throned on her hundred isles!
Childe Harold, Canto IV.   LORD BYRON.

In Venice, Tasso's echoes are no more,
    And silent rows the songless gondolier ;
Her palaces are crumbling to the shore,
    And music meets not always now the ear.
Childe Harold, Canto IV.   LORD BYRON.

O Rome! my country! city of the soul !
The orphans of the heart must turn to thee,
Lone mother of dead empires !

    .   .   .   .

The Niobe of nations ! there she stands,
Childless and crownless, in her voiceless woe ;
An empty urn within her withered hands,
Whose holy dust was scattered long ago.
Childe Harold, Canto IV.   LORD BYRON.

CLERGY.

He 'stablishes the strong, restores the weak,
    Reclaims the wanderer, binds the broken heart.
The Timepiece: The Task, Bk. II.   W. COWPER.

Do not, as some ungracious pastors do,
Show me the steep and thorny way to Heaven,
Whilst, like a puffed and reckless libertine,
Himself the primrose path of dalliance treads,
And recks not his own rede.
Hamlet, Act i. Sc. 3.   SHAKESPEARE.

Wel ought a prest ensample for to yive,
By his clennesse, how that his sheep shulde lyve.

.   .   .   .

To draw folk to heven by fairnesse
By good ensample, this was his busynesse.
Canterbury Tales: Prologue.   CHAUCER.

Of right and wrong he taught
Truths as refined as ever Athens heard ;
And (strange to tell !) he practised what he preached.
Art of Preserving Health.   J. ARMSTRONG.

CLOUD.

By unseen hands uplifted in the light
Of sunset, yonder solitary cloud
Floats, with its white apparel blown abroad,
And wafted up to heaven.
Michael Angelo, Pt. II.   H. W. LONGFELLOW.

Yonder cloud
That rises upward always higher,
And onward drags a laboring breast,
And topples round the dreary west,
A looming bastion fringed with fire.
In Memoriam, XV.   A. TENNYSON.

The Clouds consign their treasures to the fields,
And, softly shaking on the dimpled pool,
Prelusive drops, let all their moisture flow
In large effusion, o'er the freshened world.
The Seasons: Spring.   J. THOMSON.

A step,
A single step, that freed me from the skirts
Of the blind vapor, opened to my view
Glory beyond all glory ever seen
By waking sense or by the dreaming soul !
The appearance, instantaneously disclosed
Was of a mighty city,—boldly say
A wilderness of building, sinking far
And self-withdrawn into a boundless depth,
Far sinking into splendor,—without end !
Fabric it seemed of diamond and of gold,
With alabaster domes, and silver spires,
And blazing terrace upon terrace, high
Uplifted ; here, serene pavilions bright,
In avenues disposed ; there, towers begirt
With battlements that on their restless fronts
Bore stars,—illumination of all gems !
The Excursion, Bk. II.   W. WORDSWORTH.

See yonder little cloud, that, borne aloft
So tenderly by the wind, floats fast away
Over the snowy peaks !
Christus : The Golden Legend.   H. W. LONGFELLOW.

COMFORT.

Dear little head, that lies in calm content
Within the gracious hollow that God made
In every human shoulder, where He meant
Some tired head for comfort should be laid.
Song.   C. THAXTER.

Men
Can counsel and speak comfort to that grief
Which they themselves not feel.
Much Ado About Nothing, Act v. *Sc.* 1.   SHAKESPEARE.

" What is good for a bootless bene ? "
With these dark words begins my tale ;
And their meaning is, Whence can comfort spring
When Prayer is of no avail ?
Force of Prayer.   W. WORDSWORTH.

And He that doth the ravens feed,
Yea, providently caters for the sparrow,
Be comfort to my age !
As You Like It, Act ii. *Sc.* 3.   SHAKESPEARE.

Lord, dismiss us with thy blessing,
Hope, and comfort from above ;
Let us each, thy peace possessing,
Triumph in redeeming love.
Benediction.   R. S. HAWKER.

COMPLIMENT.

Current among men,
Like coin, the tinsel clink of compliment.
The Princess, Pt. II.   A. TENNYSON.

That man that hath a tongue, I say, is no man
If with his tongue he cannot win a woman.
Two Gentlemen of Verona, Act iii. *Sc.* 1.
    SHAKESPEARE.

O, thou art fairer than the evening air,
Clad in the beauty of a thousand stars.
Faustus.   C. MARLOWE.

The sweetest garland to the sweetest maid.
To a Lady ; with a Present of Flowers.   T. TICKELL.

When he shall die,
Take him and cut him out in little stars,
And he will make the face of heaven so fine,
That all the world will be in love with night,
And pay no worship to the garish sun.
Romeo and Juliet, Act iii. Sc. 2.   SHAKESPEARE.

But thy eternal summer shall not fade.
Sonnet XVIII.   SHAKESPEARE.

Be thou the rainbow to the storms of life !
The evening beam that smiles the clouds away,
And tints to-morrow with prophetic ray !
The Bride of Abydos, Canto II.   LORD BYRON.

Those curious locks so aptly twined
Whose every hair a soul doth bind.
Think not 'cause men flattering say.   T. CAREW.

And beauty draws us with a single hair.
Rape of the Lock, Canto II.   A. POPE.

When you do dance, I wish you
A wave o' th' sea, that you might ever do
Nothing but that.
Winter's Tale, Act iv. Sc. 4.   SHAKESPEARE.

Some asked me where the Rubies grew,
And nothing I did say,
But with my finger pointed to
The lips of Julia.
The Rock of Rubies, and the Quarrie of Pearls.
R. HERRICK.

Cherry ripe, ripe, ripe, I cry,
Full and fair ones,—Come and buy ;
If so be you ask me where
They do grow, I answer, there,
Where my Julia's lips do smile,
There 's the land, or cherry-isle.
Cherry Ripe.   R. HERRICK.

Where none admire, 't is useless to excel ;
Where none are beaux, 't is vain to be a belle.
Soliloquy on a Beauty in the Country.
LORD LYTTLETON.

Banish all compliments but single truth.
Faithful Shepherdess.   BEAUMONT AND FLETCHER.

What honor that,
But tedious waste of time, to sit and hear
So many hollow compliments and lies.
Paradise Regained.   MILTON.

'T was never merry world
Since lowly feigning was called compliment.
Twelfth Night, Act iii. *Sc.* 1.   SHAKESPEARE.

CONCEIT.

'T is with our judgments as our watches, none
Go just alike, yet each believes his own.
Essay on Criticism, Pt. I.   A. POPE.

To observations which ourselves we make,
We grow more partial for the observer's sake.
Moral Essays, Epistle I.   A. POPE.

In men this blunder still you find,
All think their little set mankind.
Florio, Pt. I.   HANNAH MORE.

Conceit in weakest bodies strongest works.
Hamlet, Act iii. *Sc.* 1.   SHAKESPEARE.

CONSCIENCE.

Whatever creed be taught or land be trod,
Man's conscience is the oracle of God.
The Island, Canto I.   LORD BYRON.

Oh, Conscience! Conscience! man's most faithful friend,
Him canst thou comfort, ease, relieve, defend;
But if he will thy friendly checks forego,
Thou art, oh! woe for me, his deadliest foe!
Struggles of Conscience.   G. CRABBE.

Conscience is harder than our enemies,
Knows more, accuses with more nicety.
Spanish Gypsy.   GEORGE ELIOT.

Of a' the ills that flesh can fear,
The loss o' frien's, the lack o' gear,
A yowlin' tyke, a glandered mear,
A lassie's nonsense—
There's just ae thing I cannae bear,
An' that's my conscience.
My Conscience.   R. L. STEVENSON.

My conscience hath a thousand several tongues,
And every tongue brings in a several tale,
And every tale condemns me for a villain.
K. Richard III., Act v. *Sc.* 3.   SHAKESPEARE.

4

Why should not Conscience have vacation
As well as other courts o' th' nation?
Have equal power to adjourn,
Appoint appearance and return?
Hudibras, Pt. II. Canto II.   S. BUTLER.

Soft, I did but dream.
O coward conscience, how dost thou afflict me!
K. Richard III., Act v. *Sc.* 3.   SHAKESPEARE.

Let his tormentor conscience find him out.
Paradise Regained, Bk. IV.   MILTON.

Speak no more:
Thou turn'st mine eyes into my very soul;
And there I see such black and grainèd spots
As will not leave their tinct.
Hamlet, Act iii. *Sc.* 4.   SHAKESPEARE.

Suspicion always haunts the guilty mind:
The thief doth fear each bush an officer.
K. Richard II., Act v. *Sc.* 6.   SHAKESPEARE.

Leave her to Heaven,
And to those thorns that in her bosom lodge,
To prick and sting her.
Hamlet, Act i. *Sc.* 5.   SHAKESPEARE.

Consideration, like an angel, came
And whipped the offending Adam out of him.
K. Henry V., Act i. *Sc.* 1.   SHAKESPEARE.

True, conscious Honor is to feel no sin,
He's armed without that's innocent within;
Be this thy screen, and this thy wall of Brass.
First Book of Horace, Epistle I.   A. POPE.

I know myself now; and I feel within me
A peace above all earthly dignities;
A still and quiet conscience.
K. Henry VIII., Act iii. *Sc.* 2.   SHAKESPEARE.

A quiet conscience makes one so serene!
Christians have burnt each other, quite persuaded
That all the Apostles would have done as they did.
Don Juan, Canto I.   LORD BYRON.

All is, if I have grace to use it so,
As ever in my Great Task-Master's eye.
On being arrived at his Three-and-Twentieth Year.
          MILTON.

And sure the eternal Master found
His single talent well employed.
Verses on Robert Levet.   DR. S. JOHNSON.

CONSOLATION.

With silence only as their benediction,
God's angels come
Where in the shadow of a great affliction,
The soul sits dumb !
To my Friend on the Death of his Sister.
J. G. WHITTIER.

And, as she looked around, she saw how Death the con-
soler,
Laving his hand upon many a heart, had healed it forever.
Evangeline.   H. W. LONGFELLOW.

Sprinkled along the waste of years
Full many a soft green isle appears :
Pause where we may upon the desert road,
Some shelter is in sight, some sacred safe abode.
The Christian Year. The First Sunday in Advent.
J. KEBLE.

O weary hearts ! O slumbering eyes !
O drooping souls, whose destinies
Are fraught with fear and pain,
Ye shall be loved again.
Endymion.   H. W. LONGFELLOW.

Love is indestructible :
Its holy flame forever burneth :
From Heaven it came, to Heaven returneth ;

It soweth here with toil and care,
But the harvest-time of Love is there.
Curse of Kehama, Canto X.   R. SOUTHEY.

CONSTANCY.

O heaven ! were man
But constant, he were perfect. That one error
Fills him with faults ; makes him run through all the sins :
Inconstancy falls off ere it begins.
Two Gentlemen of Verona, Act v. Sc. 4.   SHAKESPEARE.

They sin who tell us Love can die :
With Life all other passions fly,
All others are but vanity.
Curse of Kehama, Canto X.   R. SOUTHEY.

Doubt thou the stars are fire,
  Doubt that the sun doth move ;
  Doubt truth to be a liar.
  But never doubt I love.
Hamlet, Act ii. *Sc.* 2.   SHAKESPEARE.

When love begins to sicken and decay,
It useth an enforcèd ceremony.
There are no tricks in plain and simple faith.
Julius Cæsar, Act iv. *Sc.* 2.   SHAKESPEARE.

You say to me-wards your affection 's strong ;
Pray love me little, so you love me long.
Love me little, love me long.   R. HERRICK.

When change itself can give no more,
  'T is easy to be true.
Reasons for Constancy.   SIR C. SEDLEY.

If ever thou shalt love,
In the sweet pangs of it remember me ;
For such as I am all true lovers are,
Unstaid and skittish in all motions else,
Save in the constant image of the creature
That is beloved.
Twelfth Night, Act ii. *Sc.* 4.   SHAKESPEARE.

I could be well moved if I were as you ;
If I could pray to move, prayers would move me ;
But I am constant as the northern star,
Of whose true fixed and resting quality
There is no fellow in the firmament.
Julius Cæsar, Act iii. *Sc.* 1   SHAKESPEARE.

CONTENTMENT.

Happy the man, of mortals happiest he,
Whose quiet mind from vain desires is free ;
Whom neither hopes deceive, nor fears torment,
But lives at peace, within himself content ;
In thought, or act, accountable to none
But to himself, and to the gods alone.
Epistle to Mrs. Higgons.
                         LORD LANSDOWNE.

Yes ! in the poor man's garden grow,
  Far more than herbs and flowers,
Kind thoughts, contentment, peace of mind,
  And joy for weary hours.
The Poor Man's Garden.   M. HOWITT.

Whate'er the passion, knowledge, fame, or pelf,
Not one will change his neighbor with himself.
Essay on Man, Epistle II.   A. POPE.

Poor and content is rich and rich enough,
But riches, fineless, is as poor as winter
To him that ever fears he shall be poor.
Othello, Act iii. *Sc.* 3.   SHAKESPEARE.

From labor health, from health contentment spring ;
Contentment opes the source of every joy.
The Minstrel, Bk. I.   J. BEATTIE.

What happiness the rural maid attends,
In cheerful labor while each day she spends !
She gratefully receives what Heaven has sent,
And, rich in poverty, enjoys content.
Rural Sports, Canto II.   J. GAY.

My crown is in my heart, not on my head ;
Not decked with diamonds and Indian stones,
Nor to be seen : my crown is called content ;
A crown it is that seldom kings enjoy.
K. Henry VI., Pt. III. Act iii. *Sc.* 1.   SHAKESPEARE.

Shut up
In measureless content.
Macbeth, Act ii. *Sc.* 1.   SHAKESPEARE.

CONVERSATION.

Discourse, the sweeter banquet of the mind.
The Odyssey, Bk. XV.   HOMER. *Trans. of* POPE.

With good and gentle-humored hearts
I choose to chat where'er I come,
Whate'er the subject be that starts.
But if I get among the glum
I hold my tongue to tell the truth
And keep my breath to cool my broth.
Careless Content.   LORD BYRON.

But conversation, choose what theme we may,
And chiefly when religion leads the way,
Should flow, like waters after summer show'rs,
Not as if raised by mere mechanic powers.
Conversation.   W. COWPER.

In general those who nothing have to say
Contrive to spend the longest time in doing it.
An Oriental Apologue.   J. R. LOWELL.

There's nothing in this world can make me joy.
Life is as tedious as a twice-told tale,
Vexing the dull ear of a drowsy man.
King John, Act iii. *Sc.* 4.　　　　　SHAKESPEARE.

Think all you speak ; but speak not all you think :
Thoughts are your own ; your words are so no more.
Epigram.　　　　　　　　　　　H. DELAUNE.

Words learned by rote a parrot may rehearse,
But talking is not always to converse,
Not more distinct from harmony divine
The constant creaking of a country sign.
Conversation.　　　　　　　　　W. COWPER.

Just at the age 'twixt boy and youth,
When thought is speech, and speech is truth.
Marmion, Canto II.　　　　　　SIR W. SCOTT.

They never taste who always drink ;
They always talk who never think.
Upon a Passage in the Scaligerana.　　M. PRIOR.

And, when you stick on conversation's burrs,
Don't strew your pathway with those dreadful *urs.*
Urania.　　　　　　　　　　　O. W. HOLMES.

KING RICHARD.　Be eloquent in my behalf to her.
QUEEN ELIZABETH.　An honest tale speeds best, being
　　plainly told.
King Richard III., Act iv. *Sc.* 4.　　SHAKESPEARE.

O, many a shaft, at random sent,
Finds mark the archer little meant !
And many a word, at random spoken,
May soothe, or wound, a heart that's broken !
Lord of the Isles, Canto V.　　　SIR W. SCOTT.

A man in all the world's new fashion planted,
That hath a mint of phrases in his brain.
Love's Labor's Lost, Act i. *Sc.* 1.　　SHAKESPEARE.

　　　　　　　　　In his brain—
Which is as dry as the remainder biscuit
After a voyage—he hath strange places crammed
With observation, the which he vents
In mangled forms.
As You Like it, Act ii. *Sc.* 7.　　SHAKESPEARE.

Therefore, since brevity is the soul of wit,
And tediousness the limbs and outward flourishes,
I will be brief.
Hamlet, Act ii. *Sc.* 2.　　　　　SHAKESPEARE.

And I oft have heard defended,
Little said is soonest mended.
The Shepherd's Hunting.   G. WITHER.

Bid me discourse, I will enchant thine ear.
Venus and Adonis.   SHAKESPEARE.

Delivers in such apt and gracious words,
That aged ears play truant at his tales,
And younger hearings are quite ravishèd,
So sweet and voluble is his discourse,
Love's Labor's Lost, Act ii. *Sc.* 1.   SHAKESPEARE.

COQUETRY.

Or light or dark, or short or tall,
She sets a springe to snare them all:
All 's one to her—above her fan
She 'd make sweet eyes at Caliban.
Quatrains. Coquette.   T. B. ALDRICH.

Such is your cold coquette, who can't say "No."
And won't say "Yes," and keeps you on and off-ing
On a lee-shore, till it begins to blow,
Then sees your heart wrecked, with an inward scoffing.
Don Juan, Canto XII.   LORD BYRON.

And still she sits, young while the earth is old
And, subtly of herself contemplative,
Draws men to watch the bright net she can weave,
Till heart and body and life are in its hold.
Lilith.   D. G. ROSSETTI.

How happy could I be with either,
Were t' other dear charmer away!
But while ye thus tease me together,
To neither a word will I say.
Beggar's Opera, Act ii. *Sc.* 2.   J. GAY.

Ye belles, and ye flirts, and ye pert little things,
Who trip in this frolicsome round,
Pray tell me from whence this impertinence springs,
The sexes at once to confound?
Song for Ranelagh.   P. WHITEHEAD.

COUNTRIES.

AMERICA.
America! half brother of the world!
With something good and bad of every land.
Festus: Sc. The Surface.   P. J. BAILEY.

Hail Columbia! happy land!
Hail ye heroes, heaven-born band!
  Who fought and bled in freedom's cause,
  Who fought and bled in freedom's cause,
And when the storm of war was gone,
Enjoyed the peace your valor won!
  Let independence be our boast,
  Ever mindful what it cost ;
  Ever grateful for the prize,
  Let its altar reach the skies.
    Firm—united—let us be,
    Rallying round our liberty ;
    As a band of brothers joined,
    Peace and safety we shall find.
Hail Columbia.   J. HOPKINSON.

  Around I see
  The powers that be ;
I stand by Empire's primal springs ;
  And princes meet
  In every street,
And hear the tread of uncrowned kings!

.   .   .   .   .   .

  Not lightly fall
  Beyond recall
The written scrolls a breath can float ;
  The crowning fact
  The kingliest act
Of Freedom is the freeman's vote!
The Eve of Election.   J. G. WHITTIER.

Down to the Plymouth Rock, that had been to their feet
  as a doorstep
Into a world unknown,—the corner-stone of a nation!
Courtship of Miles Standish.   H. W. LONGFELLOW.

They love their land because it is their own,
  And scorn to give aught other reason why ;
Would shake hands with a king upon his throne,
  And think it kindness to his majesty.
Connecticut.   F-G. HALLECK.

How has New England's romance fled,
  Even as a vision of the morning!
Its right foredone,—its guardians dead,—
Its priestesses, bereft of dread,
  Waking the veriest urchin's scorning!

.   .   .   .   .   .

And now our modern Yankee sees
Nor omens, spells, nor mysteries ;
And naught above, below, around,

Of life or death, of sight or sound,
  Whate'er its nature, form, or look,
Excites his terror or surprise,—
All seeming to his knowing eyes
Familiar as his "catechize,"
  Or "Webster's Spelling-Book."
A New England Legend.   J. G. WHITTIER.

Long as thine Art shall love true love,
Long as thy Science truth shall know,
Long as thine Eagle harms no Dove,
Long as thy Law by law shall grow,
Long as thy God is God above,
Thy brother every man below,—
So long, dear Land of all my love,
Thy name shall shine, thy fame shall glow!
Centennial Meditation of Columbia : 1876.   S. LANIER.

His home!—the Western giant smiles,
  And turns the spotty globe to find it ;—
This little speck the British Isles?
  'T is but a freckle,—never mind it.
A Good Time Going. ·   O. W. HOLMES.

ENGLAND.

O England! model to thy inward greatness,
  Like little body with a mighty heart.
King Henry V., Act ii. *Chorus.*   SHAKESPEARE.

This royal throne of kings, this sceptred isle,
This earth of majesty, this seat of Mars,
This other Eden, demi-paradise,
This fortress built by nature for herself
Against infection and the hand of war :
This happy breed of men, this little world,
This precious stone set in the silver sea,
Which serves it in the office of a wall,
Or as a moat defensive to a house,
Against the envy of less happier lands ;
This blessed plot, this earth, this realm, this England.
  King Richard II., Act ii. *Sc.* 1.   SHAKESPEARE.

England! my country, great and free!
  Heart of the world, I leap to thee!
Festus: Sc. The Surface.   P. J. BAILEY.

We must be free or die, who speak the tongue
That Shakespeare spake ; the faith and morals hold
Which Milton held.   In everything we are sprung
Of earth's first blood, have titles manifold.
National Independence, Sonnet XVI.   W. WORDSWORTH.

Heaven (that hath placed this island to give law
To balance Europe, and her states to awe,)
In this conjunction doth on Britain smile,
The greatest leader, and the greatest isle !
Whether this portion of the world were rent,
By the rude ocean, from the continent,
Or thus created ; it was sure designed
To be the sacred refuge of mankind.
To My Lord Protector.   E. WALLER.

This England never did, nor never shall,
Lie at the proud foot of a conqueror.
King John, Act v. Sc. 7.   SHAKESPEARE.

A land of settled government,
A land of just and old renown,
Where freedom broadens slowly down,
From precedent to precedent :

Where faction seldom gathers head :
But, by degrees to fulness wrought,
The strength of some diffusive thought
Hath time and space to work and spread.
The Land of Lands.   A. TENNYSON.

Broad-based upon her people's will,
And compassed by the inviolate sea.
To the Queen.   A. TENNYSON.

SCOTLAND.

O Caledonia ! stern and wild,
Meet nurse for a poetic child !
Land of brown heath and shaggy wood,
Land of the mountain and the flood,
Land of my sires ! what mortal hand
Can e'er untie the filial band,
That knits me to thy rugged strand !
Lay of the Last Minstrel, Canto VI.   SIR W. SCOTT.

Hear, Land o' Cakes and brither Scots
Frae Maiden Kirk to Johnny Groat's.
On Capt. Grose's Peregrinations Thro' Scotland.
                                                  R. BURNS.

HOLLAND.

As when the sea breaks o'er its bounds,
And overflows the level grounds,
Those banks and dams that like a screen
Did keep it out, now keep it in.
Hudibras.   S. BUTLER.

Methinks her patient sons before me stand,
Where the broad Ocean leans against the land,
And, sedulous to stop the coming tide,
Lift the tall rampire's artificial pride.
Onward methinks, and diligently slow,
The firm connected bulwark seems to grow,
Spreads its long arms amidst the watery roar,
Scoops out an empire, and usurps the shore.
While the pent Ocean, rising o'er the pile,
Sees an amphibious world beneath him smile ;
The slow canal, the yellow-blossomed vale,
The willow-tufted bank, the gliding sail,
The crowded mart, the cultivated plain,
A new creation rescued from his reign.
The Traveller.   O. GOLDSMITH.

ITALY.

Italia !   O Italia ! thou who hast
The fatal gift of beauty, which became
A funeral dower of present woes and past,
On thy sweet brow is sorrow ploughed by shame,
And annals graved in characters of flame.
Childe Harold, Canto IV.   LORD BYRON.

Italy, my Italy !
Queen Mary's saying serves for me
     (When fortune's malice
     Lost her Calais) :
Open my heart, and you will see
     Graved inside of it, " Italy."
De Gustibus.   R. BROWNING.

COURAGE.

Courage, the highest gift, that scorns to bend
To mean devices for a sordid end.
Courage—an independent spark from Heaven's bright
     throne,
By which the soul stands raised, triumphant, high, alone.
Great in itself, not praises of the crowd,
Above all vice, it stoops not to be proud.
Courage, the mighty attribute of powers above,
By which those great in war, are great in love.
The spring of all brave acts is seated here,
As falsehoods draw their sordid birth from fear.
Love and a Bottle : Dedication.   G. FARQUHAR.

Out of this nettle, danger, we pluck this flower, safety.
King Henry IV., Pt. I. Act ii. *Sc.* 2.   SHAKESPEARE.

Write on your doors the saying wise and old,
" Be bold ! be bold ! " and everywhere—" Be bold ;
Be not too bold ! " Yet better the excess
Than the defect ; better the more than less ;
Better like Hector in the field to die,
Than like a perfumed Paris turn and fly.
Morituri Salutamus.   H. W. LONGFELLOW.

MACBETH.   If we should fail,—
LADY MACBETH.   We fail !
But screw your courage to the sticking place,
And we 'll not fail.
Macbeth, Act i. *Sc.* 7.   SHAKESPEARE.

What man dare, I dare ·
Approach thou like the rugged Russian bear,
The armed rhinoceros, or the Hyrcan tiger ;
Take any shape but that, and my firm nerves
Shall never tremble.
Macbeth, Act iii. *Sc.* 4.   SHAKESPEARE.

" Brave boys," he said, " be not dismayed,
    For the loss of one commander,
For God will be our king this day,
    And I 'll be general under."
From the Battle of the Boyne.   *Old Ballad.*

By how much unexpected, by so much
We must awake endeavor for defence,
For courage mounteth with occasion.
King John, Act ii. *Sc.* 1.   SHAKESPEARE.

Blow, wind ! come, wrack !
At least we 'll die with harness on our back.
Macbeth, Act v. *Sc.* 5.   SHAKESPEARE.

Danger knows full well
That Cæsar is more dangerous than he.
We are two lions littered in one day,
And I the elder and more terrible.
Julius Cæsar, Act ii. *Sc.* 2.   SHAKESPEARE.

No common object to your sight displays,
But what with pleasure Heaven itself surveys,
A brave man struggling in the storms of fate,
And greatly falling with a falling state.
While Cato gives his little senate laws,
What bosom beats not in his country's cause ?
Who hears him groan, and does not wish to bleed ?
Who sees him act, but envies every deed ?
Prologue to Mr. Addison's Cato.   A. POPE.

Dar'st thou, Cassius, now
Leap in with me into this angry flood,
And swim to yonder point ?—Upon the word,
Accoutred as I was, I plungèd in,
And bade him follow.
Julius Cæsar, Act i. *Sc.* 2.   SHAKESPEARE.

" You fool ! I tell you no one means you harm."
" So much the better," Juan said, " for them."
Don Juan.   LORD BYRON.

The intent and not the deed
Is in our power ; and therefore who dares greatly
Does greatly.
Barbarossa.   J. BROWN.

False Wizard, avaunt ! I have marshalled my clan,
Their swords are a thousand, their bosoms are one !
They are true to the last of their blood and their breath,
And like reapers descend to the harvest of death.
Lochiel's Warning.   T. CAMPBELL.

COURTESY.

How sweet and gracious, even in common speech,
Is that fine sense which men call Courtesy !
Wholesome as air and genial as the light,
Welcome in every clime as breath of flowers,
It transmutes aliens into trusting friends,
And gives its owner passport round the globe.
Courtesy.   J. T. FIELDS.

In thy discourse, if thou desire to please ;
All such is courteous, useful, new, or wittie :
Usefulness comes by labor, wit by ease ;
Courtesie grows in court ; news in the citie.
The Church Porch.   G. HERBERT.

I am the very pink of courtesy.
Romeo and Juliet, Act ii. *Sc.* 4.   SHAKESPEARE.

The kindest man,
The best-conditioned and unwearied spirit
In doing courtesies.
Merchant of Venice, Act iii. *Sc.* 2.   SHAKESPEARE.

Would you both please and be instructed too,
Watch well the rage of shining, to subdue ;
Hear every man upon his favorite theme,
And ever be more knowing than you seem.
        B. STILLINGFLEET.

COWARDICE.

What is danger
More than the weakness of our apprehensions?
A poor cold part o' th' blood.   Who takes it hold of?
Cowards and wicked livers : valiant minds
Were made the masters of it.
Chances.   BEAUMONT AND FLETCHER.

Alike reserved to blame, or to commend,
A timorous foe, and a suspicious friend ;
Dreading even fools, by flatteries besieged,
And so obliging that he ne'er obliged.
Satires : Prologue.   A. POPE.

Cowards are cruel, but the brave
Love mercy, and delight to save.
Fables, Pt. I. Fable I.   J. GAY.

When desp'rate ills demand a speedy cure,
Distrust is cowardice, and prudence folly.
Irene, Act iv. Sc. 1.   DR. S. JOHNSON.

He
That kills himself to avoid misery, fears it,
And, at the best, shows but a bastard valor.
This life 's a fort committed to my trust,
Which I must not yield up, till it be forced :
Nor will I.   He 's not valiant that dares die,
But he that boldly bears calamity.
Maid of Honor, Act iv. Sc. 1.   P. MASSINGER.

Thou slave, thou wretch, thou coward !
Thou little valiant, great in villany !
Thou ever strong upon the stronger side !
Thou Fortune's champion, that dost never fight
But when her humorous ladyship is by
To teach thee safety !
King John, Act iii. Sc. 1.   SHAKESPEARE.

For he who fights and runs away
May live to fight another day ;
But he who is in battle slain
Can never rise and fight again.
The Art of Poetry on a New Plan.   O. GOLDSMITH.

Cowards die many times before their deaths ;
The valiant never taste of death but once.
Julius Cæsar, Act ii. Sc. 2.   SHAKESPEARE.

CREED.

Sapping a solemn creed with solemn sneer.
Childe Harold, Canto III.   LORD BYRON.

But Faith, fanatic Faith, once wedded fast
  To some dear falsehood, hugs it to the last.
Lalla Rookh : Veiled Prophet of Khorassan. T. MOORE.

For fools are stubborn in their way,
  As coins are hardened by th' allay ;
And obstinacy 's ne'er so stiff
  As when 't is in a wrong belief.
Hudibras, Pt. III. Canto II. S. BUTLER.

You can and you can't,
  You will and you won't ;
You 'll be damned if you do,
  You 'll be damned if you don't.
Chain (Definition of Calvinism). L. DOW.

They believed—faith, I 'm puzzled—I think I may call
Their belief a believing in nothing at all,
Or something of that sort ; I know they all went
For a general union of total dissent.
A Fable for Critics. J. R. LOWELL.

We are our own fates. Our own deeds
Are our doomsmen. Man's life was made
Not for men's creeds,
  But men's actions.
Lucile, Pt. II. Canto V. LORD LYTTON (*Owen Meredith*).

Go put your creed into your deed,
  Nor speak with double tongue.
Ode : Concord, July 4, 1857. R. W. EMERSON.

CRIME.

There is a method in man's wickedness,
  It grows up by degrees.
A King and no King, Act v. Sc. 4.
  BEAUMONT AND FLETCHER.

Foul deeds will rise,
Though all the earth o'erwhelm them, to men's eyes.
Hamlet, Act i. Sc. 2. SHAKESPEARE.

Tremble, thou wretch,
  That has within thee undivulged crimes,
  Unwhipped of justice.
King Lear, Act iii. Sc. 2. SHAKESPEARE.

But many a crime deemed innocent on earth
Is registered in Heaven ; and these no doubt
Have each their record, with a curse annexed.
The Task, Bk. VI. W. COWPER.

CRITICISM.

And finds, with keen, discriminating sight,
Black 's not so black ;—nor white so *very* white.
New Morality.   G. CANNING.

In words, as fashions, the same rule will hold,
Alike fantastic if too new or old :
Be not the first by whom the new are tried,
Nor yet the last to lay the old aside.
Essay on Criticism, Pt. II.   A. POPE.

Poets lose half the praise they should have got,
Could it be known what they discreetly blot.
*Upon Roscommon's Translation of Horace's De Arte
Poetica.*   E. WALLER.

Vex not thou the poet's mind
With thy shallow wit :
Vex not thou the poet's mind ;
For thou canst not fathom it.
The Poet's Mind.   A. TENNYSON.

CUSTOM.

Man yields to custom, as he bows to fate,
In all things ruled—mind, body, and estate.
Tale III., Gentleman Farmer.   G. CRABBE.

The slaves of custom and established mode,
With pack-horse constancy we keep the road
Crooked or straight, through quags or thorny dells,
True to the jingling of our leader's bells.
Tirocinium.   W. COWPER.

Assume a virtue, if you have it not.
That monster, custom, who all sense doth eat,
Of habits devil, is angel yet in this,
That to the use of actions fair and good
He likewise gives a frock or livery,
That aptly is put on.
Hamlet, Act iii. Sc. 4.   SHAKESPEARE.

Custom calls me to 't :
What custom wills, in all things should we do 't,
The dust on antique time would lie unswept,
And mountainous error be too highly heapt
For truth to o'erpeer.
Coriolanus, Act ii. Sc. 3.   SHAKESPEARE.

Such is the custom of Branksome Hall.
The Lay of the Last Minstrel, Canto I.   SIR W. SCOTT.

The tyrant custom, most grave senators,
Hath made the flinty and steel couch of war
My thrice-driven bed of down.
Othello, Act i. *Sc.* 3.   SHAKESPEARE.

But to my mind,—though I am native here,
And to the manner born,—it is a custom
More honored in the breach, than the observance.
Hamlet, Act i. *Sc.* 4.   SHAKESPEARE.

DAY.

Day !
Faster and more fast,
O'er night's brim, day boils at last ;
Boils, pure gold, o'er the cloud-cup's brim.
Pippa Passes: Introduction.   R. BROWNING.

How troublesome is day !
It calls us from our sleep away ;
It bids us from our pleasant dreams awake,
And sends us forth to keep or break
      Our promises to pay.
How troublesome is day !
Fly-By-Night.   T. L. PEACOCK.

Blest power of sunshine !—genial day,
What balm, what life is in thy ray !
To feel there is such real bliss,
That had the world no joy but this,
To sit in sunshine calm and sweet,—
It were a world too exquisite
For man to leave it for the gloom,
The deep, cold shadow, of the tomb.
Lalla Rookh: The Fire Worshippers.   T. MOORE.

DEATH.

Death calls ye to the crowd of common men.
Cupid and Death.   J. SHIRLEY.

A worm is in the bud of youth,
      And at the root of age.
Stanza subjoined to a Bill of Mortality.   W. COWPER.

The tall, the wise, the reverend head
      Must lie as low as ours.
A Funeral Thought, Bk. II. Hymn 63.   DR. I. WATTS.

Comes at the last, and with a little pin
Bores through his castle wall, and—farewell king !
K. Richard II., Act iii. *Sc.* 2.   SHAKESPEARE.

And though mine arm should conquer twenty worlds,
There's a lean fellow beats all conquerors.
Old Fortunatus.   T. DEKKER.

Men must endure
Their going hence, even as their coming hither :
Ripeness is all.
King Lear, Act v. *Sc.* 2.   SHAKESPEARE.

This fell sergeant, death,
Is strict in his arrest.
Hamlet, Act v. *Sc.* 2.   SHAKESPEARE.

We cannot hold mortality's strong hand.
King John, Act iv. *Sc.* 2.   SHAKESPEARE.

That we shall die we know ; 't is but the time
And drawing days out, that men stand upon.
Julius Cæsar, Act iii. *Sc.* 1.   SHAKESPEARE.

Our days begin with trouble here,
Our life is but a span,
And cruel death is always near,
So frail a thing is man.
New England Primer.

Of all the wonders that I yet have heard,
It seems to me most strange that men should fear ;
Seeing that death, a necessary end,
Will come when it will come.
Julius Cæsar, Act ii. *Sc.* 2.   SHAKESPEARE.

The hour concealed, and so remote the fear,
Death still draws nearer, never seeming near.
Essay on Man, Epistle III.   A. POPE.

The tongues of dying men
Enforce attention, like deep harmony :
When words are scarce, they 're seldom spent in vain ;
For they breathe truth that breathe their words in pain.
K. Richard II., Act ii. *Sc.* 1.   SHAKESPEARE.

A death-bed 's a detector of the heart :
Here tired dissimulation drops her mask,
Through life's grimace that mistress of the scene ;
Here real and apparent are the same.
Night Thoughts, Night II.   DR. E. YOUNG.

The chamber where the good man meets his fate
Is privileged beyond the common walk
Of virtuous life, quite in the verge of heaven.
Night Thoughts, Night II.   DR. E. YOUNG.

Nothing in his life
Became him like the leaving it ; he died,
As one that had been studied in his death,
To throw away the dearest thing he owed,
As 't were a careless trifle.
Macbeth, Act i. *Sc.* 4.   SHAKESPEARE.

The bad man's death is horror ; but the just,
Keeps something of his glory in the dust.
Castara.   W. HABINGTON.

Cut off even in the blossoms of my sin,
Unhouseled, disappointed, unaneled ;
No reckoning made, but sent to my account
With all my imperfections on my head.
Hamlet, Act i. *Sc.* 1.   SHAKESPEARE.

With mortal crisis doth portend
My days to appropinque an end.
Hudibras, Pt. I. Canto III.   S. BUTLER.

Sure, 't is a serious thing to die ! . . .
Nature runs back and shudders at the sight,
And every life-string bleeds at thought of parting ;
For part they must : body and soul must part ;
Fond couple ! linked more close than wedded pair.
The Grave.   R. BLAIR.

While man is growing, life is in decrease ;
And cradles rock us nearer to the tomb.
Our birth is nothing but our death begun.
Night Thoughts, Night V.   DR. E. YOUNG.

Put out the light, and then—put out the light.
If I quench thee, thou flaming minister,
I can again thy former light restore,
Should I repent me ; but once put out thy light,
Thou cunningest pattern of excelling nature,
I know not where is that Promethean heat,
That can thy light relume.   When I have plucked thy rose
I cannot give it vital growth again,
It needs must wither.
Othello, Act v. *Sc.* 2.   SHAKESPEARE.

Death loves a shining mark, a signal blow.
Night Thoughts, Night V.   DR. E. YOUNG.

Death aims with fouler spite
At fairer marks.
Divine Poems.   F. QUARLES.

The ripest fruit first falls.
Richard II., Act ii. *Sc.* 1.   SHAKESPEARE.

The good die first,
And they whose hearts are dry as summer dust
Burn to the socket.
The Excursion, Bk. I.   W. WORDSWORTH.

Happy they !
Thrice fortunate ! who of that fragile mould,
The precious porcelain of human clay,
Break with the first fall.
Don Juan, Canto IV.   LORD BYRON.

Loveliest of lovely things are they,
On earth that soonest pass away.
The rose that lives its little hour
Is prized beyond the sculptured flower.
A Scene on the Banks of the Hudson.   W. C. BRYANT.

"Whom the gods love die young," was said of yore.
Don Juan, Canto IV.   LORD BYRON.

Ere sin could blight or sorrow fade,
Death came with friendly care ;
The opening bud to Heaven conveyed,
And bade it blossom there.
Epitaph on an Infant.   S. T. COLERIDGE.

Thank God for Death ! bright thing with dreary name.
Benedicam Dominos.
                SARAH C. WOOLSEY (*Susan Coolidge*).

But an old age serene and bright,
And lovely as a Lapland night,
Shall lead thee to thy grave.
To a Young Lady.   W. WORDSWORTH.

Death is the privilege of human nature,
And life without it were not worth our taking :
Thither the poor, the pris'ner, and the mourner
Fly for relief, and lay their burthens down.
The Fair Penitent, Act v. *Sc.* 1.   N. ROWE.

Death ! to the happy thou art terrible,
But how the wretched love to think of thee,
O thou true comforter, the friend of all
Who have no friend beside.
Joan of Arc.   R. SOUTHEY.

I would that I were low laid in my grave ;
I am not worth this coil that 's made for me.
King John, Act ii. *Sc.* 1.   SHAKESPEARE.

He gave his honors to the world again,
His blessèd part to heaven, and slept in peace.
Henry VIII., Act iv. *Sc.* 2.   SHAKESPEARE.

O, that this too, too solid flesh would melt,
Thaw, and resolve itself into a dew ;
Or that the Everlasting had not fixed
His canon 'gainst self-slaughter.
Hamlet, Act i. *Sc.* 2.   SHAKESPEARE.

Soldier, rest ! thy warfare o'er,
Dream of fighting fields no more ;
Sleep the sleep that knows not breaking,
Morn of toil, nor night of waking.

.   .   .   .

Huntsman, rest ! thy chase is done ;
Think not·of the rising sun,
For, at dawning to assail ye,
Here no bugles sound reveille.
Lady of the Lake, Canto I.   SIR W. SCOTT.

Better be with the dead,
Whom we, to gain our peace, have sent to peace,
Than on the torture of the mind to lie
In restless ecstasy.   Duncan is in his grave ;
After life's fitful fever, he sleeps well ;
Treason has done his worst : nor steel, nor poison,
Malice domestic, foreign levy, nothing,
Can touch him further !
Macbeth, Act iii. *Sc.* 2.   SHAKESPEARE.

Here may the storme-bett vessell safely ryde ;
This is the port of rest from troublous toyle,
The worlde's sweet inn from paine and wearisome turmoyle.
Faërie Queene.   E. SPENSER.

To die is landing on some silent shore,
Where billows never break, nor tempests roar ;
Ere well we feel the friendly stroke, 't is o'er.
The Dispensary, Canto III.   SIR S. GARTH.

Here lurks no treason, here no envy swells,
Here grow no damnèd grudges ; here are no storms,
No noise, but silence and eternal sleep.
Titus Andronicus, Act i. *Sc.* 2.   SHAKESPEARE.

Let guilt, or fear,
Disturb man's rest, Cato knows neither of them ;
Indifferent in his choice, to sleep or die.
Cato.   J. ADDISON.

Sleep is a death ; O make me try
By sleeping what it is to die,
And as gently lay my head
On my grave as now my bed.
Religio Medici, Pt. II. Sec. 12.   SIR T. BROWNE.

Death in itself is nothing ; but we fear
To be we know not what, we know not where.
Aurengzebe, Act iv. Sc. 1.   J. DRYDEN.

Death, so called, is a thing that makes men weep,
And yet a third of life is passed in sleep.
Don Juan, Canto XIV.   LORD BYRON.

Let no man fear to die ; we love to sleep all,
And death is but the sounder sleep.
Humorous Lieutenant.   F. BEAUMONT.

I hear a voice you cannot hear,
  Which says I must not stay,
I see a hand you cannot see,
  Which beckons me away.
Colin and Lucy.   T. TICKELL.

DECEIT.

An evil soul producing holy witness
Is like a villain with a smiling cheek ;
A goodly apple rotten at the heart :
O, what a goodly outside falsehood hath !
Merchant of Venice, Act i. Sc. 3.   SHAKESPEARE.

A man I knew who lived upon a smile,
And well it fed him ; he looked plump and fair,
While rankest venom foamed through every vein.
Night Thoughts, Night VIII.   DR. E. YOUNG.

The world is still deceived with ornament,
In law, what plea so tainted and corrupt,
But, being seasoned with a gracious voice,
Obscures the show of evil? In religion,
What damnèd error, but some sober brow
Will bless it and approve it with a text,
Hiding the grossness with fair ornament ?
Merchant of Venice, Act iii. Sc. 2.   SHAKESPEARE.

Think'st thou there are no serpents in the world
But those who slide along the grassy sod,
And sting the luckless foot that presses them ?
There are who in the path of social life
Do bask their spotted skins in Fortune's sun,
And sting the soul.
De Montford, Act i. Sc. 2.   J. BAILLIE.

Hateful to me as are the gates of hell,
Is he who, hiding one thing in his heart,
Utters another.
The Iliad, Bk. IX.   HOMER. *Trans. of* BRYANT.

Oh, that deceit should steal such gentle shapes,
And with a virtuous vizard hide foul guile !
K. Richard III., Act ii. *Sc.* 2.　　　SHAKESPEARE.

　　　　　　Our better part remains
To work in close design, by fraud or guile,
What force effected not ; that he no less
At length from us may find, who overcomes
By force hath overcome but half his foe.
Paradise Lost, Bk. I.　　　　　MILTON.

Appearances to save, his only care ;
So things seem right, no matter what they are.
Rosciad.　　　　　C. CHURCHILL.

Stamps God's own name upon a lie just made,
To turn a penny in the way of trade.
Table Talk.　　　　　W. COWPER.

DEEDS.

　　　　From this moment,
The very firstlings of my heart shall be
The firstlings of my hand.　And even now,
To crown my thoughts with acts, be it thought and done.
Macbeth, Act iv. *Sc.* 1.　　　SHAKESPEARE.

Count that day lost whose low descending sun
Views from thy hand no worthy action done.
Staniford's Art of Reading.　　*Author Unknown.*

That low man seeks a little thing to do,
　Sees it and does it ;
This high man, with a great thing to pursue,
　Dies ere he knows it.
A Grammarian's Funeral.　　　R. BROWNING.

'T is not what man Does which exalts him, but what man
　Would do.
Saul, XVIII.　　　　　R. BROWNING.

From lowest place when virtuous things proceed,
The place is dignified by the doer's deed.
All's Well that Ends Well, Act ii. *Sc.* 3.　SHAKESPEARE.

Little deeds of kindness, little words of love,
　Make our earth an Eden like the heaven above.
Little·Things.　　　　　J. A. CARNEY.

I profess not talking : only this,
　Let each man do his best.
Henry IV., Pt. I. Act v. *Sc.* 2.　　SHAKESPEARE.

Things done well,
And with a care, exempt themselves from fear ;
Things done without example, in their issue
Are to be feared.
Henry VIII. Act i. *Sc.* 2.   SHAKESPEARE.

So much one man can do,
That does both act and know.
Upon Cromwell's Return from Ireland.   A. MARVELL.

DEFEAT.

Yes, this is life ; and everywhere we meet,
Not victor crowns, but wailings of defeat.
The Unattained.   E. O. SMITH.

At a frown they in their glory die.
The painful warrior, famoused for fight,
After a thousand victories once foiled,
Is from the books of honor razèd quite,
And all the rest forgot for which he toiled.
Sonnet XXV.   SHAKESPEARE.

What though the field be lost ?
All is not lost ; the unconquerable will,
And study of revenge, immortal hate,
And courage never to submit or yield.
And what is else not to be overcome.
Paradise Lost, Bk. I.   MILTON.

Unkindness may do much ;
And his unkindness may defeat my life,
But never taint my love.
Othello, Act iv. *Sc.* 2.   SHAKESPEARE.

They never fail who die
In a great cause.
Marino Faliero, Act ii. *Sc.* 2.   LORD BYRON.

DESPAIR.

So farewell hope, and, with hope, farewell fear,
Farewell remorse : all good to me is lost ;
Evil, be thou my good.
Paradise Lost, Bk. IV.   MILTON.

No change, no pause, no hope ! Yet I endure.
Prometheus Unbound, Act i.   P. B. SHELLEY.

The strongest and the fiercest spirit
That fought in heaven, now fiercer by despair.
Paradise Lost, Bk. II.   MILTON.

I am one, my liege,
Whom the vile blows and buffets of the world
Have so incensed, that I am reckless what
I do to spite the world.
Macbeth, Act iii. *Sc.* 2.   SHAKESPEARE.

Beware of desperate steps. The darkest day,
Live till to-morrow, will have passed away.
Needless Alarm.   W. COWPER.

DEVIL.

I called the devil, and he came,
And with wonder his form did I closely scan ;
He is not ugly, and is not lame,
   But really a handsome and charming man.
A man in the prime of life is the devil,
Obliging, a man of the world, and civil ;
A diplomatist too, well skilled in debate,
He talks quite glibly of church and state.
Pictures of Travel : Return Home.   H. HEINE.

The Devil was sick, the Devil a monk would be ;
The Devil was well, the Devil a monk was he.
Works, Bk. IV.   F. RABELAIS.

He must needs go that the devil drives.
All's Well that Ends Well, Act i. *Sc.* 3. SHAKESPEARE.

The prince of darkness is a gentleman.
King Lear, Act iii. *Sc.* 4.   SHAKESPEARE.

         The devil hath power
   To assume a pleasing shape.
Hamlet, Act ii. *Sc.* 2.   SHAKESPEARE.

And oftentimes, to win us to our harm,
The instruments of darkness tell us truths ;
Win us with honest trifles, to betray us
In deepest consequence.
Macbeth, Act i. *Sc.* 3.   SHAKESPEARE.

But the trail of the serpent is over them all.
Paradise and the Peri.   T. MOORE.

DEW.

Dewdrops, Nature's tears, which she
Sheds in her own breast for the fair which die.
The sun insists on gladness ; but at night,
When he is gone, poor Nature loves to weep.
Festus : Sc. Water and Wood. Midnight. P. J. BAILEY.

Dewdrops are the gems of morning,
But the tears of mournful eve !
Youth and Age.   S. T. COLERIDGE.

The dews of the evening most carefully shun,—
Those tears of the sky for the loss of the sun.
Advice to a Lady in Autumn. EARL OF CHESTERFIELD.

With coronet of fresh and fragrant flower ;
The same dew, which sometimes on the buds
Was wont to swell, like round and orient pearls,
Stood now within the pretty flow'rets' eyes,
Like tears that did their own disgrace bewail.
Midsummer Night's Dream, Act iv. Sc. 1.

SHAKESPEARE.

I 've seen the dewdrop clinging
To the rose just newly born.
Mary of Argyle.   C. JEFFREYS.

An host
Innumerable as the stars of night,
Or stars of morning, dewdrops, which the sun
Impearls on every leaf and every flower.
Paradise Lost, Book V.   MILTON.

The dewdrops in the breeze of morn.
Trembling and sparkling on the thorn.
A Recollection of Mary F.   J. MONTGOMERY.

DISAPPOINTMENT.

Hope tells a flattering tale,
Delusive, vain, and hollow,
Ah, let not Hope prevail,
Lest disappointment follow.
The Universal Songster.   MISS WROTHER.

As distant prospects please us, but when near
We find but desert rocks and fleeting air.
The Dispensatory, Canto III.   SIR S. GARTH.

We're charmed with distant views of happiness,
But near approaches make the prospect less.
Against Enjoyment.   T. YALDEN.

The wretched are the faithful ; 't is their fate
To have all feelings, save the one, decay,
And every passion into one dilate.
Lament of Tasso.   LORD BYRON.

Alas ! the breast that inly bleeds
Hath naught to dread from outward blow :

Who falls from all he knows of bliss
Cares little into what abyss.
The Giaour.   LORD BYRON.

Full little knowest thou that hast not tried,
What hell it is in suing long to bide :
To lose good dayes, that might be better spent ;
To waste long nights in pensive discontent ;
To speed to-day, to be put back to-morrow ;
To feed on hope, to pine with feare and sorrow.
Mother Hubberd's Tale.   E. SPENSER.

A thousand years a poor man watched
Before the gate of Paradise :
But while one little nap he snatched,
It oped and shut. Ah ! was he wise?
Oriental Poetry : Swift Opportunity.   W. R. ALGER.

Defend me, therefore, common sense, say I,
From reveries so airy, from the toil
Of dropping buckets into empty wells,
And growing old in drawing nothing up.
Task, Bk. III.   W. COWPER.

Like Dead Sea fruit that tempts the eye,
But turns to ashes on the lips !
Lalla Rookh: The Fire Worshippers.   T. MOORE.

Like to the apples on the Dead Sea's shore,
All ashes to the taste.
Childe Harold, Canto III.   LORD BYRON.

At threescore winters' end I died,
A cheerless being, sole and sad ;
The nuptial knot I never tied,
And wish my father never had.
From the Greek.   W. COWPER'S *Trans.*

The cold—the changed—perchance the dead—anew,
The mourned, the loved, the lost—too many !—yet how
few !
Childe Harold, Canto IV.   LORD BYRON.

Do not drop in for an after-loss.
Ah, do not, when my heart hath 'scaped this sorrow,
Come in the rearward of a conquered woe ;
Give not a windy night a rainy morrow,
To linger out a purposed overthrow.
Sonnet XC.   SHAKESPEARE.

I have not loved the world, nor the world me.
Childe Harold, Canto III.   LORD BYRON.

DISCONTENT.

Past and to come seem best; things present worst.
King Henry IV., Pt. II. Act i. *Sc.* 3.   SHAKESPEARE.

Seldom he smiles, and smiles in such a sort
As if he mocked himself and scorned his spirit
That could be moved to smile at anything.
Julius Cæsar, Act i. *Sc.* 2.   SHAKESPEARE.

To sigh, yet feel no pain,
To weep, yet scarce know why;
To sport an hour with beauty's chain,
Then throw it idly by.
The Blue Stocking.   T. MOORE.

DISTANCE.

Why to yon mountain turns the musing eye,
Whose sunbright summit mingles with the sky?
Why do those cliffs of shadowy tint appear
More sweet than all the landscape smiling near?—
'T is distance lends enchantment to the view,
And robes the mountain in its azure hue.
Thus, with del'ght, we linger to survey
The promised joys of life's unmeasured way.
Pleasures of Hope, Pt. I.   T. CAMPBELL.

Yon foaming flood seems motionless as ice;
Its dizzy turbulence eludes the eye,
Frozen by distance.
Address to Kilchurn Castle.   W. WORDSWORTH.

How he fell
From heaven they fabled, thrown by angry Jove
Sheer o'er the crystal battlements; from morn
To noon he fell, from noon to dewy eve,
A summer's day; and with the setting sun
Dropt from the zenith like a falling star.
Paradise Lost, Bk. I.   MILTON.

What! will the line stretch out to the crack of doom?
Macbeth, Act iv. *Sc.* 1.   SHAKESPEARE.

DOUBT.

Modest doubt is called
The beacon of the wise.
Troilus and Cressida, Act ii. *Sc.* 2.   SHAKESPEARE.

Who never doubted, never half believed,
Where doubt there truth is—'t is her shadow.
Festus : Sc. A Country Town.   P. J. BAILEY.

Uncertain ways unsafest are,
And doubt a greater mischief than despair.
Cooper's Hill.   SIR J. DENHAM.

But the gods are dead—
Ay, Zeus is dead, and all the gods but Doubt,
And Doubt is brother devil to Despair !
Prometheus : Christ.   J. B. O'REILLY.

Our doubts are traitors
And make us lose the good we oft might win
By fearing to attempt.
Measure for Measure, Act i. *Sc.* 4.   SHAKESPEARE.

But now, I am cabined, cribbed, confined, bound in
To saucy doubts and fears.
Macbeth, Act iii. *Sc.* 4.   SHAKESPEARE.

Attempt the end, and never stand to doubt ;
Nothing's so hard but search will find it out.
Seek and Find.   R. HERRICK.

Dubious is such a scrupulous good man—
Yes—you may catch him tripping if you can,
He would not, with a peremptory tone,
Assert the nose upon his face his own ;
With hesitation admirably slow,
He humbly hopes—presumes—it may be so.
Conversation.   W. COWPER.

But there are wanderers o'er Eternity
Whose bark drives on and on, and anchored ne'er shall be.
Childe Harold, Canto III.   LORD BYRON.

The wound of peace is surety,
Surety secure ; but modest doubt is called
The beacon of the wise. the tent that searches
To the bottom of the worst.
Troilus and Cressida, Act ii. *Sc.* 2.   SHAKESPEARE.

DREAM.

Dreams are but interludes, which fancy makes ;
When monarch reason sleeps, this mimic wakes.
Fables : The Cock and the Fox.   J. DRYDEN.

'T was but a dream,—let it pass,—let it vanish like so many
others!
What I thought was a flower is only a weed, and is worth-
less.
Courtship of Miles Standish, Pt. VIII.
H. W. LONGFELLOW.

One of those passing rainbow dreams,
Half light, half shade, which fancy's beams
Paint on the fleeting mists that roll,
In trance or slumber, round the soul!
Lalla Rookh : Fire Worshippers.   T. MOORE.

If I may trust the flattering truth of sleep,
My dreams presage some joyful news at hand :
My bosom's lord sits lightly in his throne ;
And all this day an unaccustomed spirit
Lifts me above the ground with cheerful thoughts.
Romeo and Juliet, Act v. *Sc.* 1.   SHAKESPEARE.

And yet, as angels in some brighter dreams
Call to the soul when man doth sleep,
So some strange thoughts transcend our wonted dreams,
And into glory peep.
Ascension Hymn.   H. VAUGHAN.

When to soft Sleep we give ourselves away,
And in a dream as in a fairy bark
Drift on and on through the enchanted dark
To purple daybreak—little thought we pay
To that sweet bitter world we know by day.
Sonnet : Sleep.   T. B. ALDRICH.

Dreams are the children of an idle brain.
Romeo and Juliet, Act i. *Sc.* 4.   SHAKESPEARE.

DRESS.

Let thy attyre bee comely, but not costly.
Euphues, 1579.   J. LYLY.

The soul of this man is his clothes.
All 's Well that Ends Well, Act ii. *Sc.* 5.   SHAKESPEARE.

Costly thy habit as thy purse can buy,
But not expressed in fancy ; rich, not gaudy :
For the apparel oft proclaims the man.
Hamlet, Act i. *Sc.* 3.   SHAKESPEARE.

We 'll have a swashing and a martial outside.
As You Like It, Act i. *Sc.* 3.   SHAKESPEARE.

O fair undress, best dress! it checks no vein,
But every flowing limb in pleasure drowns,
And heightens ease with grace.
Castle of Indolence, Canto I.   J. THOMSON.

What a fine man
Hath your tailor made you!
City Madam, Act i. Sc. 2.   P. MASSINGER.

Thy gown? why, ay;—come, tailor, let us see 't.
O mercy, God! what masquing stuff is here?
What 's this? a sleeve? 't is like a demi-cannon:
What, up and down, carved like an apple-tart?
Here 's snip and nip and cut and slish and slash,
Like to a censer in a barber's shop:
Why, what i' devil's name, tailor, callest thou this!
Taming of the Shrew, Act iv. Sc. 3.   SHAKESPEARE.

With silken coats, and caps, and golden rings,
With ruffs, and cuffs, and farthingales and things;
With scarfs, and fans, and double change of bravery,
With amber bracelets, beads, and all this knavery.
Taming of the Shrew, Act iv. Sc. 3.   SHAKESPEARE.

Dress drains our cellar dry,
And keeps our larder lean; puts out our fires.
And introduces hunger, frost, and woe,
Where peace and hospitality might reign.
The Task, Bk. II.   W. COWPER.

Dwellers in huts and in marble halls—
From Shepherdess up to Queen—
Cared little for bonnets, and less for shawls,
And nothing for crinoline.
But now simplicity 's *not* the rage,
And it 's funny to think how cold
The dress they wore in the Golden Age
Would seem in the Age of Gold.
The Two Ages.   H. S. LEIGH.

DRINK.

Or merry swains, who quaff the nut-brown ale,
And sing enamored of the nut-brown maid.
The Minstrel, Bk. I.   J. BEATTIE.

Fill full! Why this is as it should be: here
Is my true realm, amidst bright eyes and faces
Happy as fair! Here sorrow cannot reach.
Sardanapalus, Act iii. Sc. 1.   LORD BYRON.

But maistly thee, the bluid o' Scots,
Frae Maidenkirk to John o' Grots,
The king o' drinks, as I conceive it,
Talisker, Isla, or Glenlivet !
For after years wi' a pockmantie
Frae Zanzibar to Alicante,
In mony a fash an' sair affliction
I gie 't as my sincere conviction—
Of a' their foreign tricks an' pliskies,
I maist abominate their whiskies.
Nae doot, themsel's, they ken it weel,
An' wi' a hash o' leemon peel,
An' ice an' siccan filth, they ettle
The stawsome kind o' goo to settle ;
Sic wersh apothecary's broos wi'
As Scotsmen scorn to fyle their moo's wi'.
The Scotman's Return from Abroad. R. L. STEVENSON.

This bottle's the sun of our table,
His beams are rosy wine ;
We planets that are not able,
Without his help to shine.
The Duenna, Act iii. Sc. 5. R. B. SHERIDAN.

Now to rivulets from the mountains
Point the rods of fortune-tellers ;
Youth perpetual dwells in fountains,
Not in flasks, and casks, and cellars.
Drinking Song. H. W. LONGFELLOW.

In vain I trusted that the flowing bowl
Would banish sorrow, and enlarge the soul.
To the late revel, and protracted feast,
Wild dreams succeeded, and disordered rest.
Solomon, Bk. II. M. PRIOR.

And now, in madness,
Being full of supper and distempering draughts,
Upon malicious bravery, dost thou come
To start my quiet.
Othello, Act i. Sc. 1. SHAKESPEARE.

He that is drunken . . .
Is outlawed by himself ; all kind of ill
Did with his liquor slide into his veins.
The Temple : The Church Porch. G. HERBERT.

A drunkard clasp his teeth, and not undo 'em,
To suffer wet damnation to run through 'em.
The Revenger's Tragedy, Act iii. Sc. 1. C. TOURNEUR.

I told you, sir, they were red-hot with drinking ;
So full of valor that they smote the air
For breathing in their faces ; beat the ground
For kissing of their feet.
Tempest, Act iv. *Sc.* 1.   SHAKESPEARE.

Of my merit
On thet point you yourself may jedge ;
All is, I never drink no sperit,
Nor I hain't never signed no pledge.
The Biglow Papers, First Series, No. VII.
                              J. R. LOWELL.

DUTY.

So nigh is grandeur to our dust,
So near is God to man,
When Duty whispers low, *Thou must,*
The youth replies, *I can.*
Voluntaries.   R. W. EMERSON.

Not once or twice in our rough island story,
The path of duty was the way to glory.
Ode: Death of the Duke of Wellington. A. TENNYSON.

When I 'm not thanked at all, I 'm thanked enough :
I 've done my duty, and I 've done no more.
Tom Thumb.   H. FIELDING.

And I read the moral—A brave endeavor
To do thy duty, whate'er its worth,
Is better than life with love forever,
And love is the sweetest thing on earth.
Sir Hugo's Choice.   J. J. ROCHE.

DYING.

The slender debt to nature 's quickly paid,
Discharged, perchance, with greater ease than made.
Emblems, Bk. II. 13.   F. QUARLES.

The sense of death is most in apprehension ;
And the poor beetle, that we tread upon,
In corporal sufferance finds a pang as great
As when a giant dies.
Measure for Measure, Act iii. *Sc.* 1.   SHAKESPEARE.

She thought our good-night kiss was given,
And like a lily her life did close ;
Angels uncurtained that repose,
And the next waking dawned in heaven.
Ballad of Babe Christabel.   G. MASSEY.

So fades a summer cloud away ;
　So sinks the gale when storms are o'er ;
So gently shuts the eye of day ;
　So dies a wave along the shore.
The Death of the Virtuous.　　　　MRS. BARBAULD.

Of no distemper, of no blast he died,
But fell like autumn fruit that mellowed long ;
Even wondered at, because he dropt no sooner.
Fate seemed to wind him up for fourscore years ;
Yet freshly ran he on ten winters more :
Till, like a clock worn out with eating time,
The wheels of weary life at last stood still.
Œdipus, Act iv. *Sc.* 1.　　　　J. DRYDEN.

EASTER.

" Christ the Lord is risen to-day,"
Sons of men and angels say.
Raise your joys and triumphs high ;
Sing, ye heavens, and earth reply.
" *Christ the Lord is risen to-day.*"　　C. WESLEY.

Yes, He is risen who is the First and Last ;
　Who was and is ; who liveth and was dead ;
Beyond the reach of death He now has passed,
　Of the one glorious Church the glorious Head.
He is Risen.　　　　H. BONAR.

Tomb, thou shalt not hold Him longer ;
Death is strong, but Life is stronger ;
Stronger than the dark, the light ;
Stronger than the wrong, the right ;
Faith and Hope triumphant say
Christ will rise on Easter Day.
An Easter Carol.　　　　PH. BROOKS.

Rise, heart ! thy Lord is risen.　Sing His praise
　　Without delays
Who takes thee by the hand, that thou likewise
　　With Him mayst rise—
That as His death calcined thee to dust,
His life may make thee gold, and much more just.
Easter.　　　　G. HERBERT.

Spring bursts to-day,
　For Christ is risen and all the earth 's at play.
An Easter Carol.　　　　C. G. ROSSETTI.

ECCLESIASTICISM.

With crosses, relics, crucifixes,
Beads, pictures, rosaries, and pixes ;
The tools of working out salvation
By mere mechanic operation.
Hudibras, Pt. III. Canto I.   S. BUTLER.

Till Peter's keys some christened Jove adorn,
And Pan to Moses lends his pagan horn.
The Dunciad, Bk. III.   A. POPE.

Christians have burnt each other, quite persuaded
That all the Apostles would have done as they did.
Don Juan, Canto I.   LORD BYRON.

To rest, the cushion and soft dean invite,
Who never mentions hell to ears polite.
Moral Essays, Epistle IV.   A. POPE.

Perverts the Prophets and purloins the Psalms.
English Bards and Scotch Reviewers.   LORD BYRON.

So shall they build me altars in their zeal,
Where knaves shall minister, and fools shall kneel :
Where faith may mutter o'er her mystic spell,
Written in blood—and Bigotry may swell
The sail he spreads for Heaven with blast from hell !
Lalla Rookh : The Veiled Prophet of Khorassan.
    T. MOORE.

In hope to merit heaven by making earth a hell.
Childe Harold, Canto I.   LORD BYRON.

When pious frauds and holy shifts
Are dispensations and gifts.
Hudibras, Pt. I. Canto III.   S. BUTLER.

Yes,—rather plunge me back in pagan night,
And take my chance with Socrates for bliss,
Than be the Christian of a faith like this,
Which builds on heavenly cant its earthly sway,
And in a convert mourns to lose a prey.
Intolerance.   T. MOORE.

And after hearing what our Church can say,
If still our reason runs another way,
That private reason 't is more just to curb,
Than by disputes the public peace disturb ;
For points obscure are of small use to learn,
But common quiet is mankind's concern.
Religio Laici.   J. DRYDEN.

ETERNITY.

The time will come when every change shall cease,
This quick revolving wheel shall rest in peace :
No summer then shall glow, nor winter freeze ;
Nothing shall be to come, and nothing past,
But an eternal now shall ever last.
The Triumph of Eternity.   PETRARCH.

Nothing is there to come, and nothing past,
But an eternal now does always last.
Davideis, Bk. I.   A. COWLEY.

This speck of life in time's great wilderness,
This narrow isthmus 'twixt two boundless seas,
The past, the future, two eternities !
Lalla Rookh : The Veiled Prophet of Khorassan.
                                   T. MOORE.

And can eternity belong to me,
Poor pensioner on the bounties of an hour ?
Night Thoughts, Night I.   DR. E. YOUNG.

'T is the divinity that stirs within us ;
'T is heaven itself, that points out an hereafter,
And indicates eternity to man.
Cato, Act v. Sc. 1.   J. ADDISON.

EVENING.

                           Sweet the coming on
Of grateful evening mild ; then silent night
With this her solemn bird and this fair moon,
And these the gems of heaven, her starry train.
Paradise Lost, Bk. IV.   MILTON.

It is the hour when from the boughs
   The nightingale's high note is heard ;
It is the hour when lovers' vows
   Seem sweet in every whispered word.
Parisina.   LORD BYRON.

O, Twilight ! Spirit that doth render birth
To dim enchantments, melting heaven with earth,
Leaving on craggy hills and running streams
A softness like the atmosphere of dreams.
Picture of Twilight.   MRS. C. NORTON.

Now came still evening on ; and twilight gray
Had in her sober livery all things clad :
Silence accompanied ; for beast and bird,

They to their grassy couch, these to their nests,
　　Were slunk, all but the wakeful nightingale.
Paradise Lost, Bk. IV.　　　　　　　　　MILTON.

　　The pale child, Eve, leading her mother, Night.
A Life Drama.　　　　　　　　　　　A. SMITH.

When on the marge of evening the last blue light is broken,
And winds of dreamy odor are loosened from afar
　When on the Marge of Evening.　　　L. I. GUINEY.

　　　When day is done, and clouds are low,
　　　　And flowers are honey-dew,
　　　And Hesper's lamp begins to glow
　　　　Along the western blue ;
　　　And homeward wing the turtle-doves,
　　　Then comes the hour the poet loves.
The Poet's Hour.　　　　　　　　　G. CROLY.

The lights begin to twinkle from the rocks :
The long day wanes : the slow moon climbs : the deep
Moans round with many voices.
Ulysses.　　　　　　　　　　　A. TENNYSON.

　　　The holy time is quiet as a Nun
　　　Breathless with adoration.
It is a Beauteous Evening.　　　W. WORDSWORTH.

EXPECTATION.

'T is expectation makes a blessing dear ;
Heaven were not heaven, if we knew what it were.
Against Fruition.　　　　　　　SIR J. SUCKLING.

　　Oft expectation fails, and most oft there
　　Where most it promises ; and oft it hits
　　Where hope is coldest, and despair most fits.
All's Well that Ends Well, Act ii. Sc. 1.　SHAKESPEARE.

　　　　　Why wish for more ?
　　Wishing, of all employments, is the worst ;
　　Philosophy's reverse and health's decay.
Night Thoughts, Night IV.　　　DR. E. YOUNG.

EYE.

　　　A gray eye is a sly eye,
　　　　And roguish is a brown one ;
　　　Turn full upon me thy eye,—
　　　　Ah, how its wavelets drown one !

A blue eye is a true eye ;
Mysterious is a dark one,
Which flashes like a spark-sun !
A black eye is the best one.
Oriental Poetry: Mirza Shaffy on Eyes.   W. R. ALGER.

O lovely eyes of azure,
Clear as the waters of a brook that run
Limpid and laughing in the summer sun !
The Masque of Pandora, Pt. I.   H. W. LONGFELLOW.

Within her tender eye
The heaven of April, with its changing light.
The Spirit of Poetry.   H. W. LONGFELLOW.

Her two blue windows faintly she up-heaveth,
Like the fair sun, when in his fresh array
He cheers the morn, and all the earth relieveth ;
And as the bright sun glorifies the sky,
So is her face illumined with her eye.
Venus and Adonis.   SHAKESPEARE.

Blue eyes shimmer with angel glances,
Like spring violets over the lea.
October's Song.   C. F. WOOLSON.

The harvest of a quiet eye,
That broods and sleeps on his own heart.
A Poet Epitaph.   W. WORDSWORTH.

Stabbed with a white wench's black eye.
Romeo and Juliet, Act ii. Sc. 4.   SHAKESPEARE.

Sometimes from her eyes
I did receive fair speechless messages.
Merchant of Venice, Act i. Sc. 1.   SHAKESPEARE.

For where is any author in the world
Teaches such beauty as a woman's eye ?
Love's Labor's Lost, Act iv. Sc. 3.   SHAKESPEARE.

Heart on her lips, and soul within her eyes,
Soft as her clime, and sunny as her skies.
Beppo.   LORD BYRON.

The fringèd curtains of thine eye advance.
The Tempest, Act i. Sc. 2.   SHAKESPEARE.

Alas ! how little can a moment show
Of an eye where feeling plays
In ten thousand dewy rays ;
A face o'er which a thousand shadows go.
The Triad.   W. WORDSWORTH.

FACE.

There 's no art
To find the mind's construction in the face.
Macbeth, Act i. *Sc.* 4.   SHAKESPEARE.

Your face, my thane, is a book where men
May read strange matters. To beguile the time,
Look like the time.
Macbeth, Act i. *Sc.* 5.   SHAKESPEARE.

Her face so faire, as flesh it seemed not,
But heavenly pourtraict of bright angels' hew,
Cleare as the skye withouten blame or blot,
Through goodly mixture of complexion's dew.
Faërie Queene, Canto III.   E. SPENSER.

The light upon her face
Shines from the windows of another world.
Saints only have such faces.
Michael Angelo.   H. W. LONGFELLOW.

Oh ! could you view the melody
Of every grace,
And music of her face.
Orpheus to Beasts.   R. LOVELACE.

A countenance more in sorrow than in anger.
Hamlet, Act i. *Sc.* 2.   SHAKESPEARE.

In each cheek appears a pretty dimple ;
Love made those hollows ; if himself were slain,
He might be buried in a tomb so simple ;
Foreknowing well, if there he came to lie,
Why, there Love lived and there he could not die.
Venus and Adonis.   SHAKESPEARE.

There Affectation, with a sickly mien,
Shows in her cheek the roses of eighteen.
Rape of the Lock, Canto IV.   A. POPE.

Sweet, pouting lips, whose color mocks the rose,
Rich, ripe, and teeming with the dew of bliss,—
The flower of love's forbidden fruit, which grows
Insidiously to tempt us with a kiss.
Tasso's Sonnets.   R. H. WILDE.

Her face betokened all things dear and good,
The light of somewhat yet to come was there
Asleep, and waiting for the opening day.
Margaret in the Xebec.   J. INGELOW.

Her face is like the Milky Way i' the sky,—
A meeting of gentle lights without a name.
Breunoralt.   SIR J. SUCKLING.

A face with gladness overspread !
Soft smiles, by human kindness bred !
To a Highland Girl.   W. WORDSWORTH,

FAIRY.

They 're fairies ! he that speaks to them shall die :
I 'll wink and couch ; no man their sports must eye.
Merry Wives of Windsor, Act v. *Sc.* 5.   SHAKESPEARE.

This is the fairy land : O, spite of spites !
We talk with goblins, owls, and elvish sprites.
Comedy of Errors, Act. ii. *Sc.* 2.   SHAKESPEARE.

In silence sad,
Trip we after the night's shade :
We the globe can compass soon,
Swifter than the wand'ring moon.
Midsummer Night's Dream, Act iv. *Sc.* 1.
                                       SHAKESPEARE.

Fairies, black, gray, green, and white,
You moonshine revellers, and shades of night.
Merry Wives of Windsor, Act v. *Sc.* 5.   SHAKESPEARE.

Fairies use flowers for their charactery.
Merry Wives of Windsor, Act v. *Sc.* 5.   SHAKESPEARE.

" Scarlet leather, sewn together,
This will make a shoe.
Left, right, pull it tight ;
Summer days are warm ;
Underground in winter,
Laughing at the storm ! "
Lay your ear close to the hill,
Do you not catch the tiny clamor,
Busy click of an elfin hammer,
Voice of the Leprecaun singing shrill
As he merrily plies his trade ?
He 's a span
And quarter in height.
Get him in sight, hold him fast,
And you 're a made
Man !
The Fairy Shoemaker.   W. ALLINGHAM.

Some say no evil thing that walks by night,
In fog, or fire. by lake or moorish fen,
Blue meagre hag, or stubborn unlaid ghost

That breaks his magic chains at curfew time,
No goblin, or swart fairy of the mine,
Hath hurtful power o'er true virginity.
Comus.   MILTON.

I took it for a faery vision
Of some gay creatures of the element,
That in the colors of the rainbow live
And play i' th' plighted clouds.
Comus.   MILTON.

Oft fairy elves,
Whose midnight revels by a forest side,
Or fountain, some belated peasant sees,
Or dreams he sees, while overhead the moon
Sits arbitress, and nearer to the earth
Wheels her pale course, they on their mirth and dance
Intent, with jocund music charm his ear ;
At once with joy and fear his heart rebounds.
Paradise Lost, Bk. I.   MILTON.

FAITH.

Faith is the subtle chain
Which binds us to the infinite ; the voice
Of a deep life within, that will remain
Until we crowd it thence.
Sonnet : Faith.   E. O. SMITH.

Nor less I deem that there are Powers
Which of themselves our minds impress ;
That we can feed this mind of ours
In a wise passiveness.
Expostulation and Reply.   W. WORDSWORTH.

One in whom persuasion and belief
Had ripened into faith, and faith become
A passionate intuition.
The Excursion, B. VII.   W. WORDSWORTH.

Faith builds a bridge across the gulf of Death,
To break the shock blind nature cannot shun,
And lands Thought smoothly on the further shore.
Night Thoughts, Night IV.   DR. E. YOUNG.

A bending staff I would not break,
A feeble faith I would not shake,
Nor even rashly pluck away
The error which some truth may stay,
Whose loss might leave the soul without
A shield against the shafts of doubt.
Questions of Life.   J. G. WHITTIER.

I stretch lame hands of faith, and grope,
And gather dust and chaff, and call
To what I feel is Lord of all,
And faintly trust the larger hope.
In Memoriam, LIV.   A. TENNYSON.

The Power that led his chosen, by pillared cloud and
flame,
Through parted sea and desert waste, that Power is still
the same ;
He fails not—He—the loyal hearts that firm on Him rely ;
So put your trust in God, my boys, and keep your powder
dry.*
Oliver's Advice.   COLONEL W. BLACKER.

If faith produce no works, I see
That faith is not a living tree.
Thus faith and works together grow ;
No separate life they e'er can know :
They 're soul and body, hand and heart :
What God hath joined, let no man part.
Dan and Jane.   H. MORE.

Whose faith has centre everywhere,
Nor cares to fix itself to form.
In Memoriam, XXXIII.   A. TENNYSON.

But who with filial confidence inspired,
Can lift to Heaven an unpresumptuous eye,
And smiling say, My Father made them all.
The Task, Bk. V. Winter Morning Walk.
                    W. COWPER.

FALSEHOOD.

I give him joy that 's awkward at a lie.
Night Thoughts, Night VIII.   DR. E. YOUNG.

For my part, if a lie may do thee grace,
I 'll gild it with the happiest terms I have.
King Henry IV., Pt. I. Act v. Sc. 4.   SHAKESPEARE.

'T is as easy as lying.
Hamlet, Act iii. Sc. 2.   SHAKESPEARE.

Some truth there was, but dashed and brewed with lies,
To please the fools, and puzzle all the wise.
Absalom and Achitophel.   J. DRYDEN.

---

* Cromwell, once when his troops were about crossing a river to at-
tack the enemy, concluded an address with these words : " Put your
trust in God ; but mind to keep your powder dry."

That a lie which is half a truth is ever the blackest of lies;
That a lie which is all a lie may be met and fought with
    outright—
But a lie which is part a truth is a harder matter to fight.
The Grandmother.   A. TENNYSON.

    Some lie beneath the churchyard stone,
        And some before the speaker.
School and Schoolfellows.   W. M. PRAED.

           Like one,
    Who having, unto truth, by telling of it,
    Made such a sinner of his memory,
    To credit his own lie.
The Tempest, Act i. *Sc.* 2.   SHAKESPEARE.

FAME.

    Fame is the shade of immortality,
    And in itself a shadow. Soon as caught,
    Contemned; it shrinks to nothing in the grasp.
Night Thoughts, Night VII.   DR. E. YOUNG.

    And what is Fame? the meanest have their day,
    The greatest can but blaze, and pass away.
First Book of Horace, Epistle VI.   A. POPE.

    What 's Fame? A fancied life in others' breath,
    A thing beyond us, e'en before our death.
Essay on Man, Epistle IV.   A. POPE.

What is the end of Fame? 't is but to fill
    A certain portion of uncertain paper:
Some liken it to climbing up a hill,
    Whose summit, like all hills, is lost in vapor:
For this men write, speak, preach, and heroes kill,
    And bards burn what they call their "midnight taper,"
To have, when the original is dust,
A name, a wretched picture, and worse bust.
Don Juan, Canto I.   LORD BYRON.

    Her house is all of Echo made
        Where never dies the sound;
    And as her brows the clouds invade,
        Her feet do strike the ground.
Fame.   B. JONSON.

    What shall I do to be forever known,
    And make the age to come my own?
The Motto.   A. COWLEY.

The best-concerted schemes men lay for fame
Die fast away : only themselves die faster.
The far-famed sculptor, and the laurelled bard,
Those bold insurancers of deathless fame,
Supply their little feeble aids in vain.
The Grave.   R. BLAIR.

By Jove !   I am not covetous for gold ;

.   .   .   .

But, if it be a sin to covet honor,
I am the most offending soul alive.
King Henry V., Act iv. *Sc.* 3.   SHAKESPEARE.

One touch of nature makes the whole world kin,—
That all with one consent praise new-born gawds,

.   .   .   .

And give to dust, that is a little gilt,
More laud than gilt o'er-dusted.
Troilus and Cressida, Act iii. *Sc.* 3.   SHAKESPEARE.

Thrice happy he whose name has been well spelt
In the despatch : I knew a man whose loss
Was printed *Grove.* although his name was Grose.
Don Juan, Canto VIII.   LORD BYRON.

Nor Fame I slight, nor for her favors call :
She comes unlooked for, if she comes at all.

.   .   .   .

Unblemished let me live, or die unknown ;
O grant an honest fame, or grant me none !
The Temple of Fame.   A. POPE.

It deserves with characters of brass
A forted residence 'gainst the tooth of time
And razure of oblivion.
Measure for Measure, Act v. *Sc.* 1.   SHAKESPEARE.

Your name is great
In mouths of wisest censure.
Othello, Act ii. *Sc.* 3.   SHAKESPEARE.

Know ye not then, said Satan, filled with scorn,—
Know ye not me?

.   .   .   .   .

Not to know me argues yourselves unknown,
The lowest of your throng.
Paradise Lost, Bk. IV.   MILTON.

The aspiring youth that fired the Ephesian dome
Outlives, in fame, the pious fool that raised it.
Shakespeare's King Richard III. (*Altered*), *Act* iii. *Sc.* 1.
C. CIBBER.

Ah! who can tell how hard it is to climb
The steep where fame's proud temple shines afar!
Ah! who can tell how many a soul sublime
Has felt the influence of malignant star,
And waged with Fortune an eternal war;
Checked by the scoff of pride, by envy's frown,
And poverty's unconquerable bar,
In life's low vale remote has pined alone,
Then dropt into the grave, unpitied and unknown!
The Minstrel, Bk. I.   J. BEATTIE.

FANCY.

This is the very coinage of your brain:
This bodiless creation ecstasy
Is very cunning in.
Hamlet, Act iii. *Sc.* 4.   SHAKESPEARE.

When I could not sleep for cold
I had fire enough in my brain,
And builded with roofs of gold
My beautiful castles in Spain!
Aladdin.   J. R. LOWELL.

Egeria! sweet creation of some heart
Which found no mortal resting-place so fair
As thine ideal breast; whate'er thou art
Or wert,—a young Aurora of the air,
The nympholepsy of some fond despair;
Or, it might be, a beauty of the earth,
Who found a more than common votary there
Too much adoring; whatsoe'er thy birth,
Thou wert a beautiful thought, and softly bodied forth.
Childe Harold, Canto IV.   LORD BYRON.

When at the close of each sad, sorrowing day,
Fancy restores what vengeance snatched away.
Eloise to Abélard.   A. POPE.

We figure to ourselves
The thing we like, and then we build it up
As chance will have it, on the rock or sand:
For Thought is tired of wandering o'er the world,
And homebound Fancy runs her bark ashore.
Philip Van Artevelde, Pt. I. Act i. *Sc.* 5.
SIR H. TAYLOR.

FAREWELL.

Farewell ! a word that must be, and hath been—
A sound which makes us linger ;—yet—farewell.
Childe Harold, Canto IV.   LORD BYRON.

All farewells should be sudden, when forever,
Else they make an eternity of moments,
And clog the last sad sands of life with tears.
Sardanapalus.   LORD BYRON.

So sweetly she bade me " Adieu,"
I thought that she bade me return.
A Pastoral.   W. SHENSTONE.

He turned him right and round about
Upon the Irish shore,
And gae his bridle reins a shake,
With Adieu for evermore,
My dear,
With Adieu for evermore.
It was a' for our Rightfu' King.   R. BURNS.

And so, without more circumstance at all,
I hold it fit, that we shake hands and part.
Hamlet, Act i. Sc. 5.   SHAKESPEARE.

Fare thee well ;
The elements be kind to thee, and make
Thy spirits all of comfort !
Antony and Cleopatra, Act iii. Sc. 2.   SHAKESPEARE.

Alas, and farewell ! But there 's no use in grieving,
For life is made up of loving and leaving.
Written in an Album.   R. W. RAYMOND.

FARMING.

Ill husbandry braggeth
To go with the best :
Good husbandry baggeth
Up gold in his chest.
Five Hundred Points of Good Husbandry, Ch. LII.
T. TUSSER.

Ye rigid Ploughmen ! bear in mind
Your labor is for future hours.
Advance ! spare not ! nor look behind !
Plough deep and straight with all your powers !
The Plough.   R. H. HORNE.

Here Ceres' gifts in waving prospect stand,
And nodding tempt the joyful reaper's hand.
Windsor Forest.   A. POPE.

When weary reapers quit the sultry field,
And, crowned with corn, their thanks to Ceres yield.
Summer.   A. POPE.

Heap high the farmer's wintry hoard !
Heap high the golden corn !
No richer gift has Autumn poured
From out her lavish horn !
The Corn-Song.   J. G. WHITTIER.

The cattle are grazing,
Their heads never raising :
There are forty feeding like one !
The Cock is Crowing.   W. WORDSWORTH.

FASHION.

Fashion—a word which knaves and fools may use,
Their knavery and folly to excuse.
Rosciad.   C. CHURCHILL.

The fashion wears out more apparel than the man.
Much Ado about Nothing, Act iii. *Sc.* 3.
                                SHAKESPEARE.

Nothing exceeds in ridicule, no doubt,
A fool in fashion, but a fool that's out ;
His passion for absurdity's so strong
He cannot bear a rival in the wrong.
Though wrong the mode. comply : more sense is shown
In wearing others' follies than our own.
Night Thoughts, Night II.   DR. E. YOUNG.

Nothing is thought rare
Which is not new, and followed ; yet we know
That what was worn some twenty years ago
Comes into grace again.
The Noble Gentleman : Prologue.
                        BEAUMONT AND FLETCHER.

I 'll be at charges for a looking-glass,
And entertain some score or two of tailors,
To study fashions to adorn my body.
King Richard III., Act i. *Sc.* 2.   SHAKESPEARE.

Let 's do it after the high Roman fashion.
Antony and Cleopatra, Act iv. *Sc.* 15.   SHAKESPEARE.

FATE.

Success, the mark no mortal wit,
Or surest hand, can always hit:
For whatsoe'er we perpetrate,
We do but row, we're steered by Fate,
Which in success oft disinherits,
For spurious causes, noblest merits.
Hudibras, Pt. I. Canto I.   S. BUTLER.

Fate holds the strings, and men like children move
But as they're led: success is from above.
Heroic Love, Act v. *Sc.* 1.   LORD LANSDOWNE.

Fate steals along with silent tread,
Found oftenest in what least we dread;
Frowns in the storm with angry brow,
But in the sunshine strikes the blow.
A Fable: Moral.   W. COWPER.

With equal pace, impartial Fate
Knocks at the palace, as the cottage gate.
Bk. I. Ode IV.   HORACE. *Trans. of* PH. FRANCIS.

Our wills and fates do so contrary run
That our devices still are overthrown;
Our thoughts are ours, their ends none of our own.
Hamlet, Act iii. *Sc.* 2.   SHAKESPEARE.

What fates impose, that men must needs abide;
It boots not to resist both wind and tide.
King Henry VI., Pt. IV. Act iv. *Sc.* 3. SHAKESPEARE.

Heaven from all creatures hides the book of fate.
Essay on Man, Epistle I.   A. POPE.

Let those deplore their doom,
Whose hope still grovels in this dark sojourn:
But lofty souls, who look beyond the tomb,
Can smile at Fate, and wonder how they mourn.
The Minstrel, Bk. I.   J. BEATTIE.

No living man can send me to the shades
Before my time; no man of woman born,
Coward or brave, can shun his destiny.
The Iliad, Bk. VI.   HOMER. *Trans. of* BRYANT.

Our remedies oft in ourselves do lie,
Which we ascribe to Heaven: the fated sky
Gives us free scope; only, doth backward pull
Our slow designs, when we ourselves are dull.
All's Well that Ends Well, Act i. *Sc.* 1. SHAKESPEARE.

I 'll make assurance doubly sure,
And take a bond of Fate.
Macbeth, Act iv. *Sc.* 1.   SHAKESPEARE.

Men at some time are masters of their fates;
The fault, dear Brutus, is not in our stars,
But in ourselves, that we are underlings.
Julius Cæsar, Act i. *Sc.* 2.   SHAKESPEARE.

Man is his own star, and the soul that can
Render an honest and a perfect man
Commands all light, all influence, all fate.
Nothing to him falls early, or too late.
Upon an Honest Man's Fortune.   J. FLETCHER.

There 's a divinity that shapes our ends,
Rough-hew them how we will.
Hamlet, Act v. *Sc.* 2.   SHAKESPEARE.

FAULT.

Roses have thorns, and silver fountains mud ;
Clouds and eclipses stain both moon and sun,
And loathsome canker lives in sweetest bud.
All men make faults.
Sonnet XXXV.   SHAKESPEARE.

Men still had faults, and men will have them still ;
He that hath none, and lives as angels do,
Must be an angel.
On Mr. Dryden's Religio Laici.   W. DILLON.

                     Go to your bosom :
Knock there, and ask your heart what it doth know
That 's like my brother's fault.
Measure for Measure, Act ii. *Sc.* 2.   SHAKESPEARE.

And oftentimes excusing of a fault
Doth make the fault the worse by the excuse,
As patches, set upon a little breach,
Discredit more in hiding of the fault
Than did the fault before it was so patched.
King John, Act iv. *Sc.* 2.   SHAKESPEARE.

Condemn the fault, and not the actor of it ?
Why, every fault's condemned ere it be done.
Mine were the very cipher of a function,
To fine the faults whose fine stands in record,
And let go by the actor.
Measure for Measure, Act ii. *Sc.* 2.   SHAKESPEARE.
7

FEAR.

Imagination frames events unknown,
In wild, fantastic shapes of hideous ruin,
And what it fears creates.
Belshazzar, Pt. II.   H. MORE.

Imagination's fool and error's wretch,
Man makes a death which nature never made ;
Then on the point of his own fancy falls ;
And feels a thousand deaths, in fearing one.
Night Thoughts, Night IV.   DR. E. YOUNG.

A lamb appears a lion, and we fear
Each bush we see 's a bear.
Emblems, Bk. I.–XIII.   F. QUARLES.

Or in the night, imagining some fear,
How easy is a bush supposed a bear !
Midsummer Night's Dream, Act v. *Sc.* 1. SHAKESPEARE.

His fear was greater than his haste :
For fear, though fleeter than the wind,
Believes 't is always left behind.
Hudibras, Pt. III. Canto III.   S. BUTLER.

His flight was madness : when our actions do not,
Our fears do make us traitors.
Macbeth, Act iv. *Sc.* 2.   SHAKESPEARE.

                    Such a numerous host
Fled not in silence through the frighted deep,
With ruin upon ruin, rout on rout,
Confusion worse confounded.
Paradise Lost, Bk. II.   MILTON.

Thou tremblest ; and the whiteness in thy cheek
Is apter than thy tongue to tell thy errand.
King Henry IV., Pt. II. Act i. *Sc.* 1. SHAKESPEARE.

To fear the foe, since fear oppresseth strength,
Gives in your weakness strength unto your foe.
King Richard II., Act iii. *Sc.* 2.   SHAKESPEARE.

                              Fear
Stared in her eyes, and chalked her face.
The Princess, IV.   A. TENNYSON.

Whose horrid image doth unfix my hair
And make my seated heart knock at my ribs,
Against the use of nature.   Present fears
Are less than horrible imaginings.
Macbeth, Act i. *Sc.* 3.   SHAKESPEARE.

LADY MACBETH. Letting *I dare not* wait upon *I would*
Like the poor cat i' the adage.
    MACBETH.   Prythee. peace :
I dare do all that may become a man ;
Who dares do more, is none.
Macbeth, Act i. *Sc.* 7.   SHAKESPEARE.

> Tender-handed stroke a nettle,
>   And it stings you for your pains ;
> Grasp it like a man of mettle,
>   And it soft as silk remains.
Verses written on a Window in Scotland.   A. HILL.

> Fain would I climb, yet fear I to fall.
Written on a Window-Pane.   SIR W. RALEIGH.

> If thy heart fails thee, climb not at all.
Written under the Above.   QUEEN ELIZABETH.

FEELING.

> Sweet sensibility ! thou keen delight !
> Unprompted moral ! sudden sense of right !
Sensibility.   H. MORE.

Feeling is deep and still ; and the word that floats on the
   surface
Is as the tossing buoy, that betrays where the anchor is
   hidden.
Evangeline, Pt. II. Sc. 2.   H. W. LONGFELLOW.

> 'T were vain to tell thee all I feel,
>   Or say for thee I'd die.
'T were Vain to Tell.   J. A. WADE.

> And inasmuch as feeling, the East's gift.
> Is quick and transient,—comes, and lo ! is gone,
> While Northern thought is slow and durable.
Luria, Act v.   R. BROWNING.

> Great thoughts, great feelings came to them,
>   Like instincts, unawares.
The Men of Old.   R. M. MILNES, LORD HOUGHTON.

FIDELITY.

> True as the needle to the pole,
> Or as the dial to the sun.
Song.   B. BOOTH.

But faithfulness can feed on suffering,
And knows no disappointment.
Spanish Gypsy, Bk. III.　　　　GEORGE ELIOT.

To God, thy countrie, and thy friend be true.
Rules and Lessons.　　　　H. VAUGHAN.

Statesman, yet friend to truth ! of soul sincere,
In action faithful, and in honor clear ;
Who broke no promise, served no private end,
Who gained no title, and who lost no friend.
Epistle to Mr. Addison.　　　　A. POPE.

FISH.

O scaly, slippery, wet, swift, staring wights,
What is 't ye do ? what life lead ? eh, dull goggles ?
How do ye vary your vile days and nights ?
How pass your Sundays ?　Are ye still but joggles
In ceaseless wash ?　Still nought but gapes and bites,
And drinks, and stares, diversified with boggles ?
Sonnets : The Fish, the Man, and the Spirit.
　　　　L. HUNT.

Our plenteous streams a various race supply,
The bright-eyed perch with fins of Tyrian dye,
The silver eel, in shining volumes rolled,
The yellow carp, in scales bedropped with gold,
Swift trouts, diversified with crimson stains,
And pikes, the tyrants of the wat'ry plains.
Windsor Forest.　　　　A. POPE.

FLATTERY.

No adulation ; 't is the death of virtue ;
Who flatters, is of all mankind the lowest
Save he who courts the flattery.
Daniel.　　　　H. MORE.

O, that men's ears should be
To counsel deaf, but not to flattery !
Timon of Athens, Act i. *Sc.* 2.　　　　SHAKESPEARE.

They do abuse the king that flatter him :
For flattery is the bellows blows up sin.
Pericles, Act i. *Sc.* 2.　　　　SHAKESPEARE.

What drink'st thou oft, instead of homage sweet,
But poisoned flattery ?
Henry V., Act iv. *Sc.* 1.　　　　SHAKESPEARE.

But flattery never seems absurd ;
The flattered always take your word :
Impossibilities seem just ;
They take the strongest praise on trust.
Hyperboles, though ne'er so great,
Will still come short of self-conceit.
The Painter who pleased Nobody and Everybody.
J. GAY.

'T is an old maxim in the schools,
That flattery 's the food of fools ;
Yet now and then your men of wit
Will condescend to take a bit.
Cadenus and Vanessa.   J. SWIFT.

He loves to hear
That unicorns may be betrayed with trees,
And bears with glasses, elephants with holes,
Lions with toils, and men with flatterers.
But when I tell him he hates flatterers,
He says he does, being then most flattered.
Julius Cæsar, Act ii. *Sc.* 1.   SHAKESPEARE.

Ne'er
Was flattery lost on Poet's ear :
A simple race ! they waste their toil
For the vain tribute of a smile.
Lay of the Last Minstrel, Canto IV.   SIR W. SCOTT.

Why should the poor be flattered ?
No, let the candied tongue lick absurd pomp,
And crook the pregnant hinges of the knee,
Where thrift may follow fawning.
Hamlet, Act iii. *Sc.* 2.   SHAKESPEARE.

His nature is too noble for the world :
He would not flatter Neptune for his trident,
Or Jove for 's power to thunder.
Coriolanus, Act iii. *Sc.* 1.   SHAKESPEARE.

FLOWERS.

No daintie flowre or herbe that growes on grownd,
No arborett with painted blossoms drest
And smelling sweete, but there it might be fownd
To bud out faire, and throwe her sweete smels al arownd.
Faërie Queene, Bk. II. Canto VI.   E. SPENSER.

" Small herbs have grace, great weeds do grow apace : "
And since, methinks, I would not grow so fast,
Because sweet flowers are slow and weeds make haste.
King Richard III., Act ii. *Sc.* 4.   SHAKESPEARE.

Ye field flowers ! the gardens eclipse you 't is true :
Yet wildings of nature, I dote upon you,
　　For ye waft me to summers of old
When the earth teemed around me with fairy delight,
And when daisies and buttercups gladdened my sight,
　　Like treasures of silver and gold.
Field Flowers.　　　　　　　　　　　T. CAMPBELL.

Loveliest of lovely things are they
On earth that soonest pass away.
The rose that lives its little hour
Is prized beyond the sculptured flower.
Scene on the Banks of the Hudson.　　W. C. BRYANT.

Sweet is the rose, but grows upon a brere ;
Sweet is the juniper, but sharp his bough ;
Sweet is the eglantine, but sticketh nere ;
Sweet is the firbloome, but its braunches rough ;
Sweet is the cypress, but its rynd is tough ;
Sweet is the nut, but bitter is his pill ;
Sweet is the broome-flowre, but yet sowre enough ;
And sweet is moly, but his root is ill.
Amoretti, Sonnet XXVI.　　　　　　E. SPENSER.

And 't is my faith that every flower
Enjoys the air it breathes.
Lines written in Early Spring.　　W. WORDSWORTH.

SPRING.

Daffy-down-dilly came up in the cold,
　　Through the brown mould
Although the March breezes blew keen on her face,
Although the white snow lay in many a place.
Daffy-Down-Dilly.　　　　　　　A. B. WARNER.

Darlings of the forest !
　　Blossoming alone
When Earth's grief is sorest
　　For her jewels gone—
Ere the last snowdrift melts, your tender buds have blown.
Trailing Arbutus.　　　　　　　R. T. COOKE.

Ring-ting ! I wish I were a primrose,
　A bright yellow primrose blowing in the spring !
　　The stooping boughs above me,
　　The wandering bee to love me,
The fern and moss to creep across,
　And the elm-tree for our king !
Wishing : A Child's Song.　　　W. ALLINGHAM.

Mild offspring of a dark and sullen sire!
Whose modest form, so delicately fine,
  Was nursed in whirling storms,
  And cradled in the winds.
Thee when young spring first questioned winter's sway,
And dared the sturdy blusterer to the fight,
  Thee on his bank he threw
  To mark his victory.
To an Early Primrose.   H. K. WHITE.

                   O Proserpina!
  For the flowers now, that, frighted, thou lett'st fall
  From Dis's wagon! daffodils,
  That come before the swallow dares, and take
  The winds of March with beauty; violets, dim,
  But sweeter than the lids of Juno's eyes,
  Or Cytherea's breath; pale primroses,
  That die unmarried ere they can behold
  Bright Phœbus in his strength.
The Winter's Tale, Act iv. *Sc.* 3.   SHAKESPEARE.

  The snowdrop and primrose our woodlands adorn,
  And violets bathe in the wet o' the morn.
My Nannie 's Awa'.   R. BURNS.

      A primrose by a river's brim
      A yellow primrose was to him.
      And it was nothing more.
Peter Bell.   W. WORDSWORTH.

  The loveliest flowers the closest cling to earth,
  And they first feel the sun: so violets blue;
  So the soft star-like primrose—drenched in dew—
  The happiest of Spring's happy, fragrant birth.
Spring Showers.   J. KEBLE.

    Primrose-eyes each morning ope
    In their cool, deep beds of grass;
    Violets make the air that pass
    Tell-tales of their fragrant slope.
Home and Travel: Ariel in the Cloven Pine.
                     B. TAYLOR.

  A spring upon whose brink the anemones
  And hooded violets and shrinking ferns
  And tremulous woodland things crowd unafraid,
  Sure of the refreshing that they always find.
Unvisited.   M. J. PRESTON.

The modest, lowly violet
In leaves of tender green is set ;
So rich she cannot hide from view,
But covers all the bank with blue.
Spring Scatters Far and Wide.   D. R. GOODALE.

Oh ! faint delicious spring-time violet,
Thine odor like a key,
Turns noiselessly in memory's wards to let
A thought of sorrow free.
The Violet.   W. W. STORY.

In kindly showers and sunshine bud
The branches of the dull gray wood ;
Out from its sunned and sheltered nooks
The blue eye of the violet looks.
Mogg Megone, Pt. III.   J. G. WHITTIER.

Come for arbutus, my dear, my dear,
The pink waxen blossoms are waking, I hear ;
We 'll gather an armful of fragrant wild cheer.
Come for arbutus, my dear, my dear,
Come for arbutus, my dear.
Come for Arbutus.   S. L. OBERHOLTZER.

A violet by a mossy stone
Half hidden from the eye !
Fair as a star when only one
Is shining in the sky.
Lucy.   W. WORDSWORTH.

Of all the months that fill the year,
Give April's month to me,
For earth and sky are then so filled
With sweet variety.

The apple blossoms' shower of pearl,
Though blent with rosier hue,
As beautiful as woman's blush,
As evanescent too.
Apple Blossoms.   L. E. LANDON.

And buttercups are coming,
And scarlet columbine,
And in the sunny meadows
The dandelions shine.
Spring.   C. THAXTER.

SUMMER.

> Ah ! Bring childhood's flower !
> The half-blown daisy bring.
> *Flowers for the Heart.*　　　　　　　J. ELLIOTT.

> There is a flower, a little flower
> 　With silver crest and golden eye,
> That welcomes every changing hour,
> 　And weathers every sky.
> *A Field Flower.*　　　　　　J. MONTGOMERY.

> We meet thee, like a pleasant thought,
> 　When such are wanted.
> *To the Daisy.*　　　　　　W. WORDSWORTH.

> Myriads of daisies have shone forth in flower
> Near the lark's nest, and in their natural hour
> Have passed away ; less happy than the one
> That, by the unwilling ploughshare, died to prove
> The tender charm of poetry and love.
> *Poems composed in the Summer of* 1833.
> 　　　　　　W. WORDSWORTH.

> With little here to do or see
> Of things that in the great world be,
> Sweet daisy ! oft I talk to thee.
> 　For thou art worthy,
> Thou unassuming commonplace
> Of nature, with that homely face,
> And yet with something of a grace
> 　Which love makes for thee !
> *To the Daisy.*　　　　　　W. WORDSWORTH.

> Here are sweet peas, on tiptoe for a flight ;
> With wings of gentle flush o'er delicate white,
> And taper fingers catching at all things,
> To bind them all about with tiny rings.
> *I Stood Tiptoe Upon a Little Hill.*　　　J. KEATS.

> All will be gay when noontide wakes anew
> The buttercups, the little children's dower.
> *Home Thoughts from Abroad.*　　　R. BROWNING.

> The buttercups, bright-eyed and bold,
> Held up their chalices of gold
> To catch the sunshine and the dew.
> *Centennial Poem.*　　　　　J. C. R. DORR.

We bring roses, beautiful fresh roses,
  Dewy as the morning and colored like the dawn ;
Little tents of odor, where the bee reposes,
  Swooning in sweetness of the bed he dreams upon.
The New Pastoral, Bk. VII.   T. B. READ.

    The amorous odors of the moveless air,—
    Jasmine and tuberose and gillyflower,
    Carnation, heliotrope, and purpling shower
    Of Persian roses.
The Picture of St. John, Bk. II.   B. TAYLOR.

    Then will I raise aloft the milk-white rose,
    With whose sweet smell the air shall be perfumed.
King Henry VI., Pt. II. Act i. *Sc.* 1.   SHAKESPEARE.

    Here eglantine embalmed the air,
    Hawthorne and hazel mingled there ;
    The primrose pale, and violet flower,
    Found in each cliff a narrow bower :
    Foxglove and nightshade, side by side,
    Emblems of punishment and pride,
    Grouped their dark hues with every stain
    The weather-beaten crags retain.
The Lady of the Lake, Canto I.   SIR W. SCOTT.

    Wild-rose, Sweetbriar, Eglantine,
    All these pretty names are mine,
    And scent in every leaf is mine,
    And a leaf for all is mine,
    And the scent—Oh, that's divine !
    Happy-sweet and pungent fine,
    Pure as dew, and picked as wine.
Songs and Chorus of the Flowers.   L. HUNT.

    Roses red and violets blew,
And all the sweetest flowres that in the forrest grew.
Faërie Queene, Bk. III. Canto VI.   E. SPENSER.

    Oh ! roses and lilies are fair to see ;
    But the wild bluebell is the flower for me.
The Bluebell.   L. A. MEREDITH.

    And the stately lilies stand
      Fair in the silvery light,
    Like saintly vestals, pale in prayer ;
    Their pure breath sanctifies the air,
      As its fragrance fills the night.
A Red Rose.   J. C. R. DORR.

And the Naiad-like lily of the vale,
Whom youth makes so fair and passion so pale,
That the light of its tremulous bells is seen,
Through their pavilions of tender green.
The Sensitive Plant.   P. B. SHELLEY.

A pure, cool lily, bending
Near the rose all flushed and warm.
Guonare.   E. L. SPROAT.

There's rosemary, that's for remembrance ; pray you,
love, remember :—and there is pansies, that's for thoughts.
Hamlet, Act iv. *Sc.* 5.   SHAKESPEARE.

Of all the bonny buds that blow
    In bright or cloudy weather,
Of all the flowers that come and go
    The whole twelve moons together,
The little purple pansy brings
Thoughts of the sweetest, saddest things.
Heart's Ease.   M. E. BRADLEY.

I send thee pansies while the year is young,
    Yellow as sunshine, purple as the night ;
Flowers of remembrance, ever fondly sung
    By all the chiefest of the Sons of Light ;
.   .   .   .   .
Take all the sweetness of a gift unsought,
    And for the pansies send me back a thought.
Pansies.   S. DOWDNEY.

I know a bank where the wild thyme blows,
Where ox-lips and the nodding violet grows,
Quite over-canopied with luscious woodbine,
With sweet musk-roses, and with eglantine.
Midsummer Night's Dream, Act ii. *Sc.* 1.
                    SHAKESPEARE.

Or o'er the sculptures, quaint and rude,
That grace my gloomy solitude,
I teach in winding wreaths to stray
Fantastic ivy's gadding spray.
Retirement.   T. WARTON.

AUTUMN.

The purple asters bloom in crowds
    In every shady nook,
And ladies' eardrops deck the banks
    Of many a babbling brook.
Autumn.   E. G. EASTMAN.

Graceful, tossing plume of glowing gold,
Waving lonely on the rocky ledge ;
Leaning seaward, lovely to behold,
Clinging to the high cliff's ragged edge.
Seaside Goldenrod.   C. THAXTER.

The aster greets us as we pass
With her faint smile.
A Day of Indian Summer.   S. H. P. WHITMAN.

Along the river's summer walk,
The withered tufts of asters nod ;
And trembles on its arid stalk
The hoar plume of the golden-rod.
And on a ground of sombre fir,
And azure-studded juniper,
The silver birch its buds of purple shows,
And scarlet berries tell where bloomed the sweet wild-
rose !
Last Walk in Autumn.   J. G. WHITTIER.

FOOL.

The right to be a cussèd fool
Is safe from all devices human,
It 's common (ez a gin'l rule)
To every critter born of woman.
The Biglow Papers, Second Series, No. 7. J. R. LOWELL.

No creature smarts so little as a fool.
Prologue to Satires.   A. POPE.

The fool hath planted in his memory
An army of good words ; and I do know
A many fools, that stand in better place,
Garnished like him, that for a tricksy word
Defy the matter.
Merchant of Venice, Act iii. *Sc.* 5.   SHAKESPEARE.

A limbo large and broad, since called
The Paradise of fools, to few unknown.
Paradise Lost, Bk. III.   MILTON.

Who are a little wise the best fools be.
The Triple Fool.   J. DONNE.

For fools rush in where angels fear to tread.
Essay on Criticism, Pt. III.   A. POPE.

In idle wishes fools supinely stay ;
Be there a will, and wisdom finds a way.
The Birth of Flattery.   G. CRABBE.

This fellow's wise enough to play the fool ;
And to do that well craves a kind of wit.
Twelfth Night, Act iii. *Sc.* 1.   SHAKESPEARE.

Some positive, persisting fools we know,
Who, if once wrong, will need be always so ;
But you with pleasure own your errors past,
And make each day a critique on the last.
Essay on Criticism, Pt. III.   A. POPE.

FORGET.

Good to forgive :
Best to forget.
La Saisiaz : Prologue.   R. BROWNING.

                              We bury love,
Forgetfulness grows over it like grass ;
That is a thing to weep for, not the dead.
A Boy's Poem.   A. SMITH.

Go, forget me—why should sorrow
    O'er that brow a shadow fling ?
Go, forget me—and to-morrow
    Brightly smile and sweetly sing.
Smile—though I shall not be near thee ;
Sing—though I shall never hear thee.
Song : Go, Forget Me !   C. WOLFE.

Forgotten ? No, we never do forget :
We let the years go ; wash them clean with tears.
Leave them to bleach out in the open day
Or lock them careful by, like dead friends' clothes,
Till we shall dare unfold them without pain,—
But we forget not, never can forget.
A Flower of a Day.   D. M. MULOCK CRAIK.

FORGIVE.

Good nature and good sense must ever join ;
To err is human, to forgive divine.
Essay on Criticism, Pt. I.   A. POPE.

Forgiveness to the injured does belong ;
But they ne'er pardon who have done the wrong.
Conquest of Granada, Pt. II. Act i. *Sc.* 2.   J. DRYDEN.

Thou whom avenging powers obey,
Cancel my debt (too great to pay)
Before the sad accounting day.
On the Day of Judgment.   W. DILLON.

Some write their wrongs in marble : he, more just,
Stooped down serene and wrote them in the dust,
Trod under foot, the sport of every wind,
Swept from the earth and blotted from his mind.
There, secret in the grave, he bade them lie.
And grieved they could not 'scape the Almighty eye.
Boulter's Monuments.   S. MADDEN.

The more we know, the better we forgive ;
Who'er feels deeply, feels for all who live.
Corinne.   MADAME DE STAËL.

FORTUNE.

Fortune, men say, doth give too much to many,
But yet she never gave enough to any.
Epigrams.   SIR J. HARRINGTON.

Are there not, dear Michal,
Two points in the adventure of the diver,
One—when, a beggar, he prepares to plunge?
One—when, a prince, he rises with his pearl?
Festus, I plunge.
Paracelsus.   R. BROWNING.

When Fortune means to men most good,
She looks upon them with a threatening eye.
King John, Act iii. *Sc. 4.*   SHAKESPEARE.

Fortune in men has some small diff'rence made,
One flaunts in rags, one flutters in brocade ;
The cobbler aproned, and the parson gowned,
The friar hooded, and the monarch crowned.
Essay on Man, Epistle IV.   A. POPE.

Who thinks that fortune cannot change her mind,
Prepares a dreadful jest for all mankind.
Second Book of Horace, Satire II.   A. POPE.

Will Fortune never come with both hands full,
But write her fair words still in foulest letters ?
She either gives a stomach, and no food,—
Such are the poor in health : or else a feast,
And takes away the stomach,—such are the rich,
That have abundance and enjoy it not.
K. Henry IV., Pt. II. Act iv. *Sc. 4.*   SHAKESPEARE.

Under heaven's high cope
Fortune is god—all you endure and do
Depends on circumstance as much as you.
Epigrams. From the Greek.   P. B. SHELLEY.

There is a tide in the affairs of men,
Which, taken at the flood, leads on to fortune ;
Omitted, all the voyage of their life
Is bound in shallows and in miseries.
On such a full sea are we now afloat ;
And we must take the current when it serves,
Or lose our ventures.
Julius Cæsar, Act iv. *Sc.* 3.   SHAKESPEARE.

Prosperity doth bewitch men, seeming clear ;
As seas do laugh, show white, when rocks are near.
White Devil, Act v. *Sc.* 6.   J. WEBSTER.

Oh, how portentous is prosperity !
How comet-like, it threatens while it shines.
Night Thoughts, Night V.   DR. E. YOUNG.

I have set my life up on a cast,
And I will stand the hazard of the die.
King Richard III., Act v. *Sc.* 4.   SHAKESPEARE.

Blessed are those
Whose blood and judgment are so well commingled,
That they are not a pipe for fortune's finger,
To sound what stop she please.
Hamlet, Act iii. *Sc.* 2.   SHAKESPEARE.

There is some soul of goodness in things evil,
Would men observingly distil it out.
King Henry V., Act iv. *Sc.* 1.   SHAKESPEARE.

FREEDOM.

Who cometh over the hills,
Her garment with morning sweet,
The dance of a thousand rills
Making music before her feet ?
Her presence freshens the air,
Sunshine steals light from her face.
The leaden footstep of Care
Leaps to the tune of her pace,
Fairness of all that is fair,
Grace at the heart of all grace !
Sweetener of hut and of hall,
Bringer of life out of naught,
Freedom, O, fairest of all
The daughters of Time and Thought !
Ode to Freedom : Centennial Anniversary of the Battle of
Concord, April 19, 1875.   J. R. LOWELL.

Of old sat Freedom on the heights,
The thunders breaking at her feet :
Above her shook the starry lights :
She heard the torrents meet.

.   .   .   .

Her open eyes desire the truth.
The wisdom of a thousand years
Is in them. May perpetual youth
Keep dry their light from tears.
Of old sat Freedom on the heights.   A. TENNYSON.

No. Freedom has a thousand charms to show,
That slaves, howe'er contented, never know.

.   .   .   .

Religion, virtue, truth, whate'er we call
A blessing—Freedom is the pledge of all.
Table Talk.   W. COWPER.

A day, an hour, of virtuous liberty
Is worth a whole eternity in bondage.
Cato, Act ii. Sc. 1.   J. ADDISON.

The love of liberty with life is given,
And life itself the inferior gift of Heaven.
Palamon and Arcite, Bk. II.   J. DRYDEN.

'T is liberty alone that gives the flower
Of fleeting life its lustre and perfume ;
And we are weeds without it.
The Task, Bk. V.   W. COWPER.

I must have liberty
Withal, as large a charter as the wind,
To blow on whom I please.
As You Like It, Act ii. Sc. 7.   SHAKESPEARE.

That bawl for freedom in their senseless mood,
And still revolt when truth would set them free.
License they mean, when they cry Liberty ;
For who loves that must first be wise and good.
*On the Detraction which followed upon my writing
Certain Treatises, II.*   MILTON.

The traitor to Humanity is the traitor most accursed ;
Man is more than Constitutions ; better rot beneath the
    sod,
Than be true to Church and State while we are doubly false
    to God.
*On the Capture of Certain Fugitive Slaves near Wash-
ington.*   J. R. LOWELL.

The sword may pierce the beaver,
Stone walls in time may sever ;
'T is mind alone,
Worth steel and stone,
That keeps men free forever.
O, the sight entrancing.　　　　　T. MOORE.

Here the free spirit of mankind, at length,
Throws its last fetters off ; and who shall place
A limit to the giant's unchained strength,
Or curb his swiftness in the forward race ?
The Ages.　　　　　W. C. BRYANT.

Yet, Freedom ! yet thy banner, torn, but flying,
Streams like the thunder-storm *against* the wind.
Childe Harold, Canto IV.　　　　LORD BYRON.

Freedom needs all her poets ; it is they
Who give her aspirations wings,
And to the wiser law of music sway
Her wild imaginings.
To the Memory of Hood.　　　　J. R. LOWELL.

Free soil, free men, free speech, free press,
Fremont and victory !
Chorus : Republican Campaign Song, 1856.
　　　　　R. R. RAYMOND.

FRIENDSHIP.

A ruddy drop of manly blood
The surging sea outweighs ;
The world uncertain comes and goes,
The lover rooted stays.
Epigraph to Friendship.　　　　R. W. EMERSON.

Friendship ! mysterious cement of the soul !
Sweet'ner of life ! and solder of society !
The Grave.　　　　　R. BLAIR.

Friendship is the cement of two minds,
As of one man the soul and body is ;
Of which one cannot sever but the other
Suffers a needful separation.
Revenge.　　　　　G. CHAPMAN.

A friendship that like love is warm,
A love like friendship steady.
How Shall I Woo ?　　　　T. MOORE.
8

Friendship 's the image of
Eternity, in which there 's nothing
Movable, nothing mischievous.
Endymion.   J. LILLY.

Flowers are lovely ; Love is flower-like ;
Friendship is a sheltering tree :
O the Joys, that came down shower-like,
Of Friendship, Love, and Liberty,
Ere I was old !
Youth and Age.   S. T. COLERIDGE.

'T is sweet, as year by year we lose
Friends out of sight, in faith to muse
How grows in Paradise our store.
Burial of the Dead.   J. KEBLE.

I praise the Frenchman,* his remark was shrewd,
How sweet, how passing sweet is solitude !
But grant me still a friend in my retreat,
Whom I may whisper, Solitude is sweet.
Retirement.   W. COWPER.

Friendship 's an abstract of love's noble flame,
'Tis love refined, and purged from all its dross,
'Tis next to angel's love, if not the same.
Friendship : A Poem.   CATH. PHILLIPS.

Heaven gives us friends to bless the present scene ;
Resumes them, to prepare us for the next.
Night Thoughts.   DR. E. YOUNG.

A day for toil, an hour for sport,
But for a friend is life too short.
Considerations by the Way.   R. W. EMERSON.

But sweeter none than voice of faithful friend ;
Sweet always, sweetest heard in loudest storm.
Some I remember, and will ne'er forget.
Course of Time, Bk. V.   R. POLLOK.

A generous friendship no cold medium knows,
Burns with one love, with one resentment glows ;
One should our interests and our passions be,
My friend must hate the man that injures me.
Iliad, Bk. IX.   HOMER.   *Trans. of* POPE.

Nor hope to find
A friend, but what has found a friend in thee.
Night Thoughts, Night II.   DR. E. YOUNG.

* La Bruyère, says *Bartlett.*

Friendship, peculiar boon of Heaven,
  The noble mind's delight and pride,
To men and angels only given,
  To all the lower world denied.
Friendship: An Ode.   DR. S. JOHNSON.

Be thou familiar, but by no means vulgar :
The friends thou hast, and their adoption tried,
Grapple them to thy soul with hoops of steel.
Hamlet, Act i. *Sc.* 3.   SHAKESPEARE.

Turn him, and see his threads : look if he be
Friend to himself, that would be friend to thee :
For that is first required, a man be his own ;
But he that 's too much that is friend to none.
Underwood.   B. JONSON.

Lay this into your breast :
Old friends, like old swords, still are trusted best.
Duchess of Malfy.   J. WEBSTER.

Talk not of wasted affection, affection never was wasted ;
If it enrich not the heart of another, its waters, returning
Back to their springs, like the rain, shall fill them full of
  refreshment ;
That which the fountain sends forth returns again to the
  fountain.
Evangeline.   H. W. LONGFELLOW.

True happiness
Consists not in the multitude of friends,
But in the worth and choice.
Cynthia's Revels.   B. JONSON.

Thou dost conspire against thy friend, Iago,
If thou but think'st him wronged, and mak'st his ear
A stranger to thy thoughts.
Othello, Act iii. *Sc.* 3.   SHAKESPEARE.

Friendship above all ties does bind the heart ;
And faith in friendship is the noblest part.
King Henry V.   EARL OF ORRERY.

Be kind to my remains ; and O, defend,
Against your judgment, your departed friend !
Epistle to Congreve.   J. DRYDEN.

O summer friendship,
Whose flattering leaves, that shadowed us in
Our prosperity, with the least gust drop off
In the autumn of adversity.
The Maid of Honor.   P. MASSINGER.

Such is the use and noble end of friendship,
To bear a part in every storm of fate.
Generous Conqueror.　　　　　　　　　　B. HIGGONS.

Friendship, like love, is but a name,
Unless to one you stint the flame.

.　　　.　　　.　　　.　　　.

'T is thus in friendships : who depend
On many, rarely find a friend.
Fables : The Hare and many Friends.　　　J. GAY.

Like summer friends,
Flies of estate and sunneshine.
The Answer.　　　　　　　　　　G. HERBERT.

What the declinèd is
He shall as soon read in the eyes of others
As feel in his own fall ; for men, like butterflies,
Show not their mealy wings but to the summer.
Troilus and Cressida, Act iii. Sc. 3.　　SHAKESPEARE.

The man that hails you Tom or Jack,
And proves, by thumping on your back,
　His sense of your great merit,
Is such a friend, that one had need
Be very much his friend indeed
　To pardon, or to bear it.
On Friendship.　　　　　　　　　　W. COWPER.

Give me the avowed, the erect, the manly foe,
Bold I can meet,—perhaps may turn his blow ;
But of all plagues, good Heaven, thy wrath can send,
Save, save, oh ! save me from the *Candid Friend !*
New Morality.　　　　　　　　　　G. CANNING.

Friendship is constant in all other things,
Save in the office and affairs of love.
Much Ado about Nothing, Act ii. Sc. 1.　SHAKESPEARE.

If I speak to thee in Friendship's name,
　Thou think'st I speak too coldly ;
If I mention Love's devoted flame,
　Thou say'st I speak too boldly.
How Shall I Woo ?　　　　　　　　　　T. MOORE.

Of all our good, of all our bad,
　This one thing only is of worth,
We held the league of heart to heart
　The only purpose of the earth.
More Songs from Vagabondia : Envoy.

R. HOVEY.

It 's an owercome sooth for age an' youth,
  And it brooks wi' nae denial,
That the dearest friends are the auldest friends
  And the young are just on trial.
Poems: In Scots.   R. L. STEVENSON.

    For friendship, of itself a holy tie,
    Is made more sacred by adversity.
The Hind and the Panther.   J. DRYDEN.

O Friendship, flavor of flowers! O lively sprite of life!
O sacred bond of blissful peace, the stalwart staunch of
    strife.
Of Friendship.   N. GRIMOALD.

FRIGHT.

I feel my sinews slacken with the fright,
And a cold sweat thrills down o'er all my limbs,
As if I were dissolving into water.
The Tempest.   J. DRYDEN.

            But that I am forbid
To tell the secrets of my prison-house,
I could a tale unfold, whose lightest word
Would harrow up thy soul, freeze thy young blood,
Make thy two eyes, like stars, start from their spheres,
Thy knotted and combinèd locks to part,
And each particular hair to stand on end,
Like quills upon the fretful porcupine:
But this eternal blazon must not be
To ears of flesh and blood.
Hamlet, Act i. *Sc.* 5.   SHAKESPEARE.

Silence that dreadful bell: it frights the isle
From her propriety.
Othello, Act ii. *Sc.* 3.   SHAKESPEARE.

FUTURE.

           Often do the spirits
Of great events stride on before the events,
And in to-day already walks to-morrow.
The Death of Wallenstein.   S. T. COLERIDGE.

When I consider life, 't is all a cheat.
Yet, fooled with hope, men favor the deceit;
Trust on, and think to-morrow will repay:
To-morrow's falser than the former day;
Lies worse; and, while it says we shall be blest
With some new joys, cuts off what we possest.

Strange cozenage ! none would live past years again,
Yet all hope pleasure in what yet remain.
Aureng-Zebe; or, The Great Mogul, Act iv. *Sc.* 1.
                                                    J. DRYDEN.

As though there were a tie,
And obligation to posterity.
We get them, bear them breed and nurse,
What has posterity done for us,
That we, lest they their rights should lose,
Should trust our necks to gripe of noose ?
McFingal, Canto II.   J. TRUMBULL.

The best of prophets of the Future is the Past.
Letter, Jan. 28, 1821.   LORD BYRON.

GENTLEMAN.

He is gentil that doth gentil dedis.
Canterbury Tales : The Wyf of Bathes Tale. CHAUCER.

The gentle minde by gentle deeds is knowne ;
For a man by nothing is so well bewrayed
As by his manners,
Faërie Queene, Bk. VI. Canto IV.   E. SPENSER.

Tho' modest, on his unembarrassed brow
Nature had written—" Gentleman."
Don Juan, Canto IX.   LORD BYRON.

I freely told you, all the wealth I had
Ran in my veins, I was a gentleman.
Merchant of Venice, Act iii. *Sc.* 2.   SHAKESPEARE.

" I am a gentleman." I 'll be sworn thou art ;
Thy tongue, thy face, thy limbs, actions and spirit,
Do give thee five-fold blazon.
Twelfth Night, Act i. *Sc.* 5.   SHAKESPEARE.

Nothing to blush for and nothing to hide,
Trust in his character felt far and wide ;
Be he a noble, or be he in trade,
This is the gentleman Nature has made.
What is a Gentleman ?   N. L. O'DONOGHUE.

And thus he bore without abuse
The grand old name of gentleman,
Defamed by every charlatan,
And soiled with all ignoble use.
In Memoriam, CX.   A. TENNYSON.

His tribe were God Almighty's gentlemen.
Absalom and Achitophel.   J. DRYDEN.

GHOST.

What beckoning ghost along the moonlight shade
Invites my steps and points to yonder glade?
To the Memory of an Unfortunate Lady. A. POPE.

What gentle ghost, besprent with April dew,
Hails me so solemnly to yonder yew?
Elegy on the Lady Jane Pawlet. B. JONSON.

By the apostle Paul, shadows to-night
Have struck more terror to the soul of Richard
Than can the substance of ten thousand soldiers.
King Richard III., Act v. *Sc.* 3. SHAKESPEARE.

And then it started, like a guilty thing
Upon a fearful summons. I have heard,
The cock, that is the trumpet to the morn,
Doth with his lofty and shrill-sounding throat
Awake the god of day; and at his warning,
Whether in sea or fire, in earth or air,
The extravagant and erring spirit hies
To his confine.
Hamlet, Act i. *Sc.* 1. SHAKESPEARE.

MACBETH. Thou canst not say I did it; never shake
Thy gory locks at me.

. . . . . .

LADY MACBETH. O proper stuff!
This is the very painting of your fear;
This is the air-drawn dagger which, you said,
Led you to Duncan.
MACBETH. Prithee, see there! behold! look! lo! how
say you?

. . . . . .

The times have been,
That, when the brains were out, the man would die,
And there an end; but now they rise again,
With twenty mortal murders on their crowns,
And push us from our stools.

. . . . .

Avaunt! and quit my sight. Let the earth hide thee!
Thy bones are marrowless, thy blood is cold;
Thou hast no speculation in those eyes,
Which thou dost glare with!

. . . . . .

Hence, horrible shadow!
Unreal mockery, hence!
Macbeth, Act iii. *Sc.* 4. SHAKESPEARE.

GLORY.

Glory is like a circle in the water,
  Which never ceaseth to enlarge itself
  Till, by broad spreading, it disperse to nought.
Henry VI., Pt. I. Act i. *Sc.* 2.   SHAKESPEARE.

Glories, like glow-worms, afar off shine bright,
  But looked to near have neither heat nor light.
The White Devil, Act v. *Sc.* 1.   J. WEBSTER.

We rise in glory, as we sink in pride :
  Where boasting ends, there dignity begins.
Night Thoughts, Night VIII.   DR. E. YOUNG.

The glory dies not, and the grief is past.
On the Death of Sir Walter Scott.   SIR S. BRYDGES.

GOD.

What is this mighty Breath, ye sages, say,
That, in powerful language, felt, not heard,
Instructs the fowls of heaven ; and through their breast
These arts of love diffuses ?   What, but God ?
Inspiring God ! who, boundless Spirit all,
And unremitting Energy, pervades,
Adjusts, sustains, and agitates the whole.
  The Seasons : Spring.   J. THOMSON.

The Somewhat which we name but cannot know,
  Ev'n as we name a star and only see
Its quenchless flashings forth, which ever show
  And ever hide him, and which are not he.
Wordsworth's Grave, I.   W. WATSON.

A Deity believed, is joy begun ;
A Deity adored, is joy advanced ;
A Deity beloved, is joy matured.
  Each branch of piety delight inspires.
Night Thoughts, Night VIII.   DR. E. YOUNG.

Thou, my all !
My theme ! my inspiration ! and my crown !
My strength in age ! my rise in low estate !
My soul's ambition, pleasure, wealth !—my world !
My light in darkness ! and my life in death !
My boast through time ! bliss through eternity !
Eternity, too short to speak thy praise !
Or fathom thy profound of love to man !
  Night Thoughts, Night IV.   DR. E. YOUNG.

Happy the man who sees a God employed
In all the good and ill that checker life.
The Task, Bk. II.   W. COWPER.

O thou, whose certain eye foresees
The fixed event of fate's remote decrees.
Odyssey, Bk. IV.   HOMER.   *Trans. of* POPE.

From thee, great God, we spring, to thee we tend,—
Path, motive, guide, original, and end.
The Rambler, No. 7.   DR. S. JOHNSON.

Whatever is, is in its causes just.
Œdipus, Act iii. Sc. 1.   J. DRYDEN.

He that doth the ravens feed
Yea, providently caters for the sparrow,
Be comfort to my age!
As You Like It, Act ii. Sc. 3.   SHAKESPEARE.

Who sees with equal eye, as God of all,
A hero perished, or a sparrow fall,
Atoms or systems into ruin hurled,
And now a bubble burst, and now a world.
Essay on Man, Epistle I.   A. POPE.

Yet I shall temper so
Justice with mercy, as may illustrate most
Them fully satisfied, and Thee appease.
Paradise Lost, Bk. X.   MILTON.

God, from a beautiful necessity, is Love.
Of Immortality.   M. F. TUPPER.

Forth from his dark and lonely hiding-place,
(Portentous sight!) the owlet Atheism,
Sailing on obscene wings athwart the noon,
Drops his blue-fringed lids, and holds them close,
And, hooting at the glorious Sun in Heaven,
Cries out, "Where is it?"
Fears in Solitude.   S. T. COLERIDGE.

God sendeth and giveth, both mouth and the meat.
Points of Good Husbandry.   T. TUSSER.

'T is Providence alone secures
In every change both mine and yours.
A Fable.   W. COWPER.

Give what thou canst, without thee we are poor;
And with thee rich, take what thou wilt away.
The Task: Winter Morning Walk.   W. COWPER.

That God, which ever lives and loves,
  One God, one law, one element,
And one far-off divine event,
  To which the whole creation moves.
In Memoriam : Conclusion.   A. TENNYSON.

GODS, THE.

Who hearkens to the gods, the gods give ear.
The Iliad, Bk. I.   HOMER. *Trans. of* BRYANT.

Shakes his ambrosial curls, and gives the nod,
The stamp of fate, and sanction of the god.
The Iliad, Bk. I.   HOMER. *Trans. of* POPE.

High in the home of the summers, the seats of the happy
  immortals,
Shrouded in knee-deep blaze, unapproachable ; there ever
  youthful
Hebè, Harmoniè, and the daughter of Jove, Aphroditè
Whirled in the white-linked dance, with the gold-crowned
  Hours and Graces.
Andromeda.   CH. KINGSLEY.

Or else flushed Ganymede, his rosy thigh
  Half buried in the eagle's down,
Sole as a flying star, shot thro' the sky,
  Above the pillared town.
Palace of Art.   A. TENNYSON.

As sweet and musical
As bright Apollo's lute, strung with his hair ;
And when Love speaks, the voice of all the gods
Makes heaven drowsy with the harmony.
Love's Labor 's Lost, Act iv. *Sc.* 2.   SHAKESPEARE.

Who knows not Circè,
The daughter of the Sun, whose charmèd cup
Whoever tasted lost his upright shape,
And downward fell into a grovelling swine ?
Comus.   MILTON.

Cupid is a knavish lad,
Thus to make poor females mad.
Midsummer Night's Dream, Act iii. *Sc.* 3. SHAKESPEARE.

This senior-junior, giant-dwarf, Dan Cupid :
Regent of love-rhymes, lord of folded arms,
The anointed sovereign of sighs and groans.
Love's Labor 's Lost, Act iii. *Sc.* 1.   SHAKESPEARE.

No wonder Cupid is a murderous boy :
A fiery archer making pain his joy.
His dam, while fond of Mars, is Vulcan's wife,
And thus 'twixt fire and sword divides her life.
Greek Anthology. MELEAGER.

The gods are just, and of our pleasant vices
Make instruments to plague us.
King Lear, Act v. Sc. 3. SHAKESPEARE.

Wilt thou draw near the nature of the gods ?
Draw near them then in being merciful ;
Sweet mercy is nobility's true badge.
Titus Andronicus, Act i. Sc. 1. SHAKESPEARE.

GOOD.

What good I see humbly I seek to do,
And live obedient to the law, in trust
That what will come, and must come, shall come well.
The Light of Asia. SIR E. ARNOLD.

There shall never be one lost good ! What was shall live
as before ;
The evil is null, is nought, is silence implying sound.
Abt Vogler, IX. R. BROWNING.

Now, at a certain time, in pleasant mood,
He tried the luxury of doing good.
Tales of the Hall, Bk. III. G. CRABBE.

'T is well said again ;
And 't is a kind of good deed to say well :
And yet words are no deeds.
King Henry VIII., Act iii. Sc. 2. SHAKESPEARE.

Look round the habitable world, how few
Know their own good, or, knowing it, pursue !
Juvenal, Satire X. J. DRYDEN.

These are thy glorious works, Parent of good !
Paradise Lost, Bk. V. MILTON.

GRATITUDE.

The still small voice of gratitude.
For Music. T. GRAY.

A grateful mind
By owing owes not, but still pays, at once
Indebted and discharged.
Paradise Lost, Bk. IV. MILTON.

I 've heard of hearts unkind, kind deeds
  With coldness still returning ;
Alas ! the gratitude of men
  Hath oftener left me mourning.
Simon Lee.   W. WORDSWORTH.

Beggar that I am, I am even poor in thanks.
Hamlet, Act ii. *Sc.* 2.   SHAKESPEARE.

GRAVE, THE.

There is a calm for those who weep,
A rest for weary pilgrims found,
They softly lie and sweetly sleep
      Low in the ground.
The Grave.   J. MONTGOMERY.

Ah, the grave 's a quiet bed :
  She shall sleep a pleasant sleep,
And the tears that you may shed
  Will not wake her—therefore weep !
The Last Scene.   W. WINTER.

O, snatched away in beauty's bloom,
On thee shall press no ponderous tomb ; .
But on thy turf shall roses rear
Their leaves, the earliest of the year,
And the wild cypress wave in tender gloom :
O, Snatched Away !   LORD BYRON.

Yet shall thy grave with rising flow'rs be dressed,
And the green turf lie lightly on thy breast ;
There shall the morn her earliest tears bestow,
There the first roses of the year shall blow.
Elegy to the Memory of an Unfortunate Lady. A. POPE.

And from his ashes may be made
The violet of his native land.
In Memoriam, XVIII.   A. TENNYSON.

Sweets to the sweet : farewell,
I hoped thou shouldst have been my Hamlet's wife :
I thought thy bride-bed to have decked, sweet maid,
And not t' have strewed thy grave.
Hamlet, Act v. *Sc.* 1.   SHAKESPEARE.

How loved, how honored once, avails thee not,
To whom related, or by whom begot ;
A heap of dust alone remains of thee ;
'T is all thou art, and all the proud shall be !
Elegy to the Memory of an Unfortunate Lady. A. POPE.

Lay her i' the earth ;
And from her fair and unpolluted flesh
May violets spring !
Hamlet, Act v. *Sc.* 1.   SHAKESPEARE.

Brave Percy, fare thee well !
Ill-weaned ambition, how much art thou shrunk :
When that this body did contain a spirit,
A kingdom for it was too small a bound ;
But now, two paces of the vilest earth
Is room enough.
King Henry VI., Pt. I. Act v. *Sc.* 4.   SHAKESPEARE.

Oft let me range the gloomy aisles alone,
Sad luxury ! to vulgar minds unknown,
Along the walls where speaking marbles show
What worthies form the hallowed mould below ;
Proud names, who once the reins of empire held,
In arms who triumphed, or in arts excelled ;
Chiefs, graced with scars, and prodigal of blood ;
Stern patriots, who for sacred freedom stood ;
Just men, by whom impartial laws were given ;
And saints, who taught and led the way to heaven.
On the Death of Mr. Addison.   T. TICKELL.

The solitary, silent, solemn scene,
Where Cæsars, heroes, peasants, hermits lie,
Blended in dust together ; where the slave
Rests from his labors ; where th' insulting proud
Resigns his powers ; the miser drops his hoard :
Where human folly sleeps.
Ruins of Rome.   J. DYER.

Then to the grave I turned me to see what therein lay ;
'T was the garment of the Christian, worn out and thrown
away.
Death and the Christian.   F. A. KRUMMACHER.

GREATNESS.

That man is great, and he alone,
Who serves a greatness not his own,
For neither praise nor pelf :
Content to know and be unknown :
Whole in himself.
A Great Man.   LORD LYTTON (*Owen Meredith*).

He fought a thousand glorious wars,
And more than half the world was his,
And somewhere, now, in yonder stars,
Can tell, mayhap, what greatness is.
The Chronicle of the Drum.   W. M. THACKERAY.

Nothing can cover his high fame but heaven ;
No pyramids set off his memories,
But the eternal substance of his greatness,—
To which I leave him.
The False One, Act ii. *Sc.* 1.

BEAUMONT AND FLETCHER.

Greatness on goodness loves to slide, not stand,
And leaves, for fortune's ice, vertue's firm land.
Turkish History.   Under a portrait of Mustapha I.
R. KNOLLES.

Such souls,
Whose sudden visitations daze the world,
Vanish like lightning, but they leave behind
A voice that in the distance far away
Wakens the slumbering ages.
Philip Van Artevelde, Pt. I. Act i. *Sc.* 7.

SIR H. TAYLOR.

GRIEF.

Every one can master grief, but he that has it.
Much Ado about Nothing, Act iii. *Sc.* 2.   SHAKESPEARE.

The grief that does not speak
Whispers the o'er-fraught heart and bids it break.
Macbeth, Act iv. *Sc.* 3.   SHAKESPEARE.

No words suffice the secret soul to show,
For truth denies all eloquence to woe.
The Corsair, Canto III.   LORD BYRON.

No greater grief than to remember days
Of joy when misery is at hand.
Inferno, Canto V.   DANTE.

I am not mad ;—I would to heaven I were !
For then, 't is like I should forget myself ;
O, if I could, what grief I should forget !
King John, Act iii. *Sc.* 4.   SHAKESPEARE.

Not to the grave, not to the grave, my soul,
    Follow thy friend beloved !
    But in the lonely hour,
    But in the evening walk,
Think that he accompanies thy solitude ;
    Think that he holds with thee
    Mysterious intercourse :
And though remembrance wake a tear,
    There will be joy in grief.
The Dead Friend.   R. SOUTHEY.

HABIT.

Habit with him was all the test of truth ;
"It must be right : I've done it from my youth."
The Borough, Letter III.   G. CRABBE.

How use doth breed a habit in a man !
This shadowy desert, unfrequented woods,
I better brook than flourishing peopled town.
Two Gentlemen of Verona, Act v. *Sc.* 4.   SHAKESPEARE.

Hackneyed in business, wearied at that oar,
Which thousands, once fast chained to, quit no more.
Retirement.   W. COWPER.

Small habits, well pursued betimes,
May reach the dignity of crimes.
Florio, Pt. I.   HANNAH MORE.

Ill habits gather by unseen degrees,
As brooks make rivers, rivers run to seas.
Metamorphoses, Bk. XV.   OVID. *Trans. of* DRYDEN.

HAIR.

Those curious locks so aptly twined,
Whose every hair a soul doth bind.
To A. L. Persuasions to Love.   T. CAREW.

Beware of her fair hair, for she excels
All women in the magic of her locks ;
And when she winds them round a young man's neck,
She will not ever set him free again.
Faust : Sc. Walpurgis Night.
       GOETHE. *Trans. of* SHELLEY.

Her glossy hair was clustered o'er a brow
Bright with intelligence, and fair, and smooth.
Don Juan, Canto I.   LORD BYRON.

It was brown with a golden gloss, Janette,
It was finer than silk of the floss, my pet ;
'T was a beautiful mist falling down to your wrist,
'T was a thing to be braided, and jewelled, and kissed—
'T was the loveliest hair in the world, my pet.
Janette's Hair.   C. G. HALPINE (*Miles O'Reilly*).

As she fled fast through sun and shade,
The happy winds upon her played,
Blowing the ringlets from the braid.
Sir Launcelot and Queen Guinevere.   A. TENNYSON.

Come let me pluck that silver hair
Which 'mid thy clustering curls I see ;
The withering type of time or care
Has nothing, sure, to do with thee.
The Grey Hair.   A. A. WATTS.

HAND.

Without the bed her other fair hand was,
On the green coverlet ; whose perfect white
Showed like an April daisy on the grass,
With pearly sweat, resembling dew of night.
Lucrece.   SHAKESPEARE.

The hand of a woman is often, in youth,
Somewhat rough, somewhat red, somewhat graceless, in
    truth ;
Does its beauty refine, as its pulses grow calm,
Or as sorrow has crossed the life line in the palm?
Lucile, Pt. I. Canto III.
                            (*Owen Meredith*). LORD LYTTON.

They may seize
On the white wonder of dear Juliet's hand.
Romeo and Juliet, Act iii. *Sc.* 3.   SHAKESPEARE.

As if the world and they were hand and glove.
Table Talk.   W. COWPER.

With an angry wafture of your hand,
Gave sign for me to leave you.
Julius Cæsar, Act ii. *Sc.* 1.   SHAKESPEARE.

Then join in hand, brave Americans all ;
By uniting we stand, by dividing we fall.
The Liberty Song (1768).   J. DICKINSON.

HAPPINESS.

Fixed to no spot is Happiness sincere :
'T is nowhere to be found, or ev'rywhere ;
'T is never to be bought, but always free.
Essay on Man, Epistle IV.   A. POPE.

We 're charmed with distant views of happiness,
But near approaches make the prospect less.
Against Enjoyment.   T. YALDEN.

For it stirs the blood in an old man's heart :
  And makes his pulses fly,
To catch the thrill of a happy voice,
  And the light of a pleasant eye.
Saturday Afternoon.   N. P. WILLIS.

True happiness ne'er entered at an eye ;
True happiness resides in things unseen.
Night Thoughts, Night VIII.   DR. E. YOUNG.

Some place the bliss in action, some in ease,
Those call it pleasure, and contentment these.
Essay on Man, Epistle IV.   A. POPE.

The spider's most attenuated thread
Is cord, is cable, to man's tender tie
On earthly bliss ; it breaks at every breeze.
Night Thoughts, Night I.   DR. E. YOUNG.

The way to bliss lies not on beds of down,
  And he that had no cross deserves no crown.
Esther.   F. QUARLES.

HATE.

Who love too much hate in the like extreme.
The Odyssey.   HOMER.   *Trans. of* POPE.

These two hated with a hate
Found only on the stage.
Don Juan, Canto IV.   LORD BYRON.

Heaven has no rage like love to hatred turned,
Nor hell a fury like a woman scorned.
The Mourning Bride, Act iii. *Sc.* 8.   W. CONGREVE.

HEART.

Oh, the heart is a free and a fetterless thing,—
A wave of the ocean, a bird on the wing.
The Captive Greek Girl.   J. PARDOE.

His heart was one of those which most enamor us,
'Wax to receive, and marble to retain.
Beppo.   LORD BYRON.

There is an evening twilight of the heart,
When its wild passion-waves are lulled to rest.
Twilight.   F-G. HALLECK.

Worse than a bloody hand is a bloody heart.
The Cenci, Act v. *Sc.* 2.   P. B. SHELLEY.
9

Who, for the poor renown of being smart,
Would leave a sting within a brother's heart?
Love of Fame, Satire II.   DR. E. YOUNG.

Nor peace nor ease the heart can know,
    Which, like the needle true,
Turns at the touch of joy or woe,
    But, turning, trembles too.
A Prayer for Indifference.   MRS. F. M. GREVILLE.

Here the heart
May give a useful lesson to the head,
And Learning wiser grow without his books.
The Task: Winter Walk at Noon.   W. COWPER.

My heart
Is true as steel.
A Midsummer Night's Dream, Act ii. *Sc.* 1.
                              SHAKESPEARE.

HEAVEN.

A heart bestowed on heaven alone.
The Corsair.   LORD BYRON.

If God hath made this world so fair,
    Where sin and death abound,
How beautiful, beyond compare,
    Will Paradise be found !
The Earth Full of God's Goodness.   J. MONTGOMERY.

This world is all a fleeting show,
    For man's illusion given ;
The smiles of joy, the tears of woe,
    Deceitful shine, deceitful flow,—
There 's nothing true but Heaven !
Sacred Songs: The world is all a fleeting show.
                              T. MOORE.

Beyond this vale of tears
    There is a life above,
Unmeasured by the flight of years ;
    And all that life is love.
The Issues of Life and Death.   J. MONTGOMERY.

No, no, I 'm sure,
My restless spirit never could endure
To brood so long upon one luxury,
Unless it did, though fearfully, espy
A hope beyond the shadow of a dream
Endymion, Bk. I.   J. KEATS.

'T is sweet, as year by year we lose
Friends out of sight, in faith to muse
How grows in Paradise our store.
Burial of the Dead.   J. KEBLE.

Nor can his blessèd soul look down from heaven,
Or break the eternal sabbath of his rest.
The Spanish Friar, Act v. Sc. 2.   J. DRYDEN.

Just are the ways of Heaven ; from Heaven proceed
The woes of man ; Heaven doomed the Greeks to bleed.
Odyssey, Bk. VIII.   HOMER. *Trans. of* POPE.

In man's most dark extremity
Oft succor dawns from Heaven.
The Lord of the Isles, Canto I.   SIR W. SCOTT.

The path of sorrow, and that path alone,
Leads to the land where sorrow is unknown.
To an Afflicted Protestant Lady.   W. COWPER.

Here bring your wounded hearts, here tell your anguish—
Earth has no sorrow that Heaven cannot heal.
Sacred Songs : Come, ye Disconsolate. T. MOORE.

HELL.

All hope abandon, ye who enter here.
Inferno, Canto III.   DANTE.

Which way shall I fly,
Infinite wrath, and infinite despair ?
Which way I fly is hell ; myself am hell ;
And, in the lowest deep, a lower deep,
Still threatening to devour me, opens wide,
To which the hell I suffer seems a heaven.
Paradise Lost, Bk. IV.   MILTON.

Long is the way
And hard, that out of hell leads up to light.
Paradise Lost, Bk. II.   MILTON.

Nor from hell
One step no more than from himself can fly
By change of place.
Paradise Lost, Bk. IV.   MILTON.

When all the world dissolves,
And every creature shall be purified,
All places shall be hell that are not heaven.
Faustus.   C. MARLOWE.

HELP.

Heav'n forming each on other to depend,
A master, or a servant, or a friend,
Bids each on other for assistance call,
Till one man's weakness grows the strength of all.
Essay on Man, Epistle II.   A. POPE.

Small service is true service while it lasts :
Of humblest friends, bright creature ! scorn not one :
The daisy, by the shadow that it casts,
Protects the lingering dewdrop from the sun.
In a Child's Album.   W. WORDSWORTH.

What's gone and what's past help
Should be past grief.
The Winter's Tale, Act iii. *Sc.* 2.   SHAKESPEARE.

Help thyself, and God will help thee.
Jaculata Prudentum.   G. HERBERT.

HEROISM.

The hero is the world-man, in whose heart
One passion stands for all, the most indulged.
Festus : Proem.   P. J. BAILEY.

The hero is not fed on sweets,
Daily his own heart he eats ;
Chambers of the great are jails,
And head-winds right for royal sails.
Essays : Heroism.   R. W. EMERSON.

Unbounded courage and compassion joined,
Tempering each other in the victor's mind,
Alternately proclaim him good and great,
And make the hero and the man complete.
The Campaign.   J. ADDISON.

See the conquering hero comes,
Sound the trumpet, beat the drums.
Orations of Joshua.   T. MORELL.

The man that is not moved at what he reads,
That takes not fire at their heroic deeds,
Unworthy of the blessings of the brave,
Is base in kind, and born to be a slave.
Table Talk.   W. COWPER.

HOME.

Domestic happiness, thou only bliss
Of paradise that has survived the fall!
The Task, Bk. III.　　　　　　　　W. COWPER.

The first sure symptom of a mind in health
Is rest of heart, and pleasure felt at home.
Night Thoughts, Night VIII.　　　　DR. E. YOUNG.

To make a happy fireside clime
To weans and wife,
That 's the true pathos and sublime
Of human life.
Epistle to Dr. Blacklock.　　　　　　R. BURNS.

For the whole world, without a native home,
Is nothing but a prison of larger room.
To the Bishop of Lincoln.　　　　　A. COWLEY.

His native home deep imaged in his soul.
Odyssey, Bk. XIII.　　HOMER.　*Trans. of* POPE.

Stay, stay at home, my heart, and rest ;
Home-keeping hearts are happiest,
For those that wander they know not where
Are full of trouble and full of care ;
To stay at home is best.
Song.　　　　　　　H. W. LONGFELLOW.

His home, the spot of earth supremely blest,
A dearer, sweeter spot than all the rest.
West Indies, Pt. III.　　　　J. MONTGOMERY.

At Christmas play, and make good cheer,
For Christmas comes but once a year.
The Farmer's Daily Diet.　　　　T. TUSSER.

He kept no Christmas-house for once a year :
Each day his boards were filled with lordly fare.
A Maiden's Dream.　　　　　R. GREENE.

Alike all ages : dames of ancient days
Have led their children through the mirthful maze ;
And the gay grandsire, skilled in gestic lore,
Has frisked beneath the burden of threescore.
The Traveller.　　　　　O. GOLDSMITH.

Now stir the fire, and close the shutters fast,
Let fall the curtains, wheel the sofa round,
And while the bubbling and loud hissing urn

Throws up a steamy column, and the cups,
That cheer but not inebriate, wait on each,
So let us welcome peaceful evening in.
The Task: Winter Evening, Bk. IV.   W. COWPER.

HOPE.

True hope is swift, and flies with swallow's wings;
Kings it makes gods, and meaner creatures kings.
King Richard III., Act v. *Sc.* 2.   SHAKESPEARE.

Know then, whatever cheerful and serene
Supports the mind, supports the body too:
Hence, the most vital movement mortals feel
Is hope, the balm and lifeblood of the soul.
Art of Preserving Health, Bk. IV.   J. ARMSTRONG.

O welcome, pure-eyed Faith, white-handed Hope,
Thou hovering angel, girt with golden wings!
Comus.   MILTON.

Hope! of all ills that men endure,
    The only cheap and universal cure!
    .   .   .   .   .   .

Hope! thou first-fruits of happiness!
Thou gentle dawning of a bright success!
    .   .   .   .   .   .

Brother of Faith! 'twixt whom and thee
The joys of Heaven and Earth divided be!
For Hope.   A. COWLEY.

Hope! thou nurse of young desire.
Love in a Village, Act i. *Sc.* 1.   I. BICKERSTAFF.

Hope, like a cordial, innocent though strong,
Man's heart at once inspirits and serenes;
Nor makes him pay his wisdom for his joys.
Night Thoughts, Night VII.   DR. E. YOUNG.

Hope, like the glimm'ring taper's light,
    Adorns and cheers the way;
And still, as darker grows the night,
    Emits a brighter ray.
The Captivity, Act ii.   O. GOLDSMITH.

Thy wish was father, Harry, to that thought.
King Henry IV., Pt. II. Act iv *Sc.* 4.   SHAKESPEARE.

Cease. every joy, to glimmer on my mind,
But leave—oh! leave the light of Hope behind!
The Pleasures of Hope, Pt. II.   T. CAMPBELL.

Hope springs eternal in the human breast:
Man never is, but always to be, blest:
The soul, uneasy and confined from home,
Rests and expatiates in a life to come.
Essay on Man, Epistle I.   A. POPE.

The wretch condemned with life to part,
     Still, still on hope relies;
And every pang that rends the heart
     Bids expectation rise.
The Captivity, Act ii.   O. GOLDSMITH.

The miserable have no other medicine,
     But only hope.
Measure for Measure, Act iii. *Sc.* 1.   SHAKESPEARE.

          To hope till hope creates
From its own wreck the thing it contemplates.
Prometheus. Act iv.   P. B. SHELLEY.

HORSEMANSHIP.

I saw young Harry, with his beaver on,
His cuisses on his thighs, gallantly armed,
Rise from the ground like feathered Mercury,
And vaulted with such ease into his seat,
As if an angel dropped down from the clouds,
To turn and wind a fiery Pegasus,
And witch the world with noble horsemanship.
King Henry IV., Pt. I. Act iv. *Sc.* 1.   SHAKESPEARE.

"Stand, Bayard, stand!" The steed obeyed,
With arching neck and bended head,
And glancing eye, and quivering ear,
As if he loved his lord to hear.
No foot Fitz-James in stirrup staid,
No grasp upon the saddle laid,
But wreathed his left hand in the mane,
And lightly bounded from the plain,
Turned on the horse his armèd heel,
And stirred his courage with the steel.
Bounded the fiery steed in air,
The rider sate erect and fair,
Then, like a bolt from steel cross-bow,
Forth launched, along the plain they go.
The Lady of the Lake, Canto V.   SIR W. SCOTT.

After many strains and heaves,
He got up to the saddle eaves,
From whence he vaulted into the seat
With so much vigor, strength, and heat,
That he had almost tumbled over
With his own weight, but did recover,
By laying hold of tail and mane,
Which oft he used instead of rein.
Hudibras.   S. BUTLER.

HOSPITALITY.

You must come home with me and be my guest ;
You will give joy to me, and I will do
All that is in my power to honor you.
Hymn to Mercury.   P. B. SHELLEY.

Sir, you are very welcome to our house :
It must appear in other ways than words,
Therefore I scant this breathing courtesy.
Merchant of Venice, Act v. Sc. 1.   SHAKESPEARE.

So saying, with despatchful looks in haste
She turns, on hospitable thoughts intent.
Paradise Lost, Bk. V.   MILTON.

This night I hold an old accustomed feast,
Whereto I have invited many a guest,
Such as I love ; and you among the store,
One more, most welcome, makes my number more.
Romeo and Juliet, Act i. Sc. 2.   SHAKESPEARE.

The atmosphere
Breathes rest and comfort and the many chambers
Seem full of welcomes.
Masque of Pandora.   H. W. LONGFELLOW.

Small cheer and great welcome makes a merry feast.
Comedy of Errors, Act iii. Sc. 1.   SHAKESPEARE.

Oh, better no doubt is a dinner of herbs,
When seasoned by love, which no rancor disturbs
And sweetened by all that is sweetest in life
Than turbot, bisque, ortolans, eaten in strife !
Lucile.   LORD LYTTON (*Owen Meredith*).

Now good digestion wait on appetite,
And health on both !
Macbeth, Act iii. Sc. 4.   SHAKESPEARE.

I 've often wished that I had clear,
For life, six hundred pounds a year,
A handsome house to lodge a friend,
A river at my garden's end.
Imitation of Horace, Bk. II. Sat. 6.   J. SWIFT.

True friendship's laws are by this rule exprest,
Welcome the coming, speed the parting guest.
Odyssey, Bk. XV.   HOMER. *Trans. of* POPE.

HUMILITY.

Humility, that low, sweet root,
From which all heavenly virtues shoot.
Loves of the Angels: The Third Angel's Story.
T. MOORE.

Content thyself to be obscurely good.
When vice prevails, and impious men bear sway,
The post of honor is a private station.
Cato, Act iv. Sc. 4.   J. ADDISON.

In a bondman's key,
With 'bated breath, and whisp'ring humbleness.
Merchant of Venice, Act i. Sc. 3.   SHAKESPEARE.

It is the witness still of excellency
To put a strange face on his own perfection.
Much Ado About Nothing, Act ii. Sc. 3. SHAKESPEARE.

God hath sworn to lift on high
Who sinks himself by true humility.
Miscellaneous Poems: At Hooker's Tomb.   J. KEBLE.

HUNTING.

Soon as Aurora drives away the night,
And edges eastern clouds with rosy light,
The healthy huntsman, with the cheerful horn,
Summons the dogs, and greets the dappled morn.
Rural Sports, Canto II.   J. GAY.

Together let us beat this ample field,
Try what the open, what the covert yield.
Essay on Man, Epistle I.   A. POPE.

My hoarse-sounding horn
Invites thee to the chase, the sport of kings ;
Image of war without its guilt.
The Chase.   W. C. SOMERVILLE.

Contusion hazarding of neck or spine,
Which rural gentlemen call sport divine.
Needless Alarm.   W. COWPER.

My hawk is tired of perch and hood,
My idle greyhound loathes his food,
My horse is weary of his stall,
And I am sick of captive thrall.
I wish I were as I have been
Hunting the hart in forests green,
With bended bow and bloodhound free,
For that 's the life is meet for me !
The Lady of the Lake : Lay of the Imprisoned Huntsman,
Canto VI.   SIR W. SCOTT.

Oh ! what delight can a mortal lack,
When he once is firm on his horse's back,
With his stirrups short, and his snaffle strong,
And the blast of the horn for his morning song !
The Hunter's Song.   B. W. PROCTER (*Barry Cornwall*).

See from the brake the whirring pheasant springs,
And mounts exulting on triumphant wings ;
Short is his joy ; he feels the fiery wound,
Flutters in blood, and panting beats the ground.
Windsor Forest.   A. POPE.

But as some muskets so contrive it,
As oft to miss the mark they drive at,
And though well aimed at duck or plover,
Bear wide, and kick their owners over.
McFingal, Canto I.   J. TRUMBULL.

HYPOCRISY.

Oh, for a *forty-parson power* to chant
   Thy praise, Hypocrisy ! Oh, for a hymn
Loud as the virtues thou dost loudly vaunt,
   Not practise !
Don Juan, Canto X.   LORD BYRON.

For neither man nor angel can discern
Hypocrisy, the only evil that walks
Invisible, except to God alone,
By his permissive will, through heaven and earth.
Paradise Lost, Bk. III.   MILTON.

Away, and mock the time with fairest show ;
False face must hide what the false heart doth know.
Macbeth, Act i. *Sc.* 7.   SHAKESPEARE.

O serpent heart, hid with a flowering face !
Did ever a dragon keep so fair a cave ?
Romeo and Juliet, Act iii. *Sc.* 2.   SHAKESPEARE.

Dissembling courtesy !   How fine this tyrant
Can tickle where she wounds !
Cymbeline, Act i. *Sc.* 1.   SHAKESPEARE.

She that asks
Her dear five hundred friends, contemns them all,
And hates their coming.
The Task, Bk. II.   W. COWPER.

He seemed
For dignity composed and high exploit :
But all was false and hollow.
Paradise Lost, Bk. II.   MILTON.

He was a man
Who stole the livery of the court of Heaven
To serve the Devil in.
Course of Time, Bk. VIII.   R. POLLOK.

The Devil can cite Scripture for his purpose.
An evil soul, producing holy witness,
Is like a villain with a smiling cheek,
A goodly apple rotten at the heart.
O, what a goodly outside falsehood hath !
Merchant of Venice, Act i. *Sc.* 3.   SHAKESPEARE.

But then I sigh, and with a piece of Scripture
Tell them that God bids us do good for evil :
And thus I clothe my naked villany
With odd old ends stol'n forth of holy writ,
And seem a saint when most I play the devil.
King Richard III., Act i. *Sc.* 3.   SHAKESPEARE.

O villain, villain, smiling damnèd villain !
My tables,—meet it is I set it down,
That one may smile, and smile, and be a villain.
Hamlet, Act i. *Sc.* 5.   SHAKESPEARE.

That practised falsehood under saintly shew,
Deep malice to conceal, couched with revenge.
Paradise Lost, Bk. IV.   MILTON.

Built God a church, and laughed his word to scorn.
Retirement.   W. COWPER.

And the devil did grin, for his darling sin
Is pride that apes humility.
The Devil's Thoughts.   S. T. COLERIDGE.

O, what may man within him hide,
Though angel on the outward side !
Measure for Measure, Act iii. *Sc.* 2.   SHAKESPEARE.

'T is too much proved—that with devotion's visage
And pious action we do sugar o'er
The devil himself.
Hamlet, Act iii. *Sc.* 1.　　　　　SHAKESPEARE.

I waive the quantum o' the sin,
　　The hazard of concealing ;
But, och ! it hardens a' within,
　　And petrifies the feeling.
Epistle to a Young Friend.　　　　　R. BURNS.

IDLENESS.

'T is the voice of the sluggard ; I heard him complain,
" You have waked me too soon, I must slumber again."
The Sluggard.　　　　　DR. I. WATTS.

Sloth views the towers of fame with envious eyes,
　　Desirous still, still impotent to rise.
The Judgment of Hercules.　　　　　W. SHENSTONE.

Their only labor was to kill the time
(And labor dire it is, and weary woe);
They sit, they loll, turn o'er some idle rhyme ;
Then, rising sudden, to the glass they go,
Or saunter forth, with tottering step and slow :
This soon too rude an exercise they find ;
Straight on the couch their limbs again they throw,
Where hours on hours they sighing lie reclined,
And court the vapory god, soft breathing in the wind.
The Castle of Indolence, Canto I.　　　J. THOMSON.

Leisure is pain ; take off our chariot wheels,
How heavily we drag the load of life !
Blest leisure is our curse ; like that of Cain,
It makes us wander, wander earth around
　　To fly that tyrant, thought.
Night Thoughts, Night II.　　　　　DR. E. YOUNG.

To sigh, yet feel no pain,
　　To weep, yet scarce know why ;
To sport an hour with Beauty's chain,
　　Then throw it idly by.
The Blue Stocking.　　　　　T. MOORE.

The keenest pangs the wretched find
　　Are rapture to the dreary void,
The leafless desert of the mind,
　　The waste of feelings unemployed.
The Giaour.　　　　　LORD BYRON.

A lazy lolling sort,
Unseen at church, at senate, or at court,
Of ever-listless idlers, that attend
No cause, no trust, no duty, and no friend.
There too, my Paridell ! she marked thee there,
Stretched on the rack of a too easy chair,
And heard thy everlasting yawn confess
The pains and penalties of idleness.
The Dunciad, Bk. IV.   A. POPE.

An idler is a watch that wants both hands ;
As useless if it goes as if it stands.
Retirement.   W. COWPER.

There is no remedy for time misspent ;
No healing for the waste of idleness,
Whose very languor is a punishment
Heavier than active souls can feel or guess.
Sonnet.   SIR A. DE VERE.

For Satan finds some mischief still
      For idle hands to do.
Song XX.   DR. I. WATTS.

ILLNESS.

As man, perhaps, the moment of his breath,
Receives the lurking principle of death,
The young disease, that must subdue at length,
Grows with his growth, and strengthens with his strength.
Essay on Man, Epistle II.   A. POPE.

Diseases desperate grown
By desperate appliance are relieved,
      Or not at all.
Hamlet, Act iv. Sc. 3.   SHAKESPEARE.

So when a raging fever burns,
We shift from side to side by turns,
And 't is a poor relief we gain
To change the place, but keep the pain.
Hymns and Spiritual Songs, Bk. II. Hymn 146.
                              DR. I. WATTS.

Long pains are light ones,
Cruel ones are brief !
Compensation.   J. G. SAXE.

Then with no throbs of fiery pain,
No cold gradations of decay,
Death broke at once the vital chain,
And freed his soul the nearest way.
Verses on Robert Levet.   DR. S. JOHNSON.

IMAGINATION.

Within the soul a faculty abides,
That with interpositions, which would hide
And darken, so can deal that they become
Contingencies of pomp ; and serve to exalt
Her native brightness.   As the ample moon,
In the deep stillness of a summer even
Rising behind a thick and lofty grove,
Burns, like an unconsuming fire of light,
In the green trees ; and, kindling on all sides
Their leafy umbrage, turns the dusky veil
Into a substance glorious as her own.
The Excursion, Bk. IV.   W. WORDSWORTH.

O for a muse of fire, that would ascend
The brightest heaven of invention !
King Henry V., Chorus.   SHAKESPEARE.

Hark, his hands the lyre explore !
Bright eyed Fancy, hovering o'er,
Scatters from her pictured urn
Thoughts that breathe and words that burn.
Progress of Poesy.   T. GRAY.

One of those passing rainbow dreams
Half light, half shade, which Fancy's beams
Paint on the fleeting mists that roll,
In trance or slumber, round the soul.
Lalla Rookh.   T. MOORE.

Of its own beauty is the mind diseased,
And fevers into false creation :—where,
Where are the forms the sculptor's soul hath seized ?
In him alone.   Can Nature show so fair ?
Where are the charms and virtues which we dare
Conceive in boyhood and pursue as men,
The unreached Paradise of our despair,
Which o'er-informs the pencil and the pen,
And overpowers the page where it would bloom again ?
Childe Harold, Canto IV.   LORD BYRON.

We figure to ourselves
The thing we like, and then we build it up
As chance will have it, on the rock or sand ;
For thought is tired of wandering o'er the world,
And home-bound Fancy runs her bark ashore.
Philip Van Artevelde, Pt. I. Act i. Sc. 5.   SIR H. TAYLOR.

HAMLET. My father,—methinks I see my father.
HORATIO. Oh! where, my lord!
HAMLET. In my mind's eye, Horatio.
Hamlet, Act i. *Sc.* 2.   SHAKESPEARE.

Presentiment is that long shadow on the lawn
Indicative that suns go down ;
The notice to the startled grass
That darkness is about to pass.
Poems.   E. DICKINSON.

IMMORTALITY.

To be no more—sad cure ; for who would lose,
Though full of pain, this intellectual being.
Those thoughts that wander through eternity,
To perish rather, swallowed up and lost
In the wide womb of uncreated night,
Devoid of sense and motion?
Paradise Lost, Bk. II.   MILTON.

Death is delightful. Death is dawn,
The waking from a weary night
Of fevers unto truth and light.
Even So.   J. MILLER.

No, no! The energy of life may be
Kept on after the grave, but not begun ;
And he who flagged not in the earthly strife,
From strength to strength advancing—only he,
His soul well-knit, and all his battles won,
Mounts, and that hardly, to eternal life.
Immortality.   M. ARNOLD.

God keeps a niche
In Heaven, to hold our idols ; and albeit
He brake them to our faces, and denied
That our close kisses should impair their white,—
I know we shall behold them raised, complete,
The dust swept from their beauty, glorified,
New Memnons singing in the great God-light.
Futurity with the Departed.   E. B. BROWNING.

The wisest men are glad to die ; no fear
Of death can touch a true philosopher.
Death sets the soul at liberty to fly.
Continuation of Lucan.   T. MAY.

Alas! for love, if thou art all,
And naught beyond, O Earth!
The Graves of a Household.   MRS. F. HEMANS.

'T is not the whole of life to live :
  Nor all of death to die.
The Issues of Life and Death.   J. MONTGOMERY.

  Since heaven's eternal year is thine.
Elegy on Mrs. Killegrew.   J. DRYDEN.

INCONSTANCY.

Look, as I blow this feather from my face,
And as the air blows it to me again,
Obeying with my wind when I do blow,
And yielding to another when it blows,
Commanded always by the greater gust :
Such is the lightness of you common men.
King Henry VI., Pt. III. Act iii. *Sc.* 1.   SHAKESPEARE.

  Sigh no more, ladies, sigh no more,
    Men were deceivers ever ;
  One foot in sea and one on shore ;
    To one thing constant never.
Much Ado about Nothing, Act ii. *Sc.* 3.   SHAKESPEARE.

  There is no music in a voice
    That is but one, and still the same ;
  Inconstancy is but a name
    To fright poor lovers from a better choice.
Shepherd's Holiday.   J. RUTTER.

  The fraud of men was ever so
  Since summer first was leafy.
Much Ado about Nothing, Act ii. *Sc.* 3.   SHAKESPEARE.

          Love ne'er should die ; . . .
  One object lost, another should succeed ;
    And all our life be love.
Pastorals.   T. BROWN.

  There are three things a wise man will not trust :
  The wind, the sunshine of an April day,
    And woman's plighted faith.
Madoc.   R. SOUTHEY.

  Who trusts himself to woman or to waves
  Should never hazard what he fears to lose.
Governor of Cyprus.   J. OLDMIXON.

  Away, away—you 're all the same,
    A fluttering, smiling, jilting throng !
  O, by my soul, I burn with shame,
    To think I 've been your slave so long !
Song.   T. MOORE.

> Frailty, thy name is woman !

Hamlet, Act i. *Sc.* 2.　　　　SHAKESPEARE.

> HAMLET.—Is this a prologue, or the posy of a ring?
> OPHELIA.—'T is brief, my lord.
> HAMLET.—As woman's love.

Hamlet, Act iii. *Sc.* 2.　　　　SHAKESPEARE.

> Framed to make women false.

Othello, Act i. *Sc.* 3.　　　　SHAKESPEARE.

> To beguile many, and be beguiled by one.

Othello, Act iv. *Sc.* 1.　　　　SHAKESPEARE.

> Or ere those shoes were old
> With which she followed my poor father's body,
> Like Niobe, all tears ;—why she, even she
> (O God ! a beast that wants discourse of reason
> Would have mourned longer) married with my uncle,
> My father's brother.

Hamlet, Act i. *Sc.* 2.　　　　SHAKESPEARE.

> Trust not a man : we are by nature false,
> Dissembling, subtle, cruel and inconstant ;
> When a man talks of love, with caution hear him ;
> But if he swears, he 'll certainly deceive thee.

The Orphan.　　　　T. OTWAY.

> Nay, women are frail too ;
> Ay, as the glasses where they view themselves ;
> Which are as easy broke as they make forms.

Measure for Measure, Act ii. *Sc.* 4.　　　　SHAKESPEARE.

> In part to blame is she,
> Which hath without consent bin only tride :
> He comes too neere that comes to be denide.

A Wife.　　　　SIR T. OVERBURY.

> The heart !—Yes, I wore it
> As sign and as token
> Of a love that once gave it,
> A vow that was spoken ;
> But a love, and a vow, and a heart,
> Can be broken.

Hearts.　　　　A. A. PROCTER.

> A love that took an early root,
> And had an early doom.

The Devil's Progress.　　　　T. K. HERVEY.

10

Or as one nail by strength drives out another,
So the remembrance of my former love
Is by a newer object quite forgotten.
Two Gentlemen of Verona, Act ii. *Sc.* 4.   SHAKESPEARE.

All love may be expelled by other love,
As poisons are by poisons.
All for Love.   J. DRYDEN.

At lovers' perjuries,
They say, Jove laughs.
Romeo and Juliet, Act ii. *Sc.* 2.   SHAKESPEARE.

Fool, not to know that love endures no tie,
And Jove but laughs at lovers' perjury.
Palamon and Arcite, Bk. II.   J. DRYDEN.

They that do change old love for new,
Pray gods, they change for worse !
The Arraignment of Paris: Cupid's Curse.   G. PEELE.

O, swear not by the moon, the inconstant moon,
That monthly changes in her circled orb,
Lest that thy love prove likewise variable.
Romeo and Juliet, Act ii. *Sc.* 2.   SHAKESPEARE.

To be once in doubt,
Is once to be resolved.
Othello, Act iii. *Sc.* 3.   SHAKESPEARE.

INGRATITUDE.

I hate ingratitude more in a man,
Than lying, vainness, babbling, drunkenness,
Or any taint of vice.
Twelfth Night, Act iii. *Sc.* 4.   SHAKESPEARE.

He that's ungrateful, has no guilt but one ;
All other crimes may pass for virtues in him.
Busiris.   DR. E. YOUNG.

Ah, how unjust to Nature and himself
Is thoughtless, thankless, inconsistent man !
Night Thoughts, Night II.   DR. E. YOUNG.

How sharper than a serpent's tooth it is
To have a thankless child !
King Lear, Act i. *Sc.* 4.   SHAKESPEARE.

INN.

Shall I not take mine ease in mine inn ?
Henry IV., Pt. I. Act iii. *Sc.* 3.   SHAKESPEARE.

Now musing o'er the changing scene
Farmers behind the tavern screen
Collect ; with elbows idly pressed
On hob, reclines the corner's guest,
Reading the news to mark again
The bankrupt lists or price of grain.
Puffing the while his red-tipt pipe
He dreams o'er troubles nearly ripe,
Yet, winter's leisure to regale,
Hopes better times, and sips his ale.
The Shepherd's Calendar.   J. CLARE.

Souls of poets dead and gone,
What Elysium have ye known,
Happy field or mossy cavern,
Choicer than the Mermaid Tavern ?
Lines on the Mermaid Tavern.   J. KEATS.

Now spurs the lated traveller apace
To gain the timely inn.
Macbeth, Act iii. *Sc.* 3.   SHAKESPEARE.

Whoe'er has travelled life's dull round,
Where'er his stages may have been,
May sigh to think he still has found
The warmest welcome at an inn.
Written on a Window of an Inn.   W. SHENSTONE.

INNOCENCE.

Hence, bashful cunning !
And prompt me, plain and holy innocence !
Tempest, Act iii. *Sc.* 1.   SHAKESPEARE.

O, white innocence,
That thou shouldst wear the mask of guilt to hide
Thine awful and serenest countenance
From those who know thee not !
The Cenci, Act v. *Sc.* 3.   P. B. SHELLEY.

I never tempted her with word too large ;
But, as a brother to his sister, showed
Bashful sincerity, and comely love.
Much Ado about Nothing, Act iv. *Sc.* 1.   SHAKESPEARE.

And dallies with the innocence of love.
Twelfth Night, Act ii. *Sc.* 4.   SHAKESPEARE.

Zealous, yet modest ; innocent, though free ;
Patient of toil ; serene amidst alarms ;
Inflexible in faith ; invincible in arms.
The Minstrel, Bk. I.   J. BEATTIE.

True, conscious honor is to feel no sin ;
He 's armed without that 's innocent within.
Imitation of Horace, Epistle I. Bk. I.   A. POPE.

INSECTS.

My banks they are furnished with bees,
Whose murmur invites one to sleep.
A Pastoral Ballad, Pt. II.   W. SHENSTONE.

Here their delicious task the fervent bees,
In swarming millions tend : around, athwart,
Through the soft air, the busy nations fly,
Cling to the bud, and with inserted tube,
Suck its pure essence, its ethereal soul ;
And oft, with bolder wing, they soaring dare
The purple heath, or where the wild thyme grows,
And yellow load them with the luscious spoil.
The Seasons : Spring.   J. THOMSON.

Inebriate of air am I,
And debauchee of dew,
Reeling, through endless summer days,
From inns of molten blue.
Poems.   E. DICKINSON.

O'er folded blooms
On swirls of musk,
The beetle booms adown the glooms
And bumps along the dusk.
The Beetle.   J. W. RILEY.

I 'd be a butterfly, born in a bower,
Where roses and lilies and violets meet.
I 'd be a Butterfly.   T. H. BAYLY.

Rose suddenly a swarm of butterflies,
On wings of white and gold and azure fire ;
And one said ; " These are flowers that seek the skies,
Loosed by the spell of their supreme desire.
Butterflies.   C. G. D. ROBERTS.

So, naturalists observe, a flea
Has smaller fleas that on him prey ;
And these have smaller still to bite 'em ;
And so proceed *ad infinitum.*
Poetry : a Rhapsody.   J. SWIFT.

I saw a flie within a beade
Of amber cleanly buried.
On a Fly buried in Amber.   R. HERRICK.

Oh! that the memories which survive us here
Were half so lovely as these wings of thine!
Pure relics of a blameless life, that shine
Now thou art gone.
On Finding a Fly Crushed in a Book.   C. T. TURNER.

When evening closes Nature's eye,
   The glow-worm lights her little spark
To captivate her favorite fly
   And tempt the rover through the dark.
The Glow-worm.   J. MONTGOMERY.

Ye living lamps, by whose dear light
   The nightingale does sit so late;
And studying all the summer night,
   Her matchless songs does meditate.
The Mower to the Glow-worm.   A. MARVEL.

Where the katydid works her chromatic reed on the wal
   nut-tree over the well.
Leaves of Grass, Pt. XXXVIII.   W. WHITMAN.

What gained we, little moth? Thy ashes,
   Thy one brief parting pang may show:
And withering thoughts for soul that dashes,
   From deep to deep, are but a death more slow.
Tragedy of the Night-Moth.   T. CARLYLE.

The spider's touch, how exquisitely fine!
Feels at each thread, and lives along the line.
Essay on Man, Epistle I.   A. POPE.

Much like a subtle spider, which doth sit
   In middle of her web, which spreadeth wide:
If aught do touch the utmost thread of it,
   She feels it instantly on every side.
Immortality of the Soul: Feeling.   SIR J. DAVIES.

INSTRUCTION.

'T is education forms the common mind;
   Just as the twig is bent the tree 's inclined.
Moral Essays, Epistle I.   A. POPE.

Men must be taught as if you taught them not,
And things unknown proposed as things forgot.
Essay on Criticism.   A. POPE.

Most wretched men
Are cradled into poetry by wrong;
They learn in suffering what they teach in song.
Julian and Maddalo.   P. B. SHELLEY.

INVENTION.

Soon shall thy arm, unconquered steam ! afar
Drag the slow barge, or drive the rapid car ;
Or on wide waving wings expanded bear
The flying-chariot through the field of air.
The Botanic Garden, Pt. I. Ch. I. [1781].   E. DARWIN.

Electric telegraphs, printing, gas,
  Tobacco, balloons, and steam,
Are little events that have come to pass
  Since the days of the old *régime.*
And, spite of Lemprière's dazzling page,
  I 'd give—though it might seem bold—
A hundred years of the Golden Age
  For a year of the Age of Gold.
The Two Ages.   H. S. LEIGH.

What cannot art and industry perform,
  When science plans the progress of their toil!
The Minstrel.   J. BEATTIE.

For out of the old fieldès, as men saithe,
Cometh al this new corne fro yere to yere,
And out of old bookès, in good faithe,
Cometh al this new science that men lere.
The Assembly of Foules.   CHAUCER.

JEALOUSY.

O, beware, my lord, of jealousy ;
It is the green-eyed monster which doth mock
The meat it feeds on. . . .
But, O, what damnèd minutes tells he o'er
Who dotes, yet doubts, suspects, yet strongly loves !
Othello, Act iii. *Sc.* 3.   SHAKESPEARE.

Trifles, light as air,
Are to the jealous confirmations strong
As proofs of holy writ.
Othello, Act iii. *Sc.* 3.   SHAKESPEARE.

With groundless fear he thus his soul deceives :
What phrenzy dictates, jealousy believes.
Diome.   J. GAY.

Nor jealousy
Was understood, the injured lover's hell.
Paradise Lost, Bk. V.   MILTON.

Good heaven, the souls of all my tribe defend
From jealousy !
Othello, Act iii. *Sc.* 3.   SHAKESPEARE.

O jealousy,
Thou ugliest fiend of hell ! thy deadly venom
Preys on my vitals, turns the healthful hue
Of my fresh cheek to haggard sallowness,
And drinks my spirit up !
David and Goliath.   H. MORE.

If I shall be condemned
Upon surmises, all proofs sleeping else
But what your jealousies awake, I tell you,
'T is rigor, and not law.
Winter's Tale, Act iii. *Sc.* 2.   SHAKESPEARE.

Though I perchance am vicious in my guess,
As, I confess, it is my nature's plague
To spy into abuses, and oft my jealousy
Shapes faults that are not.
Othello, Act iii. *Sc.* 3.   SHAKESPEARE.

But through the heart
Should Jealousy its venom once diffuse,
'T is then delightful misery no more,
But agony unmixed, incessant gall,
Corroding every thought, and blasting all
Love's paradise.
The Seasons : Spring.   J. THOMSON.

JESUS CHRIST.

Brightest and best of the sons of the morning !
Dawn on our darkness, and lend us thine aid.
Epiphany.   BISHOP R. HEBER.

He was the Word, that spake it ;
He took the bread and brake it ;
And what that Word did make it,
I do believe and take it.
Divine Poems : On the Sacrament.   DR. J. DONNE.

And so the Word had breath, and wrought
With human hands the creed of creeds
In loveliness of perfect deeds,
More strong than all poetic thought.
In Memoriam, XXXVI.   A. TENNYSON.

Some say, that ever 'gainst that season comes
Wherein our Saviour's birth is celebrated,
The bird of dawning singeth all night long :
And then, they say, no spirit dare stir abroad ;
The nights are wholesome ; then no planets strike,
No fairy takes, nor witch hath power to charm,
So hallowed and so gracious is the time.
Hamlet, Act i. *Sc.* 1.   SHAKESPEARE.

In those holy fields,
Over whose acres walked those blessèd feet
Which fourteen hundred years ago were nailed,
For our advantage, on the bitter cross.
Henry IV., Pt. I. Act i. *Sc.* 1.   SHAKESPEARE.

Lovely was the death
Of Him whose life was Love ! Holy with power,
He on the thought-benighted Skeptic beamed
Manifest Godhead.
Religious Musings.   S. T. COLERIDGE.

But chiefly Thou
Whom soft-eyed Pity once led down from Heaven
To bleed for man, to teach him how to live,
And, oh ! still harder lesson ! how to die.
Death.   B. PORTEUS.

One there is above all others,
    Well deserves the name of Friend !
His is love beyond a brother's,
    Costly, free, and knows no end :
They who once his kindness prove,
Find it everlasting love !
A Friend that Sticketh Closer than a Brother.
          J. NEWTON.

'T is done, the great transaction 's done ;
    I am my Lord's, and he is mine ;
He drew me, and I followed on,
    Charmed to confess the voice divine.

Now rest, my long-divided heart !
    Fixed on this blissful centre, rest ;
Oh, who with earth would grudge to part,
    When called with angels to be blest ?
Happy Day.   P. DODDRIDGE.

Our Friend, our Brother, and our Lord,
    What may thy service be ?—
Nor name, nor form, nor ritual word,
    But simply following thee.

We bring no ghastly holocaust,
  We pile no graven stone ;
He serves thee best who loveth most
  His brothers and thy own.
Our Master.   J. G. WHITTIER.

JEWEL.

These gems have life in them : their colors speak,
  Say what words fail of.
The Spanish Gypsy.   GEORGE ELIOT.

If that a pearl may in a toad's head dwell,
  And may be found too in an oyster shell.
Apology for his Book.   J. BUNYAN.

Some asked how pearls did grow, and where,
  Then spoke I to my girle,
To part her lips, and showed them there
  The quarelets of pearl.
The Rock of Rubies and the Quarrie of Pearl.
                  R. HERRICK.

The lively Diamond drinks thy purest rays,
  Collected light, compact.
The Seasons : Summer.   J. THOMSON.

Like stones of worth, they thinly placèd are,
  Or captain jewels in the carcanet.
Sonnet III.   SHAKESPEARE.

Than all Bocara's vaunted gold,
  Than all the gems of Samarcand.
A Persian Song of Hafiz.   SIR W. JONES.

Rich and rare were the gems she wore,
  And a bright gold ring on her wand she bore.
Song : Rich and Rare.   T. MOORE.

    I see the jewel best enamelled
Will lose his beauty ; and the gold 'bides still,
That others touch, and often touching will
  Wear gold.
Comedy of Errors, Act ii. *Sc.* 1.   SHAKESPEARE.

JOURNALISM.

He comes, the herald of a noisy world,
With spattered boots, strapped waist, and frozen locks ;
News from all nations lumbering at his back.
The Task, Bk. IV.   W. COWPER.

Trade hardly deems the busy day begun
Till his keen eye along the sheet has run ;
The blooming daughter throws her needle by,
And reads her schoolmate's marriage with a sigh ;
While the grave mother puts her glasses on,
And gives a tear to some old crony gone.
The preacher, too, his Sunday theme lays down,
To know what last new folly fills the town ;
Lively or sad, life's meanest, mightiest things,
The fate of fighting cocks, or fighting kings.
Curiosity.   C. SPRAGUE.

For evil news rides fast, while good news baits.
Samson Agonistes.   MILTON.

If there 's a hole in a' your coats,
    I rede ye tent it :
A chiel 's amang ye takin' notes,
    And, faith, he 'll prent it.
On Capt. Grose's Perigrinations Through Scotland.
                                            R. BURNS.

A would-be satirist, a hired buffoon,
A monthly scribbler of some low lampoon,
Condemned to drudge, the meanest of the mean,
And furbish falsehoods for a magazine.
English Bards and Scotch Reviewers.   LORD BYRON.

To serve thy generation, this thy fate :
" Written in water," swiftly fades thy name ;
But he who loves his kind does, first and late,
A work too great for fame.
The Journalist.   MRS. M. CLEMMER A. HUDSON.

This folio of four pages, happy work !
Which not e'en critics criticise ; that holds
Inquisitive attention while I read,

    .   .   .   .   .

What is it but a map of busy life,
Its fluctuations and its vast concerns ?
'T is pleasant, through the loop-holes of retreat,
To peep at such a world,—to see the stir
Of the great Babel, and not feel the crowd.

    .   .   .   .   .

While fancy, like the finger of a clock,
Runs the great circuit, and is still at home.
Winter Evening : The Task, Bk. IV.   W. COWPER.

Here shall the Press the People's right maintain,
Unawed by influence and unbribed by gain ;
Here Patriot Truth her glorious precepts draw,
Pledged to Religion, Liberty, and Law.
Motto of Salem (Mass.) Register.　　　　J. STORY.

JOY.

What though my wingèd hours of bliss have been,
Like angel-visits, few and far between.
Pleasures of Hope, Pt. II.　　　　T. CAMBPELL.

How fading are the joys we dote upon !
Like apparitions seen and gone ;
But those which soonest take their flight
Are the most exquisite and strong ;
Like angels' visits, short and bright,
Mortality's too weak to bear them long.
The Parting.　　　　J. NORRIS.

And these are joys, like beauty, but skin deep.
Festus, Sc. A Village Feast.　　　　P. J. BAILEY.

Joys too exquisite to last,
And yet more exquisite when past.
The Little Cloud.　　　　J. MONTGOMERY.

The joy late coming late departs.
Some Sweet Day.　　　　L. J. BATES.

There's not a joy the world can give like that it takes away.
Song : There's Not a Joy.　　　　LORD BYRON.

Base Envy withers at another's joy,
And hates that excellence it cannot reach.
The Seasons : Spring.　　　　J. THOMSON.

How sweet a thing it is to wear a crown ;
Within whose circuit is Elysium
And all that poets feign of bliss and joy.
King Henry VI., Pt. III. Act i. Sc. 2.　　SHAKESPEARE.

Sorrows remembered sweeten present joy.
The Course of Time, Bk. I.　　　　R. POLLOK.

O stay !—O stay !—
Joy so seldom weaves a chain
Like this to-night, that, oh ! 't is pain
To break its links so soon.
Fly Not Yet.　　　　T. MOORE.

KISS.

What is a kiss? Alacke ! at worst,
A single Dropp to quenche a Thirst,
Tho' oft it prooves, in happie Hour,
The first swete Dropp of our long Showre.
In the Old Time.   C. G. LELAND.

I was betrothed that day ;
I wore a troth kiss on my lips I could not give away.
The Lay of the Brown Rosary, Pt. II. E. B. BROWNING.

The kiss you take is paid by that you give :
The joy is mutual, and I 'm still in debt.
Heroic Love, Act v. Sc. 1.
                                 LORD LANDSDOWNE.

Give me a kisse, and to that kisse a score ;
Then to that twenty adde a hundred more ;
A thousand to that hundred ; so kisse on,
To make that thousand up a million ;
Treble that million, and when that is done,
Let 's kisse afresh, as when we first begun.
Hesperides to Anthea.   R. HERRICK.

Blush, happy maiden, when you feel
The lips which press love's glowing seal ;
But as the slow years darklier roll,
Grown wiser, the experienced soul
Will own as dearer far than they
The lips which kiss the tears away.
Kisses.   E. AKERS.

Teach not thy lips such scorn : for they were made
For kissing, lady, not for such contempt.
Richard III., Act i. Sc. 2.   SHAKESPEARE.

My lips till then had only known
    The kiss of mother and of sister,
But somehow, full upon her own
    Sweet, rosy, darling mouth,—I kissed her.
The Door-Step.   E. C. STEDMAN.

As in the soft and sweet eclipse,
When soul meets soul on lover's lips.
Prometheus Unbound, Act iv.   P. B. SHELLEY.

O Love ! O fire ! once he drew
With one long kiss my whole soul through
My lips, as sunlight drinketh dew.
Fatima.   A. TENNYSON.

A long, long kiss, a kiss of youth and love.
Don Juan, Canto II.   LORD BYRON.

Was this the face that launched a thousand ships,
And burnt the topless towers of Ilium ?
Sweet Helen, make me immortal with a kiss.—
Her lips suck forth my soul ; see, where it flies !—
Faustus.   C. MARLOWE.

I love the sex, and sometimes would reverse
   The tyrant's wish, " that mankind only had
One neck, which he with one fell stroke might pierce ; "
   My wish is quite as wide, but not so bad,
And much more tender on the whole than fierce ;
   It being (not *now*, but only while a lad)
That womankind had but one rosy mouth,
To kiss them all at once, from North to South.
Don Juan, Canto VI.   LORD BYRON.

                        Or ere I could
Give him that parting kiss, which I had set
Betwixt two charming words, comes in my father
And like the tyrannous breathing of the north
Shakes all our buds from growing.
Cymbeline, Act i. *Sc.* 3.   SHAKESPEARE.

              Eyes, look your last :
Arms, take your last embrace ; and lips,
                    O ! you,
The doors of breath, seal with a righteous kiss
A dateless bargain to engrossing death.
Romeo and Juliet, Act v. *Sc.* 3.   SHAKESPEARE.

KNOWLEDGE.

Knowledge is proud that he has learned so much ;
Wisdom is humble that he knows no more.
The Task, Bk. VI.   W. COWPER.

All things I thought I knew ; but now confess
The more I know I know, I know the less.
Works, Bk. VI.   J. OWEN.

In vain sedate reflections we would make
When half our knowledge we must snatch, not take.
Moral Essays, Epistle I.   A. POPE.

LABOR.

No man is born into the world whose work
Is not born with him.
A Glance Behind the Curtain.   J. R. LOWELL.

If little labor, little are our gaines :
Man's fortunes are according to his paines.
Hesperides : No Paines, No Gaines.　　R. HERRICK.

Who first invented work, and bound the free
And holiday-rejoicing spirit down

To that dry drudgery at the desk's dead wood ?

Sabbathless Satan !
Work.　　C. LAMB.

It was not by vile loitering in ease
That Greece obtained the brighter palm of art,
That soft yet ardent Athens learnt to please,
To keen the wit, and to sublime the heart,
In all supreme ! complete in every part !
It was not thence majestic Rome arose,
And o'er the nations shook her conquering dart :
For sluggard's brow the laurel never grows ;
Renown is not the child of indolent repose.

Toil, and be glad ! let Industry inspire
Into your quickened limbs her buoyant breath !
Who does not act is dead ; absorpt entire
In miry sloth, no pride, no joy he hath :
O leaden-hearted men to be in love with death !
The Castle of Indolence, Canto II.　　J. THOMSON.

My nature is subdued
To what it works in, like the dyer's hand.
Sonnet CXI.　　SHAKESPEARE.

Mechanic slaves
With greasy aprons, rules, and hammers.
Antony and Cleopatra, Act v. *Sc.* 2.　　SHAKESPEARE.

How many a rustic Milton has passed by,
Stifling the speechless longings of his heart,
In unremitting drudgery and care !
How many a vulgar Cato has compelled
His energies, no longer tameless then,
To mould a pin, or fabricate a nail !
Queen Mab, Pt. V.　　P. B. SHELLEY.

If all the year were playing holidays,
To sport would be as tedious as to work.
King Henry, Pt. I. Act i. *Sc.* 2.　　SHAKESPEARE.

MACDUFF.　I know this is a joyful trouble to you,
But yet, 't is one.
MACBETH.　The labor we delight in physics pain.
Macbeth, Act ii. *Sc.* 3.　　SHAKESPEARE.

Cheered with the view, man went to till the ground
From whence he rose ; sentenced indeed to toil,
As to a punishment, yet (even in wrath,
So merciful is heaven) this toil became
The solace of his woes, the sweet employ
Of many a livelong hour, and surest guard
Against disease and death.
Death.   B. PORTEUS.

Like a lackey, from the rise to set,
Sweats in the eye of Phœbus, and all night
Sleeps in Elysium ; next day after dawn
Doth rise and help Hyperion to his horse,
And follows so the ever-running year
With profitable labor to his grave.
And, but for ceremony, such a wretch,
Winding up days with toil and nights with sleep,
Hath the forehand and vantage of a king.
King Henry V., Act iv. *Sc.* 1.   SHAKESPEARE.

When Adam dolve, and Eve span,
Who was then the gentleman ? *
                                                      J. BALL.

Joy to the Toiler !—him that tills
    The fields with Plenty crowned ;
Him with the woodman's axe that thrills
    The wilderness profound.
Songs of the Toiler.   B. HATHAWAY.

LAW.

In the corrupted currents of this world
Offence's gilded hand may shove by justice,
And oft 't is seen the wicked prize itself
Buys out the law : but 't is not so above ;
There is no shuffling, there the action lies
In his true nature ; and we ourselves compelled,
Even to the teeth and forehead of our faults,
To give in evidence.
Hamlet, Act iii. *Sc.* 3.   SHAKESPEARE.

Press not a falling man too far ! 't is virtue :
His faults lie open to the laws ; let them,
Not you, correct him.
Henry VIII., Act iii. *Sc.* 2.   SHAKESPEARE.

Still you keep o' the windy side of the law.
Twelfth Night, Act iii. *Sc.* 4.   SHAKESPEARE.

* Lines used by John Ball, to encourage the rebels in Wat Tyler's
rebellion. Hume's *History of England*, Vol. i.

Between two hawks, which flies the higher pitch,
Between two dogs, which hath the deeper mouth,
Between two horses, which doth bear him best,
Between two girls, which hath the merriest eye,
I have, perhaps, some shallow spirit of judgment;
But in these nice sharp quillets of the law,
Good faith. I am no wiser than a daw.
King Henry VI., Pt. I. Act ii. *Sc.* 4.   SHAKESPEARE.

Mastering the lawless science of our law,
That codeless myriad of precedent,
That wilderness of single instances.
Aylmer's Field.   A. TENNYSON.

The hungry judges soon the sentence sign,
And wretches hang, that jurymen may dine.
Rape of the Lock, Canto III.   A. POPE.

In law, what plea so tainted and corrupt
But, being seasoned with a gracious voice,
Obscures the show of evil?
Merchant of Venice, Act iii. *Sc.* 2.   SHAKESPEARE.

So wise, so grave, of so perplexed a tongue
And loud withal, that could not wag, nor scarce
Lie still, without a fee.
Valpone.   B. JONSON.

While lawyers have more sober sense
Than t' argue at their own expense,
But make their best advantages
Of others' quarrels, like the Swiss.
Hudibras.   S. BUTLER.

All, all look up with reverential awe,
At crimes that 'scape, or triumph o'er the law.
Epilogue to Satire, Dialogue I.   A. POPE.

Once (says an Author; where, I need not say)
Two Trav'lers found an Oyster in their way;
Both fierce, both hungry; the dispute grew strong,
While Scale in hand Dame Justice passed along.
Before her each with clamor pleads the Laws.
Explained the matter, and would win the cause,
Dame Justice weighing long the doubtful Right,
Takes, opens, swallows it, before their sight.
The cause of strife removed so rarely well,
"There take" (says Justice), "take ye each a shell.
We thrive at Westminster on Fools like you:
'T was a fat oyster—live in peace—Adieu."
Verbatim from Boileau.   A. POPE.

We must not make a scarecrow of the law,
Setting it up to fear the birds of prey,
And let it keep one shape, till custom make it
Their perch and not their terror.
Measure for Measure, Act ii. *Sc.* 1.   SHAKESPEARE.

No man e'er felt the halter draw,
With good opinion of the law.
McFingal, Canto III.   J. TRUMBULL.

Who to himself is law, no law doth need,
Offends no law, and is a king indeed.
Bussy D'Ambois, Act ii. *Sc.* 1.   G. CHAPMAN.

LEARNING.

A little learning is a dangerous thing;
Drink deep, or taste not the Pierian spring:
There shallow draughts intoxicate the brain,
And drinking largely sobers us again.
Essay on Criticism, Pt. II.   A. POPE.

When night hath set her silver lamp on high,
Then is the time for study.
Festus, Sc. A Village Feast.   P. J. BAILEY.

BIRON.—What is the end of Study? let me know.
KING.—Why, that to know, which else we should not
    know.
BIRON.—Things hid and barred, you mean, from com-
    mon sense?
KING.—Ay, that is study's godlike recompense.
Love's Labor's Lost, Act i. *Sc.* 1.   SHAKESPEARE.

No profit grows where is no pleasure ta'en;
In brief, sir, study what you most affect.
Taming of the Shrew, Act i. *Sc.* 1.   SHAKESPEARE.

Some, for renown, on scraps of learning dote,
And think they grow immortal as they quote.
Love of Fame, Satire I.   DR. E. YOUNG.

With just enough of learning to misquote.
English Bards and Scotch Reviewers.   LORD BYRON.

Whence is thy learning? Hath thy toil
O'er books consumed the midnight oil?
Fables: The Shepherd and the Philosopher.   J. GAY.

And thou art worthy; full of power;
    As gentle; liberal-minded, great,
    Consistent; wearing all that weight
Of learning lightly like a flower.
In Memoriam : Conclusion.   A. TENNYSON.
11

Small have continual plodders ever won,
  Save base authority from others' books.
These earthly godfathers of heaven's lights,
  That give a name to every fixèd star,
Have no more profit of their shining nights
  Than those that walk, and wot not what they are.
Love's Labor's Lost, Act i. *Sc.* 1.   SHAKESPEARE.

Love seldom haunts the breast where learning lies,
And Venus sets ere Mercury can rise.
The Wife of Bath: Her Prologue.   A. POPE.

                Here the heart
  May give a useful lesson to the head,
  And learning wiser grow without his books.
The Task, Bk. VI. Winter Walk at Noon. W. COWPER.

        Learning by study must be won ;
        'T was ne'er entailed from son to son.
The Pack Horse and Carrier.   J. GAY.

Much learning shows how little mortals know ;
Much wealth, how little worldlings can enjoy.
Night Thoughts, Night VI.   DR. E. YOUNG.

Were man to live coeval with the sun,
  The patriarch-pupil would be learning still.
Night Thoughts, Night VII.   DR. E. YOUNG.

LETTERS.

Kind messages, that pass from land to land ;
  Kind letters, that betray the heart's deep history,
In which we feel the pressure of a hand,—
  One touch of fire,—and all the rest is mystery !
The Seaside and the Fireside : Dedication.
                        H. W. LONGFELLOW.

        Every day brings a ship,
        Every ship brings a word ;
        Well for those who have no fear,
        Looking seaward well assured
        That the word the vessel brings
        Is the word they wish to hear.
Letters.   R. W. EMERSON.

        And oft the pangs of absence to remove
        By letters, soft interpreters of love.
Henry and Emma.   M. PRIOR.

        Here are a few of the unpleasant'st words
        That ever blotted paper !
Merchant of Venice, Act iii. *Sc.* 2.   SHAKESPEARE.

I will touch
My mouth unto the leaves, caressingly ;
And so wilt thou. Thus from these lips of mine
My message will go kissingly to thine,
With more than Fancy's load of luxury,
And prove a true love-letter.
Sonnet (With a Letter).　　　　　J. G. SAXE.

Jove and my stars be praised ! Here is yet a postscript.
Twelfth Night, Act ii. *Sc.* 5.　　　SHAKESPEARE.

Go, little letter, apace, apace,
　　Fly ;
Fly to the light in the valley below—
Tell my wish to her dewy blue eye.
The Letter.　　　　　A. TENNYSON.

LIFE.

Let observation, with extensive view,
Survey mankind from China to Peru ;
Remark each anxious toil, each eager strife,
And watch the busy scenes of crowded life.
The Vanity of Human Wishes.　　　DR. S. JOHNSON.

It matters not how long we live, but how.
Festus, Sc. Wood and Water.　　　P. J. BAILEY.

Nor love thy life, nor hate ; but what thou liv'st
Live well ; how long or short permit to heaven.
Paradise Lost, Bk. XI.　　　MILTON.

All is concentred in a life intense,
Where not a beam, nor air, nor leaf is lost,
But hath a part of being.
Childe Harold, Canto III.　　　LORD BYRON.

Life for delays and doubts no time does give,
None ever yet made haste enough to live.
Martial, Liber II.　　　A. COWLEY.

Learn to live well, that thou may'st die so too ;
To live and die is all we have to do.
Of Prudence.　　　SIR J. DENHAM.

" Live, while you live," the epicure would say,
" And seize the pleasures of the present day ; "
" Live while you live," the sacred preacher cries,
" And give to God each moment as it flies."
" Lord, in my views let both united be ;
I live in *pleasure,* when I live to *Thee.*"
" *Dum vivimus vivamus.*" (*Motto of his Family Arms.*)
　　　　　P. DODDRIDGE.

A man's ingress into the world is naked and bare,
His progress through the world is trouble and care ;
And lastly, his egress out of the world, is nobody knows
   where.
If we do well here, we shall do well there ;
I can tell you no more if I preach a whole year.
   Eccentricities, Vol. I.   J. EDWIN.

        A little rule. a little sway,
        A sunbeam in a winter's day,
        Is all the proud and mighty have
        Between the cradle and the grave.
Grongar Hill.   J. DYER.

        So may'st thou live. till like ripe fruit thou drop
        Into thy mother's lap.
Paradise Lost, Bk. XI.   MILTON.

        Sound, sound the clarion. fill the fife !
        To all the sensual world proclaim,
        One crowded hour of glorious life
        Is worth an age without a name.
Old Mortality : Chapter Head.   SIR W. SCOTT.

        Let us (since life can little more supply
        Than just to look about us, and to die)
        Expatiate free o'er all this scene of man ;
        A mighty maze ! but not without a plan.
Essay on Man, Epistle I.   A. POPE.

        The world 's a theatre, the earth a stage
        Which God and nature do with actors fill.
Apology for Actors.   T. HEYWOOD.

        To-morrow, and to-morrow, and to-morrow,
        Creeps in this petty pace from day to day,
        To the last syllable of recorded time ;
        And all our yesterdays have lighted fools
        The way to dusty death.   Out, out, brief candle !
        Life is but a walking shadow ; a poor player,
        That struts and frets his hour upon the stage,
        And then is heard no more : it is a tale
        Told by an idiot, full of sound and fury,
        Signifying nothing.
Macbeth, Act v. Sc. 5.   SHAKESPEARE.

        The web of our life is of a mingled
        Yarn, good and ill together.
All's Well that Ends Well, Act iv. Sc. 3 . SHAKESPEARE.

And what 's a life ?—a weary pilgrimage,
Whose glory in one day doth fill the stage
With childhood, manhood, and decrepit age.
What is Life ?   F. QUARLES.

An elegant sufficiency, content,
Retirement, rural quiet, friendship, books,
Ease and alternate labor, useful life,
Progressive virtue, and approving Heaven !
The Seasons: Spring.   J. THOMSON.

On life's vast ocean diversely we sail,
Reason the card, but passion is the gale.
Essay on Man, Epistle II.   A. POPE.

I cannot tell what you and other men
Think of this life ; but, for my single self,
I had as lief not be as live to be
In awe of such a thing as I myself.
Julius Cæsar, Act i. *Sc.* 2.   SHAKESPEARE.

Why, what should be the fear ?
I do not set my life at a pin's fee.
Hamlet, Act i. *Sc.* 4.   SHAKESPEARE.

" Life is not lost," said she, " for which is bought
Endlesse renowne."
Faërie Queene, Bk. III. Canto XI.   E. SPENSER.

Our life is scarce the twinkle of a star
In God's eternal day.
Autumnal Vespers.   B. TAYLOR.

There taught us how to live ; and (oh, too high
The price for knowledge !) taught us how to die.
On the Death of Addison.   T. TICKELL.

Our life contains a thousand springs,
And dies if one be gone.
Strange ! that a harp of thousand strings
Should keep in tune so long.
Hymns and Spiritual Songs.   DR. I. WATTS.

LOSS.

For it so falls out
That what we have we prize not to the worth,
Whiles we enjoy it, but being lacked and lost,
Why, then we rack the value, then we find
The virtue that possession would not show us
Whiles it was ours.
Much Ado about Nothing, Act iv. *Sc.* 1.   SHAKESPEARE.

But over all things brooding slept
The quiet sense of something lost.
In Memoriam, LXXVIII.   A. TENNYSON.

Praising what is lost
Makes the remembrance dear.
All's Well that Ends Well, Act v. *Sc.* 3.   SHAKESPEARE.

Though lost to sight, to memory dear
Thou ever wilt remain ;
One only hope my heart can cheer,
The hope to meet again.
Song : Though Lost to Sight.   G. LINLEY.

You take my house when you do take the prop
That doth sustain my house ; you take my life
When you do take the means whereby I live.
Merchant of Venice, Act iv. *Sc.* 1.   SHAKESPEARE.

The loss of wealth is loss of dirt,
As sages in all times assert ;
The happy man 's without a shirt.
Be Merry, Friends.   J. HEYWOOD.

For 'tis a truth well known to most,
That whatsoever thing is lost,
We seek it, ere it come to light,
In every cranny but the right.
The Retired Cat.   W. COWPER.

Wise men ne'er sit and wail their loss,
But cheerly seek how to redress their harms.
King Henry VI., Pt. III. Act v. *Sc.* 4.   SHAKESPEARE.

LOVE.

What thing is love ?—for (well I wot) love is a thing.
It is a prick, it is a sting,
It is a pretty, pretty thing ;
It is a fire, it is a coal,
Whose flame creeps in at every hole !
The Hunting of Cupid.   G. PEELE.

O, love, love, love !
Love is like a dizziness ;
It winna let a poor body
Gang about his biziness !
Love is Like a Dizziness.   J. HOGG.

With a smile that glowed
Celestial rosy red, love's proper hue.
Paradise Lost, Bk. VIII.   MILTON.

Love, like death,
Levels all ranks, and lays the shepherd's crook
Beside the sceptre.
Lady of Lyons. E. BULWER-LYTTON.

Didst thou but know the inly touch of love,
Thou wouldst as soon go kindle fire with snow,
As seek to quench the fire of love with words.
Two Gentlemen of Verona, Act ii. *Sc.* 7. SHAKESPEARE.

There 's a bliss beyond all that the minstrel has told,
When two, that are linked in one heavenly tie,
With heart never changing, and brow never cold,
Love on through all ills, and love on till they die!
One hour of a passion so sacred is worth
Whole ages of heartless and wandering bliss;
And O, if there be an Elysium on earth,
It is this, it is this.
Lalla Rookh: Light of the Harem. T. MOORE.

Love is the tyrant of the heart; it darkens
Reason, confounds discretion; deaf to counsel
It runs a headlong course to desperate madness.
The Lover's Melancholy, Act iii. *Sc.* 3. J. FORD.

Ask not of me, Love, what is love?
Ask what is good of God above;
Ask of the great sun what is light;
Ask what is darkness of the night;
Ask sin of what may be forgiven;
Ask what is happiness of heaven;
Ask what is folly of the crowd;
Ask what is fashion of the shroud;
Ask what is sweetness of thy kiss;
Ask of thyself what beauty is.
Festus, Sc. Party and Entertainment. P. J. BAILEY.

All love is sweet,
Given or returned. Common as light is love,
And its familiar voice wearies not ever.
Prometheus Unbound, Act ii. *Sc.* 5. P. B. SHELLEY.

Love is a celestial harmony
Of likely hearts.
Hymn in Honor of Beauty. E. SPENSER.

There 's beggary in the love that can be reckoned.
Antony and Cleopatra, Act i. *Sc.* 1. SHAKESPEARE.

Like Dian's kiss, unasked, unsought,
Love gives itself, but is not bought.
Endymion. H. W. LONGFELLOW.

It is not virtue, wisdom, valor, wit,
Strength, comeliness of shape, or amplest merit
That woman's love can win, or long inherit.
But what it is, hard is to say,
Harder to hit.
Samson Agonistes.   MILTON.

Love sought is good, but given unsought is better.
Twelfth Night, Act ii. *Sc.* 5.   SHAKESPEARE.

Charms strike the sight, but merit wins the soul.
Rape of the Lock, Canto V.   A. POPE.

Why did she love him ?   Curious fool !—be still—
Is human love the growth of human will?
Lara, Canto II.   LORD BYRON.

                         I know not why
I love this youth ; and I have heard you say,
Love's reason 's without reason.
Cymbeline, Act iv. *Sc.* 2.   SHAKESPEARE.

Love goes toward love as school-boys from their books,
But love from love, toward school with heavy looks.
Romeo and Juliet, Act ii. *Sc.* 2.   SHAKESPEARE.

Divine is Love and scorneth worldly pelf,
And can be bought with nothing but with self.
Love the Only Price of Love.   SIR W. RALEIGH.

Love like a shadow flies when substance love pursues ;
Pursuing that that flies, and flying what pursues.
Merry Wives of Windsor, Act ii. *Sc.* 2. SHAKESPEARE.

            Love, whose month is ever May,
            Spied a blossom passing fair
            Playing in the wanton air :
            Through the velvet leaves the wind,
            All unseen can passage find ;
            That the lover, sick to death,
            Wish himself the heaven's breath.
Love's Labor's Lost, Act iv. *Sc.* 3.   SHAKESPEARE.

Affection is a coal that must be cooled ;
Else, suffered, it will set the heart on fire.
Venus and Adonis.   SHAKESPEARE.

In all amours a lover burns,
With frowns, as well as smiles, by turns ;
And hearts have been as oft with sullen,
As charming looks, surprised and stolen.
Hudibras, Pt. III. Canto I.   S. BUTLER.

Mysterious love, uncertain treasure,
Hast thou more of pain or pleasure!

.   .   .   .   .

Endless torments dwell about thee:
Yet who would live, and live without thee!
Rosamond, Act iii. Sc. 2.   J. ADDISON.

If there 's delight in love, 't is when I see
The heart, which others bleed for, bleed for me.
Way of the World, Act iii. Sc. 3.   W. CONGREVE.

Give, you gods,
Give to your boy, your Cæsar,
The rattle of a globe to play withal,
This gewgaw world, and put him cheaply off ;
I 'll not be pleased with less than Cleopatra.
All for Love, Act ii. Sc. 1.   J. DRYDEN.

Much ado there was, God wot;
He woold love, and she woold not,
She sayd, " Never man was trewe ; "
He sayes, " None was false to you."
Phillida and Corydon.   N. BRETON.

Forty thousand brothers
Could not, with all their quantity of love,
Make up my sum.
Hamlet, Act v. Sc. 1.   SHAKESPEARE.

Love, then, hath every bliss in store ;
'T is friendship, and 't is something more.
Each other every wish they give ;
Not to know love is not to live.
Plutus, Cupid, and Time.   J. GAY.

LOVE'S ARTS.

Sweet to entrance
The raptured soul by intermingling glance.
Psyche.   MRS. M. TIGHE.

Our souls sit close and silently within,
And their own web from their own entrails spin ;
And when eyes meet far off, our sense is such,
That, spider-like, we feel the tenderest touch.
Marriage à la Mode, Act ii. Sc. 1.   J. DRYDEN.

Of all the paths [that] lead to a woman's love
Pity 's the straightest.
Knight of Malta, Act i. Sc. 1.
                    BEAUMONT AND FLETCHER.

So mourned the dame of Ephesus her love ;
And thus the soldier, armed with resolution,
Told his soft tale, and was a thriving wooer.
Shakespeare's King Richard III. (Altered), Act ii. *Sc.* 1.
                                        C. CIBBER.

The Devil hath not, in all his quiver's choice,
An arrow for the heart like a sweet voice.
Don Juan, Canto XV.   LORD BYRON.

If thou dost love, pronounce it faithfully ;
Or, if thou think'st I am too quickly won,
I 'll frown, and be perverse, and say thee nay,
So thou wilt woo ; but, else, not for the world.
Romeo and Juliet, Act i'. *Sc.* 2.   SHAKESPEARE.

Read it, sweet maid, though it be done but slightly :
Who can show all his love doth love but lightly.
Sonnet.   S. DANIEL.

Love first invented verse, and formed the rhyme,
The motion measured, harmonized the chime.
Cymon and Iphigenia.   J. DRYDEN.

And you must love him, ere to you
He will seem worthy of your love.
A Poet's Epitaph.   W. WORDSWORTH.

None without hope e'er loved the brightest fair,
But love can hope where reason would despair.
Epigram.   GEORGE, LORD LYTTELTON.

LOVE'S BLINDNESS.

Love looks not with the eyes, but with the mind,
And therefore is winged Cupid painted blind.
Midsummer Night's Dream, Act i. *Sc.* 1. SHAKESPEARE.

None ever loved but at first sight they loved.
Blind Beggar of Alexandria.   G. CHAPMAN.

We only love where fate ordains we should,
And, blindly fond, oft slight superior merit.
Fall of Saguntum.   PH. FROWDE.

But love is blind, and lovers cannot see
The pretty follies that themselves commit.
Merchant of Venice, Act ii. *Sc.* 6.   SHAKESPEARE.

LOVE'S DANGERS.

And when once the young heart of a maiden is stolen,
The maiden herself will steal after it soon.
Ill Omens.   T. MOORE.

And whispering, " I will ne'er consent,"—consented.
Don Juan, Canto I.   LORD BYRON.

The fly that sips treacle is lost in the sweets.
Beggar's Opera, Act ii. *Sc.* 2.   J. GAY.

There lives within the very flame of love
A kind of wick or snuff that will abate it.
Hamlet, Act iv. *Sc.* 7.   SHAKESPEARE.

My only books
Were woman's looks,
And folly 's all they 've taught me.
The time I 've lost in wooing.   T. MOORE.

Then fly betimes, for only they
Conquer Love that run away.
Conquest by Flight.   T. CAREW.

LOVE'S CAUTIONS.

The rose that all are praising
Is not the rose for me ;
Too many eyes are gazing
Upon the costly tree ;
But there 's a rose in yonder glen
That shuns the gaze of other men,
For me its blossom raising,—
O, that 's the rose for me.
The rose that all are praising.   T. H. BAYLY.

But the fruit that can fall without shaking,
Indeed is too mellow for me.
The Answer.   LADY MARY W. MONTAGU.

Love in a hut, with water and a crust,
Is—Lord forgive us !—cinders, ashes, dust.
Lamia.   J. KEATS.

The cold in clime are cold in blood,
Their love can scarce deserve the name.
The Giaour.   LORD BYRON.

Love in your hearts as idly burns
As fire in antique Roman urns.
Hudibras, Pt. II. Canto I.   S. BUTLER.

LOVE'S DELIGHT.

All the heart was full of feeling: love had ripened into speech,
Like the sap that turns to nectar, in the velvet of the peach.
Adonais.   W. W. HARNEY.

O'er her warm cheek, and rising bosom, move
The bloom of young Desire and purple light of Love.
Progress of Poesy, i. 3.   T. GRAY.

Still amorous, and fond, and billing,
Like Philip and Mary on a shilling.
Hudibras, Pt. III. Canto I.   S. BUTLER.

Then awake !—the heavens look bright, my dear !
'T is never too late for delight, my dear !
    And the best of all ways
    To lengthen our days,
Is to steal a few hours from the night, my dear !
Young May Moon.   T. MOORE.

Lovers' hours are long, though seeming short.
Venus and Adonis.   SHAKESPEARE.

And, touched by her fair tendance, gladlier grew.
Paradise Lost, Bk. VIII.   MILTON.

Why, she would hang on him,
As if increase of appetite had grown
By what it fed on.
Hamlet, Act i. *Sc.* 2.   SHAKESPEARE.

Imparadised in one another's arms.
Paradise Lost, Bk. IV.   MILTON.

I give thee all—I can no more,
Though poor the offering be :
My heart and lute are all the store
That I can bring to thee.
My Heart and Lute.   T. MOORE.

I 've lived and loved.
Wallenstein, Pt. I. Act ii. *Sc.* 6.   S. T. COLERIDGE.

LOVE'S PAINS.

A mighty pain to love it is,
And 't is a pain that pain to miss ;
But of all pains, the greatest pain
It is to love, but love in vain.
Gold.   A. COWLEY.

The sweetest joy. the wildest woe is love ;
The taint of earth, the odor of the skies
    Is in it.
Festus, Sc. Alcove and Garden.   P. J. BAILEY.

Chords that vibrate sweetest pleasure
Thrill the deepest notes of woe.
On Sensibility. R. BURNS.

Love is like a landscape which doth stand
Smooth at a distance, rough at hand.
On Love. R. HEGGE.

Vows with so much passion, swears with so much grace,
That 't is a kind of heaven to be deluded by him.
Alexander the Great, Act i. *Sc.* 3. N. LEE.

To love you was pleasant enough,
And O, 't is delicious to hate you !
To —— T. MOORE.

LOVE'S UNITY.

Two souls with but a single thought,
Two hearts that beat as one.
Ingomar the Barbarian, Act ii.
VON M. BELLINGHAUSEN. LOVELL'S *Trans.*

Our two souls, therefore, which are one,
Though I must go, endure not yet
A breach, but an expansion,
Like gold to airy thinness beat.
If they be two, they are two so
As stiff twin compasses are two :
Thy soul, the fixt foot, makes no show
To move, but doth if the other do.
And though it in the centre sit,
Yet when the other far doth roam,
It leans and hearkens after it,
And grows erect, as that comes home.
Such wilt thou be to me, who must,
Like the other foot, obliquely run.
Thy firmness makes my circle just,
And makes me end where I begun.
A Valediction forbidding Mourning. DR. J. DONNE.

True beauty dwells in deep retreats,
Whose veil is unremoved
Till heart with heart in concord beats,
And the lover is beloved.
To —— W. WORDSWORTH.

With thee, all toils are sweet ; each clime hath charms ;
Earth—sea alike—our world within our arms.
The Bride of Abydos. LORD BYRON.

What 's mine is yours, and what is yours is mine.
Measure for Measure, Act v. *Sc.* 1. SHAKESPEARE.

He was a lover of the good old school,
Who still become more constant as they cool.
Beppo, Canto XXXIV.   LORD BYRON.

Drink ye to her that each loves best,
   And if you nurse a flame
That 's told but to her mutual breast,
   We will not ask her name.
Drink ye to her.   T. CAMPBELL.

FERDINAND.—Here 's my hand.
MIRANDA.—And mine, with my heart in 't.
Tempest, Act iii. Sc. 1.   SHAKESPEARE.

MAN.

How poor, how rich, how abject, how august,
How complicate, how wonderful, is man!
          .   .   .   .   .
A beam ethereal, sullied, and absorpt!
Though sullied and dishonored, still divine!
Dim miniature of greatness absolute!
An heir of glory! a frail child of dust!
Helpless immortal! insect infinite!
A worm! a god!
          .   .   .   .   .
What can preserve my life? or what destroy?
An angel's arm can't snatch me from the grave;
Legions of angels can't confine me there.
Night Thoughts, Night I.   DR. E. YOUNG.

Nature they say, doth dote,
   And cannot make a man
Save on some worn-out plan,
   Repeating as by rote.
Commemoration Ode.   J. R. LOWELL.

Man is the nobler growth our realms supply,
And souls are ripened in our northern sky.
The Invitation.   MRS. A. L. BARBAULD.

'T is God gives skill,
But not without men's hands: He could not make
Antonio Stradivari's violins
Without Antonio.
Stradivarius.   GEORGE ELIOT.

Not two strong men the enormous weight could raise;
Such men as live in these degenerate days.
Iliad, Bk. V.   HOMER. *Trans. of* POPE.

Be wise with speed :
A fool at forty is a fool indeed.
Love of Fame, Satire II. ⌐ DR. E. YOUNG.

What tho' short thy date ?
Virtue, not rolling suns, the mind matures.
That life is long which answers life's great end.
The time that bears no fruit deserves no name.
The man of wisdom is the man of years.
In hoary youth Methusalems may die ;
O, how misdated on their flatt'ring tombs !
Night Thoughts, Night V. DR. E. YOUNG.

Man !
Thou pendulum betwixt a smile and tear.
Childe Harold, Canto IV. LORD BYRON.

Like leaves on trees the race of man is found,
Now green in youth. now withering on the ground :
Another race the following spring supplies ;
They fall successive, and successive rise.
Iliad, Bk. VI. HOMER. *Trans. of* POPE.

Know then thyself, presume not God to scan ;
The proper study of mankind is man.

.   .   .   .

Created half to rise, and half to fall ;
Great lord of all things, yet a prey to all ;
Sole judge of truth, in endless error hurled ;
The glory, jest, and riddle of the world !
Essay on Man, Epistle II. A. POPE.

MANNERS.

Those graceful acts,
Those thousand decencies that daily flow
From all her words and actions.
Paradise Lost, Bk. VIII. MILTON.

Of manners gentle, of affections mild ;
In wit a man, simplicity a child.

.   .   .   .

A safe companion and an easy friend
Unblamed through life, lamented in thy end.
Epitaph on Gay. A. POPE.

Her air, her manners, all who saw admired ;
Courteous though coy, and gentle though retired :
The joy of youth and health her eyes displayed,
And ease of heart her every look conveyed.
Parish Register, Pt. II. G. CRABBE.

Be thou familiar, but by no means vulgar.
Hamlet, Act i. *Sc.* 3.   SHAKESPEARE.

What would you have ? your gentleness shall force
More than your force move us to gentleness.
As You Like It, Act ii. *Sc.* 7.   SHAKESPEARE.

'T is not enough your counsel still be true ;
Blunt truths more mischief than nice falsehoods do.
Essay on Criticism, Pt. III.   A. POPE.

Fit for the mountains and the barb'rous caves,
  Where manners ne'er weré preached.
Twelfth Night, Act iv. *Sc.* 1.   SHAKESPEARE.

He was the mildest mannered man
  That ever scuttled ship or cut a throat.
Don Juan, Canto III.   LORD BYRON.

Men's evil manners live in brass ; their virtues
  We write in water.
King Henry VIII., Act iv. *Sc.* 2.   SHAKESPEARE.

Manners with fortunes, humors turn with climes,
Tenets with books, and principles with times.
Moral Essays, Epistle I.   A. POPE.

Plain living and high thinking are no more.
The homely beauty of the good old cause
Is gone ; our peace, our fearful innocence,
And pure religion breathing household laws.
Written in London, September, 1802. W. WORDSWORTH.

Eye Nature's walks, shoot folly as it flies,
And catch the manners living as they rise ;
Laugh where we must, be candid where we can,
But vindicate the ways of God to man.
Essay on Man, Epistle I.   A. POPE.

MATRIMONY.

True Love is but a humble, low-born thing,
And hath its food served up in earthen ware ;
It is a thing to walk with, hand in hand,
Through the every-dayness of this work-day world,
         .   .   .   .   .
A simple, fireside thing, whose quiet smile
Can warm earth's poorest hovel to a home.
Love.   J. R. LOWELL.

He is the half part of a blessed man,
Left to be finished by such as she ;
And she a fair divided excellence,
Whose fulness of perfection lies in him ;
King John, Act ii. *Sc.* 1.   SHAKESPEARE.

As unto the bow the cord is,
So unto the man is woman ;
Though she bends him she obeys him ;
Though she draws him, yet she follows,
Useless each without the other !
Hiawatha, Pt. X.   H. W. LONGFELLOW.

Man is but half without woman ; and
As do idolaters their heavenly gods,
We deify the things that we adore.
Festus.   P. J. BAILEY.

        Let still the woman take
An elder than herself : so wears she to him,
So sways she level in her husband's heart,
For, boy, however we do praise ourselves,
Our fancies are more giddy and unfirm,
More longing, wavering, sooner lost and won,
Than women's are.

   .   .   .   .

Then let thy love be younger than thyself,
Or thy affection cannot hold the bent.
Twelfth Night, Act ii. *Sc.* 4.   SHAKESPEARE.

Such duty as the subject owes the prince,
Even such a woman oweth to her husband.
Taming of the Shrew, Act v. *Sc.* 2.   SHAKESPEARE.

And truant husband should return, and say,
"My dear, I was the first who came away."
Don Juan, Canto I.   LORD BYRON.

With thee conversing I forget all time ;
All seasons and their change, all please alike.

   .   .   .   .

But neither breath of morn when she ascends
With charm of earliest birds, nor rising sun
On this delightful land, nor herb, fruit, flower,
Glistering with dew, nor fragrance after showers,
Nor grateful evening mild, nor silent night
With this her solemn bird, nor walk by moon,
Or glittering starlight, without thee is sweet.
Paradise Lost, Bk. IV.   MILTON.
12

So loving to my mother,
That he might not beteem the winds of heaven
Visit her face too roughly.
Hamlet, Act i. *Sc.* 2.   SHAKESPEARE.

Dear as the vital warmth that feeds my life ;
Dear as these eyes, that weep in fondness o'er thee.
Venice Preserved, Act v. *Sc.* 1.   T. OTWAY.

Maidens like moths are ever caught by glare,
And Mammon wins his way where seraphs might despair.
English Bards and Scotch Reviewers.   LORD BYRON.

So, with decorum all things carry'd ;
Miss frowned, and blushed, and then was—married.
The Double Transformation.   O. GOLDSMITH.

For talk six times with the same single lady,
And you may get the wedding dresses ready.
Don Juan, Canto XII.   LORD BRYON.

Why don't the men propose, mamma,
Why don't the men propose ?
Why don't the men propose ?   T. H. BAYLY.

There swims no goose so gray, but soon or late
She finds some honest gander for her mate.
Chaucer's Wife of Bath : Prologue.   A. POPE.

Under this window in stormy weather
I marry this man and woman together ;
Let none but Him who rules the thunder
Put this man and woman asunder.
Marriage Service from his Chamber Window.
                                          J. SWIFT.

This house is to be let for life or years ;
Her rent is sorrow, and her income tears ;
Cupid, 't has long stood void ; her bills make known,
She must be dearly let, or let alone.
Emblems, Bk. II. 10.   F. QUARLES.

Look ere thou leap, see ere thou go.
Of Wiving and Thriving.   T. TUSSER.

Thus grief still treads upon the heels of pleasure ;
Married in haste, we may repent at leisure.
The Old Bachelor, Act v. *Sc.* 1.   W. CONGREVE.

Men are April when they woo, December when they wed.
As You Like It, Act iv. *Sc.* 1.   SHAKESPEARE.

And oft the careless find it to their cost,
The lover in the husband may be lost.
Advice to a Lady.   LORD LYTTELTON.

Wedlock, indeed, hath oft comparèd been
To public feasts, where meet a public rout,
Where they that are without would fain go in,
And they that are within would fain go out.
Contention betwixt a Wife, etc.   SIR J. DAVIES.

O fie upon this single life ! forego it.
Duchess of Malfy.   J. WEBSTER.

1. That man must lead a happy life
2. Who is directed by a wife ;
3. Who's free from matrimonial chains
4. Is sure to suffer for his pains.

5. Adam could find no solid peace
6. Till he beheld a woman's face ;
7. When Eve was given for a mate,
8. Adam was in a happy state.
Epigram on Matrimony : Read alternate lines,—1, 3 ; 2,
4 ; 5, 7 ; 6, 8.

The kindest and the happiest pair
Will find occasion to forbear ;
And something every day they live
To pity and perhaps forgive.
Mutual Forbearance.   W. COWPER.

But happy they, the happiest of their kind !
Whom gentler stars unite, and in one fate
Their hearts, their fortunes, and their beings blend.
Seasons : Spring.   J. THOMSON.

And when with envy Time, transported,
Shall think to rob us of our joys.
You'll in your girls again be courted,
And I'll go wooing in my boys.
Winifreda.   T. PERCY.

Cling closer, closer, life to life,
Cling closer, heart to heart ;
The time will come, my own wed Wife,
When you and I must part !
Let nothing break our band but Death,
For in the world above
'T is the breaker Death that soldereth
Our ring of Wedded Love.
On a Wedding Day.   G. MASSEY.

MEDICINE.

You tell your doctor, that y' are ill ;
And what does he, but write a bill ?
Of which you need not read one letter ;
The worse the scrawl, the dose the better.
For if you knew but what you take,
Though you recover, he must break.
Alma, Canto III.   M. PRIOR.

But when ill indeed,
E'en dismissing the doctor don't always succeed.
Lodgings for Single Gentlemen. G. COLEMAN, *the Younger.*

" Is there no hope ? " the sick man said.
The silent doctor shook his head
And took his leave with signs of sorrow,
Despairing of his fee to-morrow.
The Sick Man and the Angel.   J. GAY.

I do remember an apothecary.

.   .   .   .

Sharp misery had worn him to the bones :
And in his needy shop a tortoise hung,
An alligator stuffed, and other skins
Of ill-shaped fishes ; and about his shelves
A beggarly account of empty boxes.
Romeo and Juliet, Act v. *Sc.* 1.   SHAKESPEARE.

With us ther was a Doctour of Phisik,
In al this world ne was ther non him lyk
To speke of phisik and of surgerye.

.   .   .

He knew the cause of every maladye,
Were it of hoot or colde, or moyste or drye,
And wher engendered and of what humour ;
He was a verrey parfight practisour.
Canterbury Tales : Prologue.   CHAUCER.

'T is not amiss, ere ye 're giv'n o'er.
To try one desp'rate med'cine more ;
For where your case can be no worse,
The desp'rat'st is the wisest course.
Hudibras to Sidrophel.   S. BUTLER.

Take a little rum,
   The less you take the better,
Pour it in the lakes
   Of Wener or of Wetter.

Dip a spoonful out
And mind you don't get groggy,
Pour it in the lake
Of Winnipissiogie.

Stir the mixture well
Lest it prove inferior,
Then put half a drop
Into Lake Superior.

Every other day
Take a drop in water,
You 'll be better soon—
Or at least you oughter.

Lines on Homœopathy.   BISHOP G. W. DOANE.

By medicine life may be prolonged, yet death
Will seize the doctor too.

Cymbeline, Act v. Sc. 5.   SHAKESPEARE.

MELANCHOLY.

Melancholy
Is not, as you conceive, indisposition
Of body, but the mind's disease.

The Lover's Melancholy, Act iii. Sc. 1.   J. FORD.

Go—you may call it madness, folly,
You shall not chase my gloom away.
There 's such a charm in melancholy,
I would not, if I could, be gay !

To ——   S. ROGERS.

There is a mood
(I sing not to the vacant and the young),
There is a kindly mood of melancholy
That wings the soul and points her to the skies.

Ruins of Rome.   J. DYER.

MEMORY.

And, when the stream
Which overflowed the soul was passed away,
A consciousness remained that it had left,
Deposited upon the silent shore
Of memory, images and precious thoughts
That shall not die, and cannot be destroyed.

The Excursion, Bk. VII.   W. WORDSWORTH.

I cannot but remember such things were,
That were most precious to me.

Macbeth, Act iv. Sc. 3.   SHAKESPEARE.

This memory brightens o'er the past,
As when the sun concealed
Behind some cloud that near us hangs,
Shines on a distant field.
A Gleam of Sunshine.   H. W. LONGFELLOW.

I count myself in nothing else so happy
As in a soul rememb'ring my good friends;
And, as my fortune ripens with thy love,
It shall be still thy true love's recompense.
Richard II., Act ii. *Sc.* 3.   SHAKESPEARE.

The sweet remembrance of the just
Shall flourish when he sleeps in dust.
Psalm CXII.   TATE AND BRADY.

When he shall hear she died upon his words,
Th' idea of her life shall sweetly creep
Into his study of imagination,
And every lovely organ of her life
Shall come apparelled in more precious habit,
More moving-delicate, and full of life,
Into the eye and prospect of his soul,
Than when she lived indeed.
Much Ado about Nothing, Act iv. *Sc.* 1. SHAKESPEARE.

Thou, thou alone, shall dwell forever.
And still shall recollection trace
In fancy's mirror, ever near,
Each smile, each tear, upon that face—
Though lost to sight, to memory dear.
Though Lost to Sight, to Memory Dear.   T. MOORE.

Joy's recollection is no longer joy,
While sorrow's memory is a sorrow still.
Doge of Venice.   LORD BYRON.

Of joys departed,
Not to return, how painful the remembrance!
The Grave.   R. BLAIR.

He that is strucken blind cannot forget
The precious treasure of his eyesight lost.
Romeo and Juliet, Act i. *Sc.* 1.   SHAKESPEARE.

Oh, how cruelly sweet are the echoes that start
When Memory plays an old tune on the heart!
Old Dobbin.   E. COOK.

What peaceful hours I once enjoyed!
How sweet their memory still!
But they have left an aching void
The world can never fill.
Walking with God.   W. COWPER.

While memory holds a seat
In this distracted globe.   Remember thee?
Yea, from the table of my memory
I'll wipe away all trivial fond records,
All saws of books, all forms, all pressures past,
That youth and observation copied there ;
And thy commandment all alone shall live
Within the book and volume of my brain.
Hamlet, Act i. *Sc.* 5.   SHAKESPEARE.

The leaves of memory seem to make
A mournful rustling in the dark.
The Fire of Driftwood.   H. W. LONGFELLOW.

My memory now is but the tomb of joys long past.
The Giaour.   LORD BYRON.

Remembrance and reflection how allied !
What thin partitions sense from thought divide !
Essay on Man, Epistle I.   A. POPE.

And memory, like a drop that night and day
Falls cold and ceaseless, wore my heart away !
Lalla Rookh.   T. MOORE.

Of all affliction taught the lover yet,
'T is sure the hardest science to forget.
Eloisa to Abélard.   A. POPE.

Ere such a soul regains its peaceful state,
How often must it love. how often hate,
How often hope, despair, resent, regret,
Conceal, disdain,—do all things but forget.
Eloisa to Abélard.   A. POPE.

To live with them is far less sweet
Than to remember thee !
I saw thy form.   T. MOORE.

The heart hath its own memory, like the mind
And in it are enshrined
The precious keepsakes, into which is wrought
The giver's loving thought.
From my Arm-chair.   H. W. LONGFELLOW.

MERCY.

The quality of mercy is not strained,—
It droppeth as the gentle rain from heaven
Upon the place beneath : it is twice blessed,—
It blesseth him that gives, and him that takes :

'T is mightiest in the mightiest : it becomes
The thronèd monarch better than his crown ;
His sceptre shows the force of temporal power,
The attribute to awe and majesty,
Wherein doth sit the dread and fear of kings :
But mercy is above this sceptred sway,—
It is enthronèd in the hearts of kings,
It is an attribute to God himself ;
And earthly power doth then show likest God's,
When mercy seasons justice. . . .

We do pray for mercy ;
And that same prayer doth teach us all to render
The deeds of mercy.
Merchant of Venice, Act iv. *Sc.* 1.   SHAKESPEARE.

Who will not mercie unto others show,
How can he mercie ever hope to have ?
Faërie Queene, Bk. VI. Canto I.   E. SPENSER.

No ceremony that to great ones 'longs,
Not the king's crown, nor the deputed sword,
The marshal's truncheon, nor the judge's robe,
Become them with one half so good a grace
As mercy does.
Measure for Measure, Act ii. *Sc.* 2.   SHAKESPEARE.

Sweet mercy is nobility's true badge.
Titus Andronicus, Act i. *Sc.* 2.   SHAKESPEARE.

Yet I shall temper so
Justice with mercy, as may illustrate most
Them fully satisfied, and Thee appease.
Paradise Lost, Bk. X.   MILTON.

MERRIMENT.

Gold that buys health can never be ill spent,
Nor hours laid out in harmless merriment.
Westward Ho, Act v. *Sc.* 3.   J. WEBSTER.

Merrily, merrily, shall I live now
Under the blossom that hangs on the bough.
Tempest, Act v. *Sc.* 1.   SHAKESPEARE.

The glad circles round them yield their souls
To festive mirth, and wit that knows no gall.
The Seasons : Summer.   J. THOMSON.

As merry as the day is long.
Much Ado about Nothing, Act ii. *Sc.* 1. SHAKESPEARE.

And frame your mind to mirth and merriment,
Which bars a thousand harms and lengthens life.
Taming of the Shrew : Induction, Sc. 2. SHAKESPEARE.

A merrier man,
Within the limit of becoming mirth,
I never spent an hour's talk withal.
His eye begets occasion for his wit.
For every object that the one doth catch,
The other turns to a mirth-loving jest.
Love's Labor's Lost, Act ii. Sc. 1. SHAKESPEARE.

Jog on, jog, on the footpath way,
And merrily hent the stile-a :
A merry heart goes all the day,
Your sad tires in a mile-a.
The Winter's Tale, Act iv. Sc. 3. SHAKESPEARE.

Care to our coffin adds a nail, no doubt,
And every grin, so merry, draws one out.
Expostulatory Odes, XV. DR. J. WOLCOTT (*Peter Pindar*).

And yet, methinks, the older that one grows,
Inclines us more to laugh than scold, tho' laughter
Leaves us so doubly serious shortly after.
Beppo. LORD BYRON.

There's not a string attuned to mirth
But has its chord in melancholy.
Ode to Melancholy. T. HOOD.

Low gurgling laughter, as sweet
As the swallow's song i' the South,
And a ripple of dimples that, dancing, meet
By the curves of a perfect mouth.
Ariel. P. H. HAYNE.

Fight Virtue's cause, stand up in Wit's defence,
Win us from vice and laugh us into sense.
On the Prospect of Peace. T. TICKELL.

Let me play the fool :
With mirth and laughter let old wrinkles come ;
And let my liver rather heat with wine,
Than my heart cool with mortifying groans.
Why should a man whose blood is warm within,
Sit like his grandsire cut in alabaster?
Sleep when he wakes? and creep into the jaundice
By being peevish?
Merchant of Venice, Act i. Sc. 1. SHAKESPEARE.

MIND.

We had not walked
But for Tradition ; we walk evermore
To higher paths by brightening Reason's lamp.
Spanish Gypsy, Bk. II.   GEORGE ELIOT.

He that of such a height hath built his mind,
And reared the dwelling of his thoughts so strong,
As neither fear nor hope can shake the frame
Of his resolvèd powers ; nor all the wind
Of vanity or malice pierce to wrong
His settled peace, or to disturb the same ;
What a fair seat hath he, from whence he may
The boundless wastes and wilds of man survey ?

.   .   .   .   .

Unless above himself he can
Erect himself, how poor a thing is man !
To the Countess of Cumberland.   S. DANIEL.

The mind is its own place, and in itself
Can make a heaven of hell, a hell of heaven.
Paradise Lost, Bk. I.   MILTON.

Sure, He that made us with such large discourse,
Looking before and after, gave us not
That capability and godlike reason,
To fust in us unused.
Hamlet, Act iv. Sc. 4.   SHAKESPEARE.

How rarely reason guides the stubborn choice,
Rules the bold hand, or prompts the suppliant voice.
The Vanity of Human Wishes.   DR. S. JOHNSON.

How small, of all that human hearts endure,
That part which laws or kings can cause or cure !
Still to ourselves in every place consigned,
Our own felicity we make or find.
With secret course, which no loud storms annoy,
Glides the smooth current of domestic joy.
Lines added to Goldsmith's Traveller.   DR. S. JOHNSON.

Now see that noble and most sovereign reason,
Like sweet bells jangled, out of tune and harsh.
Hamlet, Act iii. Sc. 1.   SHAKESPEARE.

Measure your mind's height by the shade it casts !
Paracelsus.   R. BROWNING.

Were I so tall to reach the pole,
Or grasp the ocean with my span,
I must be measured by my soul :
The mind 's the standard of the man.
Horæ Lyricæ, Bk. II. : False Greatness.   DR. I. WATTS.

Who reasons wisely is not therefore wise ;
His pride in reasoning, not in acting, lies.
Moral Essays, Epistle I.   A. POPE.

While Reason drew the plan, the Heart informed
The moral page and Fancy lent it grace.
Liberty, Pt. IV.   J. THOMSON.

Minds that have nothing to confer
Find little to perceive.
Yes ! Thou art Fair.   WORDSWORTH.

Cried, " 'T is resolved, for Nature pleads that he
Should only rule who most resembles me.
Shadwell alone my perfect image bears.
Mature in dulness from his tender years ;
Shadwell alone of all my sons is he
Who stands confirmed in full stupidity.
The rest to some faint meaning make pretence,
But Shadwell never deviates into sense.
Some beams of wit on other souls may fall,
Strike through and make a lucid interval ;
But Shadwell's genuine night admits no ray."
Mac Flecknoe.   J. DRYDEN.

MISSIONS.

Onward, ye men of prayer !
Scatter in rich exuberance the seed,
Whose fruit is living bread, and all your need
  Will God supply ; his harvest ye shall share.

Seek ye the far-off isle ;
The sullied jewel of the deep,
O'er whose remembered beauty angels weep,
  Restore its lustre and to God give spoil.
Missionaries.   W. B. TAPPAN.

When they reach the land of strangers,
  And the prospect dark appears,
Nothing seen but toils and dangers,
  Nothing felt but doubts and fears ;
    Be thou with them !
  Hear their sighs, and count their tears.
Departing Missionaries.   T. KELLY.

Shall we, whose souls are lighted
  With wisdom from on high,
Shall we to men benighted
  The Lamp of life deny ?
Salvation !   O Salvation !
  The joyful sound proclaim,
Till earth's remotest nation
  Has learned Messiah's name.
From Greenland's Icy Mountains.   BISHOP R. HEBER.

Blest river of salvation,
  Pursue thy onward way ;
Flow thou to every nation,
  Nor in thy richness stay :
Stay not till all the lowly
  Triumphant reach their home ;
Stay not till all the holy
  Proclaim, " The Lord is come ! "
Success of the Gospel.   S. F. SMITH.

Nor shall thy spreading gospel rest,
  Till through the world thy truth has run :
Till Christ has all the nations blessed
  That see the light, or feel the sun.
God's Word and Works.   DR. I. WATTS.

MODERATION.

Reason's whole pleasure, all the joys of sense,
Lie in three words,--health, peace, and competence.
But health consists with temperance alone,
And peace, O Virtue ! peace is all thine own.
Essay on Man, Epistle IV.   A. POPE.

These violent delights have violent ends,
  And in their triumph die ; like fire and powder,
Which as they kiss consume.
          .   .   .   .   .
Therefore love moderately ; long love doth so ;
Too swift arrives as tardy as too slow.
Romeo and Juliet, Act ii. *Sc.* 6.   SHAKESPEARE.

They surfeited with honey ; and began
To loathe the taste of sweetness, whereof a little
More than a little is by much too much.
King Henry IV., Pt. I. Act iii. *Sc.* 2.   SHAKESPEARE.

And for my means, I 'll husband them so well
They shall go far with little.
Hamlet, Act iv. *Sc.* 5.   SHAKESPEARE.

He that holds fast the golden mean,
And lives contentedly between
  The little and the great,
Feels not the wants that pinch the poor,
Nor plagues that haunt the rich man's door.
Translation of Horace, Bk. II. Ode X.   w. COWPER.

Take this at least, this last advice, my son :
Keep a stiff rein, and move but gently on :
The coursers of themselves will run too fast,
Your art must be to moderate their haste.
Metamorphoses : Phaeton, Bk. II.
               OVID. *Trans. of* ADDISON.

    Have more than thou showest,
    Speak less than thou knowest,
    Lend less than thou owest,
    Ride more than thou goest,
    Learn more than thou trowest,
    Set less than thou throwest.
King Lear, Act i. *Sc.* 4.   SHAKESPEARE.

MOON.

The night is come, but not too soon ;
  And sinking silently,
All silently, the little moon
  Drops down behind the sky.
The Light of Stars.   H. W. LONGFELLOW.

See yonder fire ! it is the moon
Slow rising o'er the eastern hill.
It glimmers on the forest tips,
And through the dewy foliage drips
In little rivulets of light,
And makes the heart in love with night.
Christus : The Golden Legend, Pt. VI.
              H. W. LONGFELLOW.

How like a queen comes forth the lonely Moon
From the slow opening curtains of the clouds ;
  Walking in beauty to her midnight throne !
Diana.   G. CROLY.

The Moon arose : she shone upon the lake,
Which lay one smooth expanse of silver light ;
She shone upon the hills and rocks, and cast
Upon their hollows and their hidden glens
A blacker depth of shade.
Madoc, Pt. II.   R. SOUTHEY.

No rest—no dark.
Hour after hour that passionless bright face
Climbs up the desolate blue.
Moon-struck.   D. M. MULOCK CRAIK.

Mother of light! how fairly dost thou go
    Over those hoary crests, divinely led!
Art thou that huntress of the silver bow
    Fabled of old?   Or rather dost thou tread
Those cloudy summits thence to gaze below,
Like the wild chamois from her Alpine snow,
    Where hunters never climbed—secure from dread?
Ode to the Moon.   T. HOOD.

And thou didst shine, thou rolling moon. upon
All this, and cast a wide and tender light,
Which softened down the hoar austerity
Of rugged desolation, and filled up,
As 't were anew, the gaps of centuries,
Leaving that beautiful which still was so,
And making that which was not, till the place
Became religion, and the heart ran o'er
With silent worship of the great of old!—
The dead, but sceptred sovereigns,who still rule
Our spirits from their urns.
Manfred, Act iii. *Sc.* 4 (*The Coliseum*).   LORD BYRON.

When the moon shone, we did not see the candle ;
So doth the greater glory dim the less.
Merchant of Venice, Act v. *Sc.* 1.   SHAKESPEARE.

            The moon looks
            On many brooks,
    " The brook can see no moon but this."
While gazing on the moon's light.   T. MOORE.

    I see them on their winding way,
    Above their ranks the moonbeams play.
        .   .   .   .
    And waving arms and banners bright
    Are glancing in the mellow light.
Lines written to a March.   BISHOP R. HEBER.

The devil 's in the moon for mischief ; they
Who called her chaste, methinks, began too soon
    Their nomenclature ; there is not a day,
The longest, not the twenty-first of June,
    Sees half the business in a wicked way,
On which three single hours of moonshine smile—
And then she looks so modest all the while !
Don Juan, Canto I.   LORD BYRON.

                              Faëry elves,
    Whose midnight revels, by a forest-side,
    Or fountain, some belated peasant sees,
    Or dreams he sees, while overhead the moon
    Sits arbitress, and nearer to the earth
    Wheels her pale course.
Paradise Lost, Bk. I.   MILTON.

    Day glimmered in the east, and the white Moon
    Hung like a vapor in the cloudless sky.
Italy : Lake of Geneva.   S. ROGERS.

MORNING.

    But soft ! methinks I scent the morning air.
Hamlet, Act i. *Sc.* 5.   SHAKESPEARE.

    The glow-worm shows the matin to be near,
    And 'gins to pale his uneffectual fire.
Hamlet, Act i. *Sc.* 5.   SHAKESPEARE.

                    Look, the gentle day,
    Before the wheels of Phœbus, roundabout,
    Dapples the drowsy east with spots of gray.
Much Ado about Nothing, Act v. *Sc.* 3.   SHAKESPEARE.

                    '   Till morning fair
    Came forth with pilgrim steps in amice gray.
Paradise Regained, Bk. IV.   MILTON.

    The gray-eyed morn smiles on the frowning night,
    Checkering the eastern clouds with streaks of light.
Romeo and Juliet, Act ii. *Sc.* 3.   SHAKESPEARE.

    Clothing the palpable and familiar
    With golden exhalations of the dawn.
The Death of Wallenstein, Act i. *Sc.*1.   S. T. COLERIDGE.

Night wanes,—the vapors round the mountains curled
Melt into morn, and light awakes the world.
Lara.   LORD BYRON.

    Night's candles are burnt out, and jocund day
    Stands tiptoe on the misty mountain-tops.
Romeo and Juliet, Act iii. *Sc.* 5.   SHAKESPEARE.

                Night's sun was driving
                His golden-haired horses up ;
                Over the eastern firths
                High flashed their manes.
The Longbeard's Saga.   C. KINGSLEY.

Slow buds the pink dawn like a rose
From out night's gray and cloudy sheath;
Softly and still it grows and grows,
Petal by petal, leaf by leaf.
The Morning Comes Before the Sun.
S. C. WOOLSEY (*Susan Coolidge*).

The charm dissolves apace,
And as the morning steals upon the night,
Melting the darkness, so their rising senses
Begin to chase the ignorant fumes that mantle
Their clearer reason.
Tempest, Act v. *Sc.* 1.   SHAKESPEARE.

An hour before the worshipped sun
Peered forth the golden window of the east.
Romeo and Juliet, Act i. *Sc.* 1.   SHAKESPEARE.

The morn is up again, the dewy morn,
With breath all incense, and with cheek all bloom,
Laughing the clouds away with playful scorn,
And living as if earth contained no tomb,—
And glowing into day.
Childe Harold, Canto III.   LORD BYRON.

Hail, gentle dawn! mild blushing goddess, hail!
Rejoiced I see thy purple mantle spread
O'er half the skies, gems pave thy radiant way,
And orient pearls from ev'ry shrub depend.
The Chase, Bk. II.   W. C. SOMERVILLE.

Morn in the white wake of the morning star
Came furrowing all the orient into gold.
The Princess.   A. TENNYSON.

The meek-eyed Morn appears, mother of dews.
The Seasons: Summer.   J. THOMSON.

Sweet is the breath of morn, her rising sweet
With charms of earliest birds; pleasant the sun,
When first on this delightful land he spreads
His orient beams, on herb, tree, fruit, and flower,
Glistering with dew.
Paradise Lost, Bk. IV.   MILTON.

This morning, like the spirit of a youth
That means to be of note, begins betimes.
Antony and Cleopatra, Act iv. *Sc.* 4.   SHAKESPEARE.

Morn,
Waked by the circling hours, with rosy hand
Unbarred the gates of light.
Paradise Lost, Bk. VI.   MILTON.

Now morn, her rosy steps in the eastern clime
Advancing, sowed the earth with orient pearl,
When Adam waked, so customed, for his sleep
Was aery-light, from pure digestion bred.
Paradise Lost, Bk. V.   MILTON.

At last, the golden orientall gate
Of greatest heaven gan to open fayre,
And Phœbus, fresh as brydegrome to his mate,
Came dauncing forth, shaking his dewie hayre ;
And hurls his glistring beams through gloomy ayre.
Faërie Queene, Bk. I. Canto V.   E. SPENSER.

But yonder comes the powerful King of Day
Rejoicing in the east.
The Seasons : Summer.   J. THOMSON.

'T is always morning somewhere in the world,
And Eos rises, circling constantly
The varied regions of mankind. No pause
Of renovation and of freshening rays
She knows.
Orion, Bk. III. Canto III.   R. H. HORNE.

MOTHER.

The only love which, on this teeming earth,
Asks no return for passion's wayward birth.
The Dream.   HON. MRS. NORTON.

A mother's love,—how sweet the name !
    What is a mother's love ?—
A noble, pure, and tender flame,
    Enkindled from above,
To bless a heart of earthly mould ;
The warmest love that can grow cold ;—
    This is a mother's love.
A Mother's Love.   J. MONTGOMERY.

Hath he set bounds between their love and me ?
I am their mother ; who shall bar me from them ?
King Richard III., Act iv. Sc. 1.   SHAKESPEARE.

                    The poor wren,
The most diminutive of birds, will fight,
Her young ones in her nest, against the owl.
Macbeth, Act iv. Sc. 2.   SHAKESPEARE.

Where yet was ever found a mother
Who 'd give her booby for another ?
Fables : The Mother, the Nurse, and the Fairy. J. GAY.
13

Women know
The way to rear up children (to be just) ;
They know a simple, merry, tender knack
Of tying sashes, fitting baby-shoes,
And stringing pretty words that make no sense,
And kissing full sense into empty words ;
Which things are corals to cut life upon,
Although such trifles.
Aurora Leigh, Bk. I.   E. B. BROWNING.

They say that man is mighty,
    He governs land and sea,
He wields a mighty scepter
    O'er lesser powers that be ;
But a mightier power and stronger
    Man from his throne has hurled,
For the hand that rocks the cradle
    Is the hand that rules the world.
What Rules the World.   W. R. WALLACE.

Who ran to help me when I fell,
And would some pretty story tell,
Or kiss the place to make it well ?
        My mother.
My Mother.   JANE TAYLOR.

Happy he
With such a mother ! faith in womankind
Beats with his blood, and trust in all things high
Comes easy to him, and though he trip and fall,
He shall not blind his soul with clay.
The Princess, Canto VII.   A. TENNYSON.

A mother is a mother still,
The holiest thing alive.
The Three Graces.   S. T. COLERIDGE.

MOUNTAIN.

Two voices are there ; one is of the sea,
One of the mountains ; each a mighty Voice.
Thought of a Briton on the Subjugation of Switzerland.
                    W. WORDSWORTH.

Who first beholds those everlasting clouds,
Seedtime and harvest, morning, noon, and night,
Still where they were, steadfast, immovable ;
Who first beholds the Alps—that mighty chain

Of mountains, stretching on from east to west,
So massive, yet so shadowy, so ethereal,
As to belong rather to heaven than earth—
But instantly receives into his soul
A sense, a feeling that he loses not,
A something that informs him 't is a moment
Whence he may date henceforward and forever !
Italy. S. ROGERS.

The avalanche—the thunderbolt of snow !—
All that expands the spirit, yet appalls,
Gather around these summits, as to show
How earth may pierce to Heaven, yet leave vain man below.
Childe Harold, Canto III. LORD BYRON.

Mountains interposed
Make enemies of nations, who had else
Like kindred drops been mingled into one.
The Task, Bk. II. W. COWPER.

Over the hills and far away.
The Beggar's Opera, Act i. *Sc.* 1. J. GAY.

Mont Blanc is the monarch of mountains ;
They crowned him long ago
On a throne of rocks, in a robe of clouds,
With a diadem of snow.
Manfred, Act i. *Sc.*1. LORD BYRON.

MOURNING.

They truly mourn, that mourn without a witness.
Mirza. R. BARON.

He mourns the dead who lives as they desire.
Night Thoughts, Night II. DR. E. YOUNG.

Each lonely scene shall thee restore ;
For thee the tear be duly shed ;
Beloved till life can charm no more,
And mourned till Pity's self be dead.
Dirge in Cymbeline. W. COLLINS.

Those that he loved so long and sees no more,
Loved and still loves,—not dead, but gone before,—
He gathers round him.
Human Life. S. ROGERS.

Give sorrow words ; the grief that does not speak
Whispers the o'erfraught heart, and bids it break.
Macbeth, Act iv. *Sc.* 3. SHAKESPEARE.

Praising what is lost
Makes the remembrance dear.
All's Well that Ends Well, Act v. *Sc.* 3. SHAKESPEARE.

We bear it calmly, though a ponderous woe,
And still adore the hand that gives the blow.
Verses to his Friend under Affliction. J. POMFRET.

My grief lies all within ;
And these external manners of laments
Are merely shadows to the unseen grief
That swells with silence in the tortured soul.
King Richard II., Act iv. *Sc.* 1. SHAKESPEARE.

What though no friends in sable weeds appear.
Grieve for an hour, perhaps, then mourn a year,
And bear about the mockery of woe
To midnight dances and the public show !
To the Memory of an Unfortunate Lady. A. POPE.

He first deceased ; she for a little tried
To live without him, liked it not, and died.
Upon the Death of Sir Albert Morton's Wife.
SIR H. WOTTON.

Poor Jack, farewell !
I could have better spared a better man.
King Henry IV., Pt. I. Act v. *Sc.* 4. SHAKESPEARE.

So may he rest : his faults lie gently on him !
King Henry VIII., Act iv. *Sc.* 2. SHAKESPEARE.

He that lacks time to mourn, lacks time to mend.
Eternity mourns that. 'T is an ill cure
For life's worst ills to have no time to feel them.
Philip Van Artevelde, Pt. I. Act i. *Sc.* 5. H. TAYLOR.

The very cypress droops to death—
Dark tree, still sad when others' grief is fled,
The only constant mourner o'er the dead.
The Giaour. LORD BYRON.

MURDER.

O blissful God, that art so just and trewe !
Lo, howe that thou biwreyest mordre alway !
Mordre wol out, that se we day by day.
The Nonnes Preestes Tale. CHAUCER.

Blood, though it sleep a time, yet never dies.
The gods on murtherers fix revengeful eyes.
The Widow's Tears. G. CHAPMAN.

Murder may pass unpunished for a time,
But tardy justice will o'ertake the crime.
The Cock and the Fox.   J. DRYDEN.

For murder, though it have no tongue, will speak
With most miraculous organ.
Hamlet, Act ii. *Sc.* 1.   SHAKESPEARE.

MUSIC.

God is its author, and not man ; he laid
The key-note of all harmonies ; he planned
All perfect combinations, and he made
Us so that we could hear and understand.
Music.   J. G. C. BRAINARD.

There 's music in the sighing of a reed ;
    There 's music in the gushing of a rill ;
There 's music in all things, if men had ears :
    Their earth is but an echo of the spheres.
Don Juan, Canto XV.   LORD BYRON.

With melting airs, or martial, brisk, or grave ;
Some chord in unison with what we hear
Is touched within us, and the heart replies.
The Task, Bk. VI.: Winter Walk at Noon. W. COWPER.

A velvet flute-note fell down pleasantly,
Upon the bosom of that harmony,
And sailed and sailed incessantly,
As if a petal from a wild-rose blown
Had fluttered down upon that pool of tone,
And boatwise dropped o' the convex side
And floated down the glassy tide
And clarified and glorified
The solemn spaces where the shadows bide.
The Symphony.   S. LANIER.

Can any mortal mixture of earth's mould
Breathe such divine enchanting ravishment ?
Sure something holy lodges in that breast,
And with these raptures moves the vocal air
To testify his hidden residence.
How sweetly did they float upon the wings
Of silence, through the empty-vaulted night,
At every fall smoothing the raven down
Of darkness till it smiled.
Comus.   MILTON.

Though music oft hath such a charm
To make bad good, and good provoke to harm.
Measure for Measure, Act iv. *Sc.* 1.   SHAKESPEARE.

If music be the food of love, play on ;
Give me excess of it, that, surfeiting,
The appetite may sicken, and so die.—
That strain again—it had a dying fall :
O, it came o'er my ear like the sweet south,
That breathes upon a bank of violets,
Stealing and giving odor.
Twelfth Night, Act i. *Sc.* 1.   SHAKESPEARE.

Where music dwells
Lingering and wandering on. as loath to die,
Like thoughts whose very sweetness yieldeth proof
That they were born for immortality.
Ecclesiastical Sonnets, Pt. III. xliii. W. WORDSWORTH.

Music hath charms to soothe a savage breast,
To soften rocks, or bend a knotted oak.
I 've read that things inanimate have moved,
And, as with living souls, have been informed
By magic numbers and persuasive sound.
The Mourning Bride, Act i. *Sc.* 1.   W. CONGREVE.

There is a charm, a power, that sways the breast ;
Bids every passion revel or be still ;
Inspires with rage, or all our cares dissolves ;
Can soothe distraction, and almost despair.
Art of Preserving Health.   J. ARMSTRONG.

The soul of music slumbers in the shell,
Till waked and kindled by the Master's spell ;
And feeling hearts—touch them but lightly—pour
A thousand melodies unheard before !
Human Life.   S. ROGERS.

Give me some music : music, moody food
Of us that trade in love.
Antony and Cleopatra, Act ii. *Sc.* 5.   SHAKESPEARE.

See to their desks Apollo's sons repair,
Swift rides the rosin o'er the horse's hair !
In unison their various tones to tune,
Murmurs the hautboy, growls the hoarse bassoon ;
In soft vibration sighs the whispering lute,
Tang goes the harpsichord, too-too the flute,
Brays the loud trumpet, squeaks the fiddle sharp,
Winds the French-horn, and twangs the tingling harp ;
Till, like great Jove, the leader, figuring in,
Attunes to order the chaotic din.
Rejected Addresses : The Theatre.   H. AND J. SMITH.

'T is believed that this harp which I wake now for thee
Was a siren of old who sung under the sea.
The Origin of the Harp.   T. MOORE.

And wheresoever, in his rich creation,
  Sweet music breathes—in wave, or bird, or soul—
'T is but the faint and far reverberation
Of that great tune to which the planets roll !
Music.   F. S. OSGOOD.

He touched his harp, and nations heard, entranced ;
As some vast river of unfailing source,
Rapid, exhaustless, deep, his numbers flowed,
And opened new fountains in the human heart.
Course of Time, Bk. IV.   R. POLLOK.

Music resembles poetry : in each
Are nameless graces which no methods teach,
And which a master-hand alone can reach.
Essay on Criticism.   A. POPE.

NAME.

Who hath not owned, with rapture-smitten frame,
The power of grace, the magic of a name ?
Pleasures of Hope, Pt. II.   T. CAMPBELL.

Wherever the bright sun of heaven shall shine,
His honor and the greatness of his name
Shall be, and make new nations.
King Henry VIII., Act iv. Sc. 2.   SHAKESPEARE.

Halloo your name to the reverberate hills
And make the babbling gossip of the air
  Cry out.
Twelfth Night, Act i. Sc. 5.   SHAKESPEARE.

My name is Norval ; on the Grampian hills
My father feeds his flocks ; a frugal swain,
Whose constant cares were to increase his store,
And keep his only son, myself, at home.
Douglas, Act ii. Sc. 1.   J. HOME.

And if his name be George, I 'll call him Peter ;
For new-made honor doth forget men's names.
King John, Act i. Sc. 1.   SHAKESPEARE.

What woful stuff this madrigal would be
If some starved hackney sonneteer, or me,
But let a lord once own the happy lines,
How the wit brightens ! how the style refines !
Essay on Criticism, Pt. II.   A. POPE.

'T is from high life high characters are drawn ;
A saint in crape is twice a saint in lawn.
Moral Essays, Epistle I.   A. POPE.

Oh! Amos Cottle !* Phœbus! What a name
To fill the speaking trump of future fame !
English Bards and Scotch Reviewers.   LORD BYRON.

NATURE.

The fall of kings,
The rage of nations, and the crush of states,
Move not the man, who, from the world escaped,
In still retreats, and flowery solitudes,
To nature's voice attends, from month to month,
And day to day, through the revolving year.
The Seasons : Autumn.   J. THOMSON.

When that the monthe of May
Is comen, and that I hear the foules synge,
And that the floures gynnen for to sprynge,
Farwel my boke, and my devocion.
Legende of Goode Women : Prologue.   CHAUCER.

To one who has been long in city pent,
'T is very sweet to look into the fair
And open face of heaven.—to breathe a prayer
Full in the smile of the blue firmament.
Sonnet XIV.   J. KEATS.

What more felicitie can fall to creature
Than to enjoy delight with libertie,
And to be lord of all the workes of Nature,
To raine in th' aire from earth to highest skie,
To feed on flowres and weeds of glorious feature !
The Fate of the Butterfly.   E. SPENSER.

Warms in the sun, refreshes in the breeze,
Glows in the stars, and blossoms in the trees.
Essay on Man, Epistle I.   A. POPE.

In such green palaces the first kings reigned,
Slept in their shades, and angels entertained ;
With such old counsellors they did advise,
And by frequenting sacred groves grew wise.
On St. James' Park.   E. WALLER

* " Mr. Cottle, Amos or Joseph, I don't know which, but one or both,
once sellers of books they did not write, but now writers of books that
do not sell, have published a pair of epics."--THE AUTHOR.

And recognizes ever and anon
The breeze of Nature stirring in his soul.
The Excursion, Bk. IV.   W. WORDSWORTH.

Nature ! great parent ! whose unceasing hand
Rolls round the seasons of the changeful year ;
How mighty, how majestic are thy works !
The Seasons : Winter.   J. THOMSON.

Every sound is sweet ;
Myriads of rivulets hurrying through the lawn,
The moan of doves in immemorial elms,
And murmuring of innumerable bees.
The Princess, Canto VII.   A. TENNYSON.

I trust in Nature for the stable laws
Of beauty and utility. Spring shall plant
And Autumn garner to the end of time.
I trust in God—the right shall be the right
And other than the wrong, while he endures ;
I trust in my own soul, that can perceive
The outward and the inward, Nature's good
And God's.
A Soul Tragedy, Act i.   R. BROWNING.

I care not, Fortune, what you me deny ;
You cannot rob me of free Nature's grace,
You cannot shut the windows of the sky,
Through which Aurora shows her brightening face ;
You cannot bar my constant feet to trace
The woods and lawns, by living stream, at eve.
The Castle of Indolence, Canto II.   J. THOMSON.

Who can paint
Like Nature ? Can imagination boast,
Amid its gay creation, hues like hers ?
The Seasons : Spring.   J. THOMSON.

For Art may err, but Nature cannot miss.
The Cock and Fox.   J. DRYDEN.

The course of nature is the art of God.
Night Thoughts, Night IX.   DR. E. YOUNG.

'T is elder Scripture, writ by God's own hand :
Scripture authentic ! uncorrupt by man.
Night Thoughts, Night IX.   DR. E. YOUNG.

Nature, the vicar of the almightie Lord.
Assembly of Foules.   CHAUCER.

To the solid ground
Of nature trusts the Mind that builds for aye.
Miscellaneous Sonnets.   W. WORDSWORTH.

NIGHT.

Darkness now rose,
As daylight sunk, and brought in low'ring Night,
Her shadowy offspring.
Paradise Regained, Bk. IV.   MILTON.

Now black and deep the Night begins to fall,
A shade immense ! Sunk in the quenching gloom,
Magnificent and vast, are heaven and earth.
Order confounded lies ; all beauty void,
Distinction lost, and gay variety
One universal blot : such the fair power
Of light, to kindle and create the whole.
The Seasons : Autumn.   J. THOMSON.

How beautiful is night !
A dewy freshness fills the silent air ;
No mist obscures, nor cloud, nor speck, nor stain,
Breaks the serene of heaven :
In full-orbed glory, yonder moon divine
Rolls through the dark-blue depths.
Beneath her steady ray
The desert-circle spreads.
Like the round ocean, girdled with the sky.
How beautiful is night !
Thalaba.   R. SOUTHEY.

This sacred shade and solitude, what is it ?
'T is the felt presence of the Deity.
  .   .   .   .   .   .
By night an atheist half believes a God.
Night Thoughts, Night V.   DR. E. YOUNG.

Night, sable goddess ! from her ebon throne,
In rayless majesty, now stretches forth
Her leaden sceptre o'er a slumbering world.
Night Thoughts, Night I.   DR. E. YOUNG.

All is gentle ; naught
Stirs rudely ; but, congenial with the night,
Whatever walks is gliding like a spirit.
Doge of Venice.   LORD BYRON.

O radiant Dark ! O darkly fostered ray !
Thou hast a joy too deep for shallow Day.
The Spanish Gypsy, Bk. I.   GEORGE ELIOT.

I linger yet with Nature. for the night
Hath been to me a more familiar face
Than that of man ; and in her starry shade
Of dim and solitary loveliness,
I learned the language of another world.
Manfred, Act iii. *Sc.* 4.　　　　　LORD BYRON.

Night is the time for rest ;
　How sweet, when labors close,
To gather round an aching breast
　The curtain of repose,
Stretch the tired limbs. and lay the head
Down on our own delightful bed !
Night.　　　　　J. MONTGOMERY.

Now the hungry lion roars,
　And the wolf behowls the moon ;
Whilst the heavy ploughman snores,
　All with weary task foredone.
Midsummer Night's Dream, Act v. *Sc.* 1.　SHAKESPEARE.

Quiet night, that brings
Rest to the laborer, is the outlaw's day,
In which he rises early to do wrong,
And when his work is ended dares not sleep.
The Guardian, Act ii. *Sc.* 4.　　　P. MASSINGER.

I must become a borrower of the night
For a dark hour or twain.
Macbeth, Act iii. *Sc.* 1.　　　　SHAKESPEARE.

All was so still, so soft, in earth and air,
You scarce would start to meet a spirit there
Secure that nought of evil could delight
To walk in such a scene, on such a night !
Lara.　　　　　LORD BYRON.

Soon as midnight brought on the dusky hour
Friendliest to sleep and silence.
Paradise Lost, Bk. V.　　　　MILTON.

The iron tongue of midnight hath told twelve ;
Lovers, to bed ; 't is almost fairy time.
Midsummer Night's Dream, Act v. *Sc.* 1.　SHAKESPEARE.

In the dead vast and middle of the night.
Hamlet, Act i. *Sc.* 2.　　　　SHAKESPEARE.

'T is now the very witching time of night,
When churchyards yawn, and Hell itself breathes out
Contagion to this world.
Hamlet, Act iii. *Sc.* 2.　　　　SHAKESPEARE.

O wild and wondrous midnight,
There is a might in thee
To make the charmèd body
Almost like spirit be,
And give it some faint glimpses
Of immortality !

Midnight.   J. R. LOWELL.

NOBILITY.

Be noble ! and the nobleness that lies
In other men, sleeping, but never dead,
Will rise in majesty to meet thine own.
Sonnet IV.   J. R. LOWELL.

His nature is too noble for the world :
He would not flatter Neptune for his trident,
Or Jove for 's power to thunder.
Coriolanus, Act iii. *Sc.* 1.   SHAKESPEARE.

This was the noblest Roman of them all :
All the conspirators save only he
Did that they did in envy of great Cæsar ;
He only, in a general honest thought
And common good to all, made one of them.
Julius Cæsar, Act v. *Sc.* 5.   SHAKESPEARE.

OPINION.

For most men (till by losing rendered sager)
Will back their own opinions by a wager.
Beppo.   LORD BYRON.

Some praise at morning what they blame at night,
But always think the last opinion right.
Essay on Criticism, Pt. II.   A. POPE.

He that complies against his will
Is of his own opinion still.
Hudibras, Canto III.   S. BUTLER.

OPPORTUNITY.

Who seeks. and will not take when once 't is offered,
Shall never find it more.
Antony and Cleopatra, Act ii. *Sc.* 7.   SHAKESPEARE.

This could but have happened once,
And we missed it, lost it forever.
Youth and Art.   R. BROWNING.

He that will not when he may,
When he will he shall have nay.
Quoted in Anatomy of Melancholy.   R. BURTON.

He that would not when he might,
He shall not when he wolda.
Reliques: The Baffled Knight.   BISHOP T. PERCY.

Urge them while their souls
Are capable of this ambition,
Lest zeal, nor melted by the windy breath
Of soft petitions, pity and remorse,
Cool and congeal again to what it was.
King John, Act ii. Sc. 2.   SHAKESPEARE.

Turning, for them who pass, the common dust
Of servile opportunity to gold.
Desultory Stanzas.   W. WORDSWORTH.

ORATORY.

But, spite of all the criticising elves,
Those who would make us feel—must feel themselves.
The Rosciad.   C. CHURCHILL.

Words that weep and tears that speak.
The Prophet.   A. COWLEY.

Thence to the famous orators repair,
Those ancient, whose resistless eloquence
Wielded at will that fierce democratie.
Shook the arsenal, and fulmined over Greece,
To Macedon, and Artaxerxes' throne.
Paradise Regained, Bk. IV.   MILTON.

Where nature's end of language is declined,
And men talk only to conceal the mind.
Love of Fame, Satire II.   DR. E. YOUNG.

What means this passionate discourse,
This peroration with such circumstance?
Henry VI., Pt. II. Act i. Sc. 1.   SHAKESPEARE.

Frank, haughty, rash,—the Rupert of debate.
The New Timon, Pt. I.   E. BULWER-LYTTON.

For rhetoric, he could not ope
His mouth, but out there flew a trope.

.   .   .   .

For all a rhetorician's rules
Teach nothing but to name his tools.
Hudibras, Pt. I. Canto I.   S. BUTLER.

" I wonder if Brougham thinks as much as he talks,"
    Said a punster, perusing a trial ;
" I vow, since his lordship was made Baron Vaux,
    He's been *Vaux et præterea nihil !* "
A Voice and Nothing More.   ANONYMOUS.

ORDER.

Confusion heard his voice, and wild uproar
Stood ruled, stood vast infinitude confined ;
Till at his second bidding darkness fled,
Light shone, and order from disorder sprung.
Paradise Lost, Bk. III.   MILTON.

For the world was built in order
    And the atoms march in tune :
Rhyme the pipe, and Time the warder,
    The sun obeys them, and the moon.
Monadnock.   R. W. EMERSON.

Mark what unvaried laws preserve each state,
Laws wise as Nature, and as fixed as Fate.
Essay on Man, Epistle III.   A. POPE.

The heavens themselves, the planets and this centre
Observe degree, priority and place,
Insisture, course, proportion, season, form,
Office and custom, in all line of order.
Troilus and Cressida, Act i. *Sc.* 2.   SHAKESPEARE.

PAIN.

The scourge of life, and death's extreme disgrace,
The smoke of Hell, that monster callèd Paine.
Sidera : Paine.   SIR P. SIDNEY.

Nothing begins, and nothing ends,
    That is not paid with moan ;
For we are born in others' pain,
    And perish in our own.
Daisy.   F. THOMPSON.

Pain is no longer pain when it is past.
Nature's Lesson.   M. J. PRESTON.

Why, all delights are vain ; but that most vain,
Which, with pain purchased, doth inherit pain.
Love's Labor's Lost. Act i. *Sc.* 1.   SHAKESPEARE.

Alas ! by some degree of woe
We every bliss must gain ;
The heart can ne'er a transport know
That never feels a pain.
Song.   LORD LYTTELTON.

PAINTING.

The glowing portraits, fresh from life, that bring
Home to our hearts the truth from which they spring.
Monody on the Death of the Rt. Hon. R. B. Sheridan.
LORD BYRON.

Hard features every bungler can command :
To draw true beauty shows a master's hand.
To Mr. Lee, on his Alexander.   J. DRYDEN.

A flattering painter, who made it his care
To draw men as they ought to be, not as they are.
Retaliation.   O. GOLDSMITH.

Lely on animated canvas stole
The sleepy eye, that spoke the melting soul.
Horace, Bk. II. Epistle I.   A. POPE.

I will say of it,
It tutors nature : artificial strife
Lives in these touches, livelier than life.
Timon of Athens, Act i. Sc. 1.   SHAKESPEARE.

With hue like that when some great painter dips
His pencil in the gloom of earthquake and eclipse.
The Revolt of Islam.   P. B. SHELLEY.

PARTING.

To know, to esteem, to love,—and then to part,
Makes up life's tale to many a feeling heart.
On Taking Leave of ——.   S. T. COLERIDGE.

Forever, Fortune, wilt thou prove
An unrelenting foe to love ;
And, when we meet a mutual heart,
Come in between and bid us part ?
Song.   J. THOMSON.

Two lives that once part, are as ships that divide
When, moment on moment, there rushes between
The one and the other, a sea ;—
Ah, never can fall from the days that have been
A gleam on the years that shall be !
A Lament.   E. BULWER-LYTTON.

Such partings break the heart they fondly hope to heal.
Childe Harold, Canto I.   LORD BYRON.

We twain have met like the ships upon the sea.
Who hold an hour's converse, so short, so sweet ;
One little hour ! and then, away they speed
On lonely paths, through mist, and cloud, and foam,
To meet no more.
Life Drama, Sc. 4.   A. SMITH.

He did keep
The deck, with glove, or hat, or handkerchief,
Still waving as the fits and stirs of his mind
Could best express how slow his soul sailed on,—
How swift his ship.
Cymbeline, Act i. *Sc. 4.*   SHAKESPEARE.

But in vain she did conjure him,
To depart her presence so,
Having a thousand tongues t' allure him
And but one to bid him go.
When lips invite,
And eyes delight,
And cheeks as fresh as rose in June
Persuade delay,—
What boots to say
Forego me now, come to me soon ?
Dulcina.   SIR W. RALEIGH.

Good night, good night : parting is such sweet sorrow,
That I shall say good night till it be morrow.
Romeo and Juliet, Act ii. *Sc. 2.*   SHAKESPEARE.

JULIET.—O, think'st thou we shall ever meet again ?
ROMEO.—I doubt it not ; and all these woes shall serve
For sweet discourses in our time to come.
Romeo and Juliet, Act iii. *Sc. 5.*   SHAKESPEARE.

In the hope to meet
Shortly again, and make our absence sweet.
Underwoods.   B. JONSON.

When we two parted
In silence and tears,
Half broken-hearted,
To sever for years,
Pale grew thy cheek and cold,
Colder thy kiss :
Truly that hour foretold
Sorrow to this !
When we two parted.   LORD BYRON.

BRUTUS.—Whether we shall meet again I know not.
Therefore our everlasting farewell take ;
For ever, and for ever, farewell. Cassius !
If we do meet again, why, we shall smile ;
If not, why, then this parting was well made.
    CASSIUS.—For ever, and for ever, farewell. Brutus !
Julius Cæsar, Act v. *Sc.* 1.   SHAKESPEARE.

PASSION.

            Take heed lest passion sway
Thy judgment to do aught, which else free will
Would not admit.
Paradise Lost, Bk. VIII.   MILTON.

    In men, we various ruling passions find ;
    In women two almost divide the kind ;
    Those only fixed, they first or last obey,
    The love of pleasure, and the love of sway.
Moral Essays, Epistle II.   A. POPE.

    Passions are likened best to floods and streams,
    The shallow murmur, but the deep are dumb.
The Silent Lover.   SIR W. RALEIGH.

    A little fire is quickly trodden out ;
    Which, being suffered, rivers cannot quench.
Henry VI., Pt. III. Act iv. *Sc.* 8.   SHAKESPEARE.

    The ruling passion, be it what it will,
    The ruling passion conquers reason still.

       .   .   .   .

    Hear then the truth : 'T is Heav'n each passion sends,
    And different men directs to different ends.
    Extremes in nature equal good produce ;
    Extremes in man concur to general use.
Moral Essays, Epistle III.   A. POPE.

    And hence one master-passion in the breast,
    Like Aaron's serpent, swallows up the rest.
Essay on Man, Epistle II.   A. POPE.

PAST, THE.

    O, call back yesterday, bid time return.

       .   .   .   .

    To-day, unhappy day, too late.
King Richard II., Act iii. *Sc.* 2.   SHAKESPEARE.
14

Not heaven itself upon the past has power ;
But what has been, has been, and I have had my hour.
Imitation of Horace, Bk. I. Ode XXIX.   J. DRYDEN.

Things without all remedy
Should be without regard : what 's done is done.
Macbeth, Act iii. *Sc.* 2.   SHAKESPEARE.

Gone, glimmering through the dream of things that were,

    .   .   .   .   .

A school-boy's tale, the wonder of an hour !
Childe Harold, Canto II.   LORD BYRON.

This is the place.   Stand still, my steed,
    Let me review the scene,
And summon from the shadowy Past
    The forms that once have been.
A Gleam of Sunshine.   H. W. LONGFELLOW.

Applause
To that blest son of foresight ; lord of fate !
That awful independent on to-morrow
Whose work is done ; who triumphs in the past ;
Whose yesterdays look backwards with a smile.
Night Thoughts, Night II.   DR. E. YOUNG.

For time is like a fashionable host,
That slightly shakes his parting guest by the hand,
And with his arms outstretched, as he would fly,
Grasps-in the comer.   Welcome ever smiles,
And farewell goes out sighing.
Troilus and Cressida, Act iii. *Sc.* 3.   SHAKESPEARE.

PATIENCE.

Endurance is the crowning quality,
    And patience all the passion of great hearts.
Columbus.   J. R. LOWELL.

His patient soul endures what Heav'n ordains,
    But neither feels nor fears ideal pains.
The Borough.   G. CRABBE.

'T is all men's office to speak patience
To those that ring under the load of sorrow,
But no man's virtue nor sufficiency
To be so moral when he shall endure
The like himself.
Much Ado about Nothing. Act v. *Sc.* 1.   SHAKESPEARE.

And I must bear
What is ordained with patience, being aware
Necessity doth front the universe
With an invincible gesture.
Prometheus Bound.   E. B. BROWNING.

How poor are they that have not patience !
What wound did ever heal but by degrees ?
Othello, Act ii. *Sc.* 3.   SHAKESPEARE.

I will with patience hear, and find a time
Both meet to hear and answer such high things.
Julius Cæsar, Act i. *Sc.* 2.   SHAKESPEARE.

I worked with patience, which means almost power.
Aurora Leigh, Bk. III.   E. B. BROWNING.

Or arm th' obdured breast
With stubborn patience as with triple steel.
Paradise Lost, Bk. II.   MILTON.

Patience, sov'reign o'er transmuted ill.
The Vanity of Human Wishes.   DR. S. JOHNSON.

Patience, my lord ! why, 't is the soul of peace ;
Of all the virtues 't is nearest kin to heaven ;
It makes men look like gods.   The best of men
That e'er wore earth about him was a sufferer,
A soft, meek, patient, humble, tranquil spirit,
The first true gentleman that ever breathed.
The Honest Whore, Pt. I. Act i. *Sc.* 12.   T. DEKKER.

PATRIOTISM.

They love their land, because it is their own,
And scorn to give aught other reason why.
Connecticut.   F-G. HALLECK.

No factious voice
Called them unto the field of generous fame,
But the pure consecrated love of home ;
No deeper feeling sways us, when it wakes
In all its greatness.
The Graves of the Patriots.   J. G. PERCIVAL.

The worst of rebels never arm
To do their king and country harm,
But draw their swords to do them good,
As doctors use, by letting blood.
Hudibras.   S. BUTLER.

Hail! Independence, hail! Heaven's next best gift,
To that of life and an immortal soul!
Liberty, Pt. V.   J. THOMSON.

The inextinguishable spark, which fires
The soul of patriots.
Leonidas.   R. GLOVER.

I do love
My country's good with a respect more tender,
More holy and profound, than mine own life.
Coriolanus, Act iii. Sc. 3.   SHAKESPEARE.

What pity is it
That we can die but once to save our country!
Cato, Act iv. Sc. 4.   J. ADDISON.

PEACE.

O Peace! thou source and soul of social life;
Beneath whose calm inspiring influence
Science his views enlarges, Art refines,
And swelling Commerce opens all her ports.
Britannia.   J. THOMSON.

Ay, but give me worship and quietness;
I like it better than a dangerous honor.
King Henry VI., Pt. III. Act iv. Sc. 3.   SHAKESPEARE.

This hand, to tyrants ever sworn the foe,
For freedom only deals the deadly blow;
Then sheathes in calm repose the vengeful blade,
For gentle peace in freedom's hallowed shade.
Written in an Album.   J. Q. ADAMS.

To reap the harvest of perpetual peace,
By this one bloody trial of sharp war.
King Richard III., Act v. Sc. 2.   SHAKESPEARE.

Take away the sword;
States can be saved without it.
Richelieu, Act ii. Sc. 2.   E. BULWER-LYTTON.

A peace is of the nature of a conquest;
For then both parties nobly are subdued,
And neither party loser.
King Henry IV., Pt. II. Act iv. Sc. 2.   SHAKESPEARE.

His helmet now shall make a hive for bees,
And lover's sonnets turned to holy psalms;
A man at arms must now serve on his knees,
And feed on prayers, which are his age's alms.
Polyhymnia.   G. PEELE.

Ne'er to meet, or ne'er to part, is peace.
Night Thoughts, Night V.   DR. E. YOUNG.

Till each man finds his own in all men's good,
And all men work in noble brotherhood,
Breaking their mailèd fleets and armèd towers,
And ruling by obeying Nature's powers,
And gathering all the fruits of peace and crowned with
     all her flowers.
Ode, sung at the Opening of the International Exhibition.
                     A. TENNYSON.

PEN.

Beneath the rule of men entirely great
The pen is mightier than the sword.
Richelieu, Act ii. Sc. 2.   E. BULWER-LYTTON.

The feather, whence the pen
Was shaped that traced the lives of these good men,
Dropped from an Angel's wing.
Ecclesiastical Sonnets, Pt. III., v. Walton's Book of Lives.
                 W. WORDSWORTH.

Whose noble praise
Deserves a quill pluckt from an angel's wing.
Sonnet.   DOROTHY BERRY.

You still shall live—such virtue hath my pen,
Where breath most breathes, even in the mouths of men.
Sonnet, LXXXI.   SHAKESPEARE.

Oh ! nature's noblest gift—my gray-goose quill !
Slave of my thoughts, obedient to my will,
Torn from thy parent-bird to form a pen,
That mighty instrument of little men !
English Bards and Scotch Reviewers.   LORD BYRON.

PEOPLE, THE.

Who o'er the herd would wish to reign,
Fantastic, fickle, fierce, and vain !—
Vain as the leaf upon the stream,
And fickle as a changeful dream ;
Fantastic as a woman's mood,
And fierce as Frenzy's fevered blood.
Thou many-headed monster thing,
O, who would wish to be thy king !
Lady of the Lake, Canto V.   SIR W. SCOTT.

I have bought
Golden opinions from all sorts of people.
Macbeth, Act i. Sc. 7.   SHAKESPEARE.

He that depends
Upon your favors swims with fins of lead,
And hews down oaks with rushes. Hang ye! Trust ye?
With every minute you do change a mind:
And call him noble that was now your hate,
Him vile that was your garland.
Coriolanus, Act i. *Sc.* 1.   SHAKESPEARE.

The scum
That rises upmost when the nation boils.
Don Sebastian.   J. DRYDEN.

Rumor is a pipe
Blown by surmises, jealousies, conjectures,
And of so easy and so plain a stop
That the blunt monster with uncounted heads,
The still-discordant wavering multitude,
Can play upon it.
King Henry IV., Pt. II. Act i. *Induction.*
           SHAKESPEARE.

The people's voice is odd,
It is, and it is not, the voice of God.
To Augustus.   A. POPE.

Through all disguise, form, place or name,
Beneath the flaunting robes of sin,
Through poverty and squalid shame,
Thou lookest on the man within.

On man, as man, retaining yet,
Howe'er debased, and soiled, and dim,
The crown upon his forehead set—
The immortal gift of God to him.
Democracy.   J. G. WHITTIER.

PERFECTION.

To gild refinèd gold, to paint the lily,
To throw a perfume on the violet,
To smooth the ice, or add another hue
Unto the rainbow, or with taper-light
To seek the beauteous eye of heaven to garnish,
Is wasteful and ridiculous excess.
King John, Act iv. *Sc.* 2.   SHAKESPEARE.

How many things by season seasoned are
To their right praise and true perfection!
Merchant of Venice, Act v. *Sc.* 1.   SHAKESPEARE.

Those about her
From her shall read the perfect ways of honor.
King Henry VIII., Act v. *Sc.* 5.   SHAKESPEARE.

Whoever thinks a faultless piece to see,
Thinks what ne'er was, nor is, nor e'er shall be.
Essay on Criticism, Pt. II.   A. POPE.

PERFUME.

And the ripe harvest of the new-mown hay
Gives it a sweet and wholesome odor.
Richard III. (Altered), Act v. Sc. 3.   C. CIBBER.

Perfume for a lady's chamber.
Winter's Tale, Act iv. Sc. 4.   SHAKESPEARE.

Take your paper, too,
And let me have them very well perfumed,
For she is sweeter than perfume itself
To whom they go to.
Taming of the Shrew, Act i. Sc. 2.   SHAKESPEARE.

Sabean odors from the spicy shore
Of Arabie the blest.
Paradise Lost, Bk. IV.   MILTON.

And all Arabia breathes from yonder box.
Rape of the Lock, Canto I.   A. POPE.

A violet in the youth of primy nature,
Forward, not permanent, sweet, not lasting,
The perfume and suppliance of a minute.
Hamlet, Act i. Sc. 3.   SHAKESPEARE.

I cannot talk with civet in the room,
A fine puss-gentleman that 's all perfume.
Conversation.   W. COWPER.

PERSONAL.

CHAUCER.

As that renownèd poet them compyled
With warlike numbers and heroicke sound,
Dan Chaucer, well of English undefyled,
On Fame's eternall beadroll worthie to be fyled.
Faërie Queene, Bk. IV. Canto II.   E. SPENSER.

EARL OF WARWICK.

Peace, impudent and shameless Warwick!
Proud setter-up and puller-down of kings.
King Henry VI., Part III. Act iii. Sc. 3. SHAKESPEARE.

GALILEO.

> The starry Galileo, with his woes.
> *Childe Harold, Canto IV.*   LORD BYRON.

SIR PHILIP SIDNEY.

> The admired mirror, glory of our isle,
> Thou far, far more than mortal man, whose style
> Struck more men dumb to hearken to thy song
> Than Orpheus' harp, or Tully's golden tongue.
> To him, as right, for wit's deep quintessence,
> For honor, valor, virtue, excellence,
> Be all the garlands, crown his tomb with bay,
> Who spake as much as e'er our tongue can say.
> *Britannia's Pastorals, Bk. II. Song 2.*   W. BROWNE.

EDMUND SPENSER.

> Divinest Spenser, heaven-bred, happy Muse!
> Would any power into my brain infuse
> Thy worth, or all that poets had before,
> I could not praise till thou deserv'st no more.
> *Britannia's Pastorals, Bk. II. Song 1.*   W. BROWNE.

FRANCIS, LORD BACON.

> If parts allure thee, think how Bacon shined,
> The wisest, brightest, meanest of mankind!
> *Essay on Man, Epistle IV.*   A. POPE.

BEN JONSON.

> O rare Ben Jonson!
> *Epitaph.*   SIR J. YOUNG.

> What things have we seen
> Done at the Mermaid! heard words that have been
> So nimble, and so full of subtle flame,
> As if that every one from whence they came
> Had meant to put his whole wit in a jest,
> And had resolved to live a fool the rest
> Of his dull life: then when there hath been thrown
> Wit able enough to justify the town
> For three days past; wit that might warrant be
> For the whole city to talk foolishly
> Till that were cancelled; and when that was gone,
> We left an air behind us, which alone
> Was able to make the two next companies
> (Right witty, though but downright fools) more wise.
> *Letter to Ben Jonson.*   F. BEAUMONT.

WILLIAM SHAKESPEARE.

Renownèd Spenser, lie a thought more nigh
To learnèd Chaucer, and rare Beaumont lie
A little nearer Spenser, to make room
For Shakespeare in your threefold, fourfold tomb,
On Shakespeare.   W. BASSE.

ABRAHAM COWLEY.

Old mother-wit and nature gave
Shakespeare and Fletcher all they have ;
In Spenser and in Jonson art
Of slower nature got the start ;
But both in him so equal are,
None knows which bears the happiest share ;
To him no author was unknown,
Yet what he wrote was all his own.
Elegy on Cowley.   SIR J. DENHAM.

EARL OF MARLBOROUGH.

[Lord President of the Council to King James I. Parliament was dissolved March 10, and he died March 14, 1628.]

Till the sad breaking of that Parliament
Broke him. . . .
Killed with report that old man eloquent.
To the Lady Margaret Ley.   MILTON.

JOHN WICKLIFFE.

As thou these ashes, little Brook ! wilt bear
Into the Avon, Avon to the tide
Of Severn, Severn to the narrow seas,
Into main ocean they, this deed accursed
An emblem yields to friends and enemies,
How the bold Teacher's doctrine, sanctified
By truth, shall spread, throughout the world dispersed.
Ecclesiastical Sonnets, Part II. xvii.   *To Wickliffe.*
                              W. WORDSWORTH.

[Bartlett quotes, in this connection, the following :]

" Some prophet of that day said :
     ' The Avon to the Severn runs,
        The Severn to the sea ;
     And Wickliffe's dust shall spread abroad,
        Wide as the waters be.' "
From Address before the " Sons of New Hampshire" (1849).
                              D. WEBSTER.

JOHN MILTON.

> Nor second he, that rode sublime
> Upon the seraph-wings of ecstasy,
> The secrets of the abyss to spy.
>   He passed the flaming bounds of place and time,
> The living throne. the sapphire blaze,
> Where angels tremble while they gaze,
> He saw ; but, blasted with excess of light,
> Closed his eyes in endless night.
> *Progress of Poesy.*   T. GRAY.

OLIVER CROMWELL.

> His grandeur he derived from Heaven alone ;
>   For he was great, ere fortune made him so :
> And wars, like mists that rise against the sun,
>   Made him but greater seem, not greater grow.
> *Oliver Cromwell.*   J. DRYDEN.

> Or, ravished with the whistling of a name,
>   See Cromwell, damned to everlasting fame !
> *Essay on Man, Epistle IV.*   A. POPE.

KING CHARLES II.

> Here lies our sovereign lord the king,
>   Whose word no man relies on ;
> He never says a foolish thing,
>   Nor ever does a wise one.
> *Written on the Bedchamber Door of Charles II.*
>   EARL OF ROCHESTER.

MARTIN LUTHER.

> The solitary monk who shook the world
> From pagan slumber, when the gospel trump
> Thundered its challenge from his dauntless lips
> In peals of truth.
> *Luther.*   R. MONTGOMERY.

THOMAS CHATTERTON.

> I thought of Chatterton, the marvellous Boy,
> The sleepless soul that perished in his pride.
> *Resolution and Independence.*   W. WORDSWORTH.

JAMES THOMSON.

> A bard here dwelt, more fat than bard beseems,
> Who. void of envy. guile. and lust of gain,
> On virtue still, and Nature's pleasing themes,
> Poured forth his unpremeditated strain :

The world forsaking with a calm disdain,
Here laughed he careless in his easy seat ;
Here quaffed, encircled with the joyous train,
Oft moralizing sage : his ditty sweet
He lothèd much to write, ne carèd to repeat.
Stanza introduced into Thomson's " Castle of Indolence."
Canto I.   LORD LYTTELTON.

In yonder grave a Druid lies.
Where slowly winds the stealing wave ;
The year's best sweets shall duteous rise
To deck its poet's sylvan grave.
Ode on the Death of Thomson.   W. COLLINS.

WILLIAM HOGARTH.

The hand of him here torpid lies
That drew the essential form of grace ;
Here closed in death the attentive eyes
That saw the manners in the face.
Epitaph.   DR. S. JOHNSON.

SIR ISAAC NEWTON.

Nature and Nature's laws lay hid in night :
God said, " Let Newton be ! " and all was light.
Epitaph.   A. POPE.

DAVID GARRICK.

Here lies David Garrick—describe me, who can.
An abridgement of all that was pleasant in man.
As an actor, confessed without rival to shine ;
As a wit, if not first, in the very first line.
Retaliation.   O. GOLDSMITH.

EDMUND BURKE.

Here lies our good Edmund, whose genius was such,
We scarcely can praise it, or blame it, too much ;
Who, born for the universe, narrowed his mind.
And to party gave up what was meant for mankind.
Though fraught with all learning, yet straining his throat,
To persuade Tommy Townshend to lend him a vote :
Who, too deep for his hearers, still went on refining.
And thought of convincing, while they thought of dining ;
Though equal to all things, for all things unfit,
Too nice for a statesman, too proud for a wit ;
For a patriot too cool ; for a drudge disobedient ;
And too fond of the *right* to pursue the *expedient.*
In short, 't was his fate, unemployed, or in place, sir,
To eat mutton cold, and cut blocks with a razor.
Retaliation.   O. GOLDSMITH.

Richard Brinsley Sheridan.

Whose humor, as gay as the firefly's light,
　Played round every subject, and shone as it played ;—
Whose wit, in the combat. as gentle as bright,
　Ne'er carried a heart-stain away on its blade ;—
Whose eloquence—brightening whatever it tried,
　Whether reason or fancy, the gay or the grave—
Was as rapid, as deep, and as brilliant a tide,
　As ever bore freedom aloft on its wave !
Lines on the Death of Sheridan.　　　　T. MOORE.

Long shall we seek his likeness,—long in vain,
And turn to all of him which may remain,
Sighing that Nature formed but one such man,
And broke the die—in moulding Sheridan !
Monody on the Death of Sheridan.　　　LORD BYRON.

George Washington.

While Washington 's a watchword, such as ne'er
Shall sink while there 's an echo left to air.
Age of Bronze.　　　　　　　　LORD BYRON.

Duke of Wellington.

O good gray head which all men knew,
O voice from which their omens all men drew,
O iron nerve to true occasion true,
O fallen at length that tower of strength
Which stood four-square to all the winds that blew !
Such was he whom we deplore.
The long self-sacrifice of life is o'er.
The great World-victor's victor will be seen no more.
On the Death of the Duke of Wellington. A. TENNYSON.

Oliver Wendell Holmes.

His nature 's a glass of champagne with the foam on 't,
As tender as Fletcher, as witty as Beaumont ;
So his best things are done in the flash of the moment.
A Fable for Critics.　　　　　　J. R. LOWELL.

Nathaniel Hawthorne.

There in seclusion and remote from men
　The wizard hand lies cold,
Which at its topmost speed let fall the pen,
　And left the tale half told.

Ah ! who shall lift that wand of magic power,
　And the lost clew regain ?
The unfinished window in Aladdin's tower
　Unfinished must remain !
Hawthorne, May 23, 1864.　　　H. W. LONGFELLOW.

RALPH WALDO EMERSON.

A Greek head on right Yankee shoulders, whose range
Has Olympus for one pole, for t' other the Exchange ;
He seems, to my thinking (although I 'm afraid
The comparison must, long ere this, have been made).
A Plotinus-Montaigne, where the Egyptian's gold mist
And the Gascon's shrewd wit cheek-by-jowl coexist.
A Fable for Critics.   J. R. LOWELL.

CARLYLE AND EMERSON.

C. 's the Titan, as shaggy of mind as of limb,—
E. the clear-eyed Olympian, rapid and slim ;
The one 's two thirds Norseman, the other half Greek,
Where the one 's most abounding, the other 's to seek ;
C. 's generals require to be seen in the mass,—
E. 's specialties gain if enlarged by the glass ;
C. gives nature and God his own fits of the blues,
And rims common-sense things with mystical hues,—
E. sits in a mystery calm and intense,
And looks coolly around him with sharp common-sense.
A Fable for Critics.   J. R. LOWELL.

EDGAR ALLAN POE.

There comes Poe, with his raven, like Barnaby Rudge,
Three-fifths of him genius and two-fifths sheer fudge,
Who talks like a book of iambs and pentameters,
In a way to make people of common sense damn metres,
Who has written some things quite the best of their kind,
But the heart somehow seems all squeezed out by the mind.
A Fable for Critics.   J. R. LOWELL.

JOHN GREENLEAF WHITTIER.

There is Whittier, whose swelling and vehement heart
Strains the strait-breasted drab of the Quaker apart,
And reveals the live Man, still supreme and erect,
Underneath the bemummying wrappers of sect ;
There was ne'er a man born who had more of the swing
Of the true lyric bard and all that kind of thing ;

  . . . . .

Our Quaker leads off metaphorical fights
For reform and whatever they call human rights,
Both singing and striking in front of the war,
And hitting his foes with the mallet of Thor.
A Fable for Critics.   J. R. LOWELL.

PHILOSOPHY.

The intellectual power, through words and things,
Went sounding on, a dim and perilous way !
The Excursion, Bk. III.   W. WORDSWORTH.

How charming is divine philosophy !
Not harsh, and crabbèd, as dull fools suppose,
But musical as is Apollo's lute,
And a perpetual feast of nectared sweets,
Where no crude surfeit reigns.
Comus.   MILTON.

In discourse more sweet,
(For eloquence the soul, song charms the sense,)
Others apart sat on a hill retired,
In thoughts more elevate, and reasoned high
Of providence, foreknowledge, will, and fate,
Fixed fate, free will, foreknowledge absolute ;
And found no end, in wand'ring mazes lost.
Of good and evil much they argued then,
Of happiness and final misery,
Passion and apathy, and glory and shame ;
Vain wisdom all, and false philosophy.
Paradise Lost, Bk. II.   MILTON.

Sublime Philosophy !
Thou art the patriarch's ladder, reaching heaven,
And bright with beckoning angels ;—but alas !
We see thee, like the patriarch, but in dreams.
By the first step,—dull slumbering on the earth.
Richelieu, Act iii. Sc. 1.   E. BULWER-LYTTON.

Not so the son ; he marked this oversight,
And then mistook reverse of wrong for right ;
(For What to shun, will no great knowledge need,
But What to follow, is a task indeed !)
Moral Essays, Epistle III.   A. POPE.

He knew what 's what, and that 's as high
As metaphysic wit can fly.
Hudibras, Pt. I.   DR. S. BUTLER.

His cogitative faculties immersed
In cogibundity of cogitation.
Chronon, Act i. Sc. 1.   H. CAREY.

When Bishop Berkeley said "there was no matter,"
And proved it—'t was no matter what he said.
Don Juan, Canto XI.   LORD BYRON.

Thinking is but an idle waste of thought,
And naught is everything and everything is naught.
Rejected Addresses : Cui Bono ?   H. AND J. SMITH.

HORATIO.—O day and night, but this is wondrous strange!
HAMLET.—And therefore as a stranger give it welcome.
There are more things in heaven and earth, Horatio,
Than are dreamt of in your philosophy.
   Hamlet, Act i. *Sc.* 5.   SHAKESPEARE.

PITY.

Pity 's akin to love ; and every thought
Of that soft kind is welcome to my soul.
Oroonoko, Act ii. *Sc.* 2.   T. SOUTHERNE.

My friend, I spy some pity in thy looks ;
O, if thine eye be not a flatterer,
Come thou on my side, and entreat for me,
As you would beg, were you in my distress :
A begging prince what beggar pities not?
King Richard IV., Act i. *Sc.* 4.   SHAKESPEARE.

My pity hath been balm to heal their wounds,
My mildness hath allayed their swelling griefs.
King Henry VI., Pt. III. Act iv. *Sc.* 8. SHAKESPEARE.

Pity is the virtue of the law,
And none but tyrants use it cruelly.
Timon of Athens, Act iii. *Sc.* 5.   SHAKESPEARE.

Soft pity never leaves the gentle breast
Where love has been received a welcome guest.
The Duenna, Act ii. *Sc.* 3.   R. B. SHERIDAN.

PLEASURE.

Pleasures lie thickest where no pleasures seem ;
There 's not a leaf that falls upon the ground
But holds some joy of silence or of sound,
Some sprite begotten of a summer dream.
Hidden Joys.   L. BLANCHARD.

Pleasure admitted in undue degree
Enslaves the will, nor leaves the judgment free.
Progress of Error.   W. COWPER.

Sure as night follows day,
Death treads in Pleasure's footsteps round the world,
When Pleasure treads the paths which Reason shuns.
Night Thoughts, Night V.   DR. E. YOUNG.

To frown at pleasure, and to smile in pain.
Night Thoughts, Night VIII.   DR. E. YOUNG.

A man of pleasure is a man of pains.
Night Thoughts, Night V.   DR. E. YOUNG.

Who mixed reason with pleasure and wisdom with mirth.
Retaliation.   O. GOLDSMITH.

Never to blend our pleasure or our pride
With sorrow of the meanest thing that feels.
Resolution and Independence.   W. WORDSWORTH.

Reason's whole pleasure, all the joys of sense,
Lie in three words—health, peace, and competence. •
Essay on Man, Epistle IV.   A. POPE.

POET, THE.

We call those poets who are first to mark
    Through earth's dull mist the coming of the dawn,—
Who see in twilight's gloom the first pale spark,
    While others only note that day is gone.
Shakespeare.   O. W. HOLMES.

Sweet are the pleasures that to verse belong,
And doubly sweet a brotherhood in song.
Epistle to G. F. Mathews.   J. KEATS.

Most joyful let the poet be;
    It is through him that all men see.
The Poet of the Old and New Times.   W. E. CHANNING.

God's prophets of the beautiful.
Vision of Poets.   E. B. BROWNING.

For that fine madness still he did retain,
    Which rightly should possess a poet's brain.
Of Poets and Poesy: (Christopher Marlowe).
                                M. DRAYTON.

But he, the bard of every age and clime,
Of genius fruitful, and of soul sublime,
Who, from the glowing mint of fancy, pours
No spurious metal, fused from common ores,
But gold, to matchless purity refin'd,
And stamp'd with all the godhead in his mind.
Juvenal.   W. GIFFORD.

Most wretched men
Are cradled into poetry by wrong;
They learn in suffering what they teach in song.
Julian and Maddalo.   P. B. SHELLEY.

Here at the fountain's sliding foot,
Or at some fruit-tree's mossy root,
Casting the body's vest aside,
My soul into the boughs does glide:

There, like a bird, it sits and sings,
Then whets and claps its silver wings,
And, till prepared for longer flight,
Waves in its plumes the various light.
The Garden (Translated).　　　　A. MARVELL.

In his own verse the poet still we find,
In his own page his memory lives enshrined,
As in their amber sweets the smothered bees,—
As the fair cedar, fallen before the breeze,
Lies self-embalmed amidst the mouldering trees.
Bryant's Seventieth Birthday.　　　O. W. HOLMES.

There is a pleasure in poetic pains
Which only poets know.
The Timepiece: The Task, Bk. II.　　　W. COWPER.

While pensive poets painful vigils keep,
Sleepless themselves to give their readers sleep.
The Dunciad.　　　　　　A. POPE.

Deem not the framing of a deathless lay
The pastime of a drowsy summer day.
　But gather all thy powers,
And wreak them on the verse that thou wouldst weave.
The Poet.　　　　　　W. C. BRYANT.

From his chaste Muse employed her heaven-taught lyre
None but the noblest passions to inspire,
Not one immoral, one corrupted thought,
One line which, dying, he could wish to blot.
Prologue to Thomson's Coriolanus.　LORD LYTTELTON.

I can no more believe old Homer blind,
Than those who say the sun hath never shined ;
The age wherein he lived was dark, but he
Could not want sight who taught the world to see.
Progress of Learning.　　　SIR J. DENHAM.

Read Homer once, and you can read no more,
For all books else appear so mean, so poor ;
Verse may seem prose ; but still persist to read,
And Homer will be all the books you need.
Essay on Poetry.
　　　　SHEFFIELD, DUKE OF BUCKINGHAMSHIRE.

15

The poet in a golden clime was born,
  With golden stars above ;
Dowered with the hate of hate, the scorn of scorn,
  The love of love.
The Poet.   A. TENNYSON.

Happy who in his verse can gently steer
From grave to light, from pleasant to severe.
The Art of Poetry.   J. DRYDEN.

But those that write in rhyme still make
The one verse for the other's sake :
  For one for sense, and one for rhyme,
  I think 's sufficient at one time.
Hudibras, Pt. II.   DR. S. BUTLER.

For rhyme the rudder is of verses,
With which, like ships, they steer their courses.
Hudibras, Pt. I.   DR. S. BUTLER.

And he whose fustian 's so sublimely bad,
It is not poetry, but prose run mad.
Prologue to Satires.   A. POPE.

I had rather be a kitten, and cry, mew,
Than one of these same metre ballad-mongers ;
I had rather hear a brazen can'stick turned,
Or a dry wheel grate on the axle-tree ;
And that would set my teeth nothing on edge,
Nothing so much as mincing poetry :
'T is like the forced gait of a shuffling nag.
King Henry IV., Pt. I. Act iii. Sc. 1.   SHAKESPEARE.

Poets, like painters, thus unskilled to trace
The naked nature and the living grace,
With gold and jewels cover every part,
And hide with ornaments their want of art.
True wit is nature to advantage dressed,
What oft was thought, but ne'er so well expressed.
Essay on Criticism, Pt. II.   A. POPE.

Unjustly poets we asperse :
Truth shines the brighter clad in verse,
And all the fictions they pursue
Do but insinuate what is true.
To Stella.   J. SWIFT.

Blessings be with them, and eternal praise,
Who gave us nobler loves and nobler cares,—
The Poets ! who on earth have made us heirs
Of truth and pure delight by heavenly lays !
Personal Talk.   W. WORDSWORTH.

POETRY.

Wisdom married to immortal verse.
The Excursion, Bk. VII.   W. WORDSWORTH.

Of all those arts in which the wise excel,
Nature's chief masterpiece is writing well ;
No writing lifts exalted man so high
As sacred and soul-moving poesy.
Essay on Poetry.
SHEFFIELD, DUKE OF BUCKINGHAMSHIRE.

Poetry is itself a thing of God ;
He made his prophets poets ; and the more
We feel of poesie do we become
Like God in love and power,—under-makers.
Festus : Proem.   P. J. BAILEY.

Go boldly forth, my simple lay,
Whose accents flow with artless ease,
Like orient pearls at random strung.
A Persian Song of Hafiz.   SIR W. JONES.

One simile that solitary shines
In the dry desert of a thousand lines.
Imitations of Horace. Epistle I. Bk. II.   A. POPE.

Read, meditate, reflect, grow wise—in vain ;
Try every help, force fire from every spark ;
Yet shall you ne'er the poet's power attain,
If heaven ne'er stamped you with the muses' mark.
The Poet.   A. HILL.

Jewels five-words long,
That on the stretched forefinger of all time
Sparkle forever.
The Princess, Canto II.   A. TENNYSON.

Choice word and measured phrase above the reach
Of ordinary men.
Resolution and Independence.   W. WORDSWORTH.

The varying verse, the full resounding line,
The long majestic march, and energy divine.
Imitations of Horace, Bk. II. Epistle I.   A. POPE.

Myriads of daisies have shone forth in flower
Near the lark's nest, or in their natural hour
Have passed away ; less happy than the one
That, by the unwilling ploughshare, died to prove
The tender charm of poetry and love.
Poems in Summer of 1833, XXXVII.
W. WORDSWORTH.

Thanks untraced to lips unknown
Shall greet me like the odors blown
From unseen meadows newly mown,
Or lilies floating in some pond,
Wood-fringed, the wayside gaze beyond ;
The traveller owns the grateful sense
Of sweetness near, he knows not whence,
And, pausing, takes with forehead bare
The benediction of the air.
Snow-Bound.   J. G. WHITTIER.

Give me that growth which some perchance deem sleep,
Wherewith the steadfast coral-stems arise,
Which, by the toil of gathering energies,
Their upward way into clear sunshine keep
Until, by Heaven's sweetest influences,
Slowly and slowly spreads a speck of green
Into a pleasant island in the seas,
Where, mid tall palms, the cane-roofed home is seen,
And wearied men shall sit at sunset's hour,
Hearing the leaves and loving God's dear power.
Sonnet VII.   J. R. LOWELL.

A drainless shower
Of light is poesy : 't is the supreme of power ;
'T is might half slumbering on its own right arm.
Sleep and Poetry.   J. KEATS.

For dear to gods and men is sacred song.
Self-taught I sing ; by Heaven and Heaven alone,
The genuine seeds of poesy are sown.
Odyssey, Bk. XXII.   HOMER. *Trans. of* POPE.

Still govern thou my song,
Urania, and fit audience find, though few.
Paradise Lost, Bk. VII.   MILTON.

POLITICS.

The freeman casting, with unpurchased hand,
The vote that shakes the turrets of the land.
Poetry.   O. W. HOLMES.

A weapon that comes down as still
As snowflakes fall upon the sod ;
But executes a freeman's will.
As lightning does the will of God :
And from its force, nor doors nor locks
Can shield you ;—'t is the ballot-box.
A Word from a Petitioner.   J. PIERPONT.

What is a Communist? One who has yearnings
For equal division of unequal earnings.
Epigram. E. ELLIOTT.

Measures, not men, have always been my mark.
The Good-natured Man, Act ii. O. GOLDSMITH.

Coffee, which makes the politician wise,
And see through all things with his half shut eyes.
Rape of the Lock, Canto III. A. POPE.

Get thee glass eyes;
And, like a scurvy politician, seem
To see the things thou dost not.
King Lear, Act iv. *Sc.* 6. SHAKESPEARE.

Here and there some stern, high patriot stood,
Who could not get the place for which he sued.
Don Juan, Canto XIII. LORD BYRON.

Get place and wealth; if possible, with grace;
If not, by any means get wealth and place.
Epistles of Horace, Epistle I. A. POPE.

O, that estates, degrees, and offices
Were not derived corruptly, and that clear honor
Were purchased by the merit of the wearer!
Merchant of Venice, Act ii. *Sc.* 9. SHAKESPEARE.

POSSESSION.

When I behold what pleasure is pursuit,
  What life, what glorious eagerness it is,
  Then mark how full possession falls from this,
How fairer seem the blossoms than the fruit,—
I am perplext, and often stricken mute,
  Wondering which attained the higher bliss,
  The wingèd insect, or the chrysalis
It thrust aside with unreluctant foot.
Pursuit and Possession. T. B. ALDRICH.

Bliss in possession will not last;
Remembered joys are never past;
At once the fountain, stream, and sea,
They were, they are, they yet shall be.
The Little Cloud. J. MONTGOMERY.

But 'midst the crowd, the hum, the shock of men,
  To hear, to see, to feel, and to possess,
And roam along, the world's tired denizen,
  With none who bless us, none whom we can bless.
Childe Harold, Canto II. LORD BYRON.

I die,—but first I have possessed,
And come what may, I *have been* blessed.
The Giaour.   LORD BYRON.

POVERTY.

I am as poor as Job, my lord, but not so patient.
King Henry IV., Pt. II. Act i. *Sc.* 2.   SHAKESPEARE.

Yon friendless man, at whose dejected eye
Th' unfeeling proud one looks, and passes by,
Condemned on penury's barren path to roam,
Scorned by the world, and left without a home.
Pleasures of Hope.   T. CAMPBELL.

Through tattered clothes small vices do appear ;
Robes and furred gowns hide all.
King Lear, Act iv. *Sc.* 6.   SHAKESPEARE.

Take physic, Pomp ;
Expose thyself to feel what wretches feel.
King Lear, Act iii. *Sc.* 4.   SHAKESPEARE.

O world ! how apt the poor are to be proud !
Twelfth Night, Act iii. *Sc.* 1.   SHAKESPEARE.

This mournful truth is everywhere confessed,
Slow rises worth by poverty oppressed.
Vanity of Human Wishes.   DR. S. JOHNSON.

And rustic life and poverty
Grow beautiful beneath his touch.
Burns.   T. CAMPBELL.

Evermore thanks, the exchequer of the poor.
King Richard II., Act ii. *Sc.* 1.   SHAKESPEARE.

POWER.

Power, like a desolating pestilence,
Pollutes whate'er it touches ; and obedience,
Bane of all genius, virtue, freedom, truth,
Makes slaves of men, and of the human frame.
A mechanized automaton.
Queen Mab, Pt. III.   P. B. SHELLEY.

Because the good old rule
Sufficeth them, the simple plan,
That they should take who have the power,
And they should keep who can.
Rob Roy's Grave.   W. WORDSWORTH.

For what can power give more than food and drink,
To live at ease, and not be bound to think ?
Medal.   J. DRYDEN.

Patience and gentleness is power.
On a Lock of Milton's Hair.   L. HUNT.

Some novel power
Sprang up forever at a touch,
And hope could never hope too much,
In watching thee from hour to hour.
In Memoriam, CXI.   A. TENNYSON.

A power is passing from the earth.
On the Expected Dissolution of Mr. Fox.
                                    W. WORDSWORTH.

He hath no power that hath not power to use.
Festus, Sc. A Visit.   P. J. BAILEY.

PRAISE.

The love of praise, howe'er concealed by art,
Reigns more or less, and glows in every heart.
Love of Fame, Satire I.   DR. E. YOUNG.

One good deed dying tongueless
Slaughters a thousand waiting upon that.
Our praises are our wages.
Winter's Tale, Act i. Sc. 2.   SHAKESPEARE.

O Popular Applause ! what heart of man
Is proof against thy sweet, seducing charms ?
The Task, Bk. II.   W. COWPER.

I would applaud thee to the very echo,
That should applaud again.
Macbeth, Act v. Sc. 3.   SHAKESPEARE.

To things of sale a seller's praise belongs.
Love's Labor's Lost, Act iv. Sc. 3.   SHAKESPEARE.

If matters not how false or forced,
So the best things be said o' the worst.
Hudibras, Pt. II.   S. BUTLER.

Of whom to be dispraised were no small praise.
Paradise Regained, Bk. III.   MILTON.

Praise from a friend, or censure from a foe,
Are lost on hearers that our merits know.
Iliad, Bk. X.   HOMER. *Trans. of* POPE.

Not in the clamor of the crowded street,
Not in the shouts and plaudits of the throng,
But in ourselves, are triumph and defeat.
The Poets.   H. W. LONGFELLOW.

PRAYER.

Prayer moves the Hand which moves the world.
There is an Eye that Never Sleeps.   J. A. WALLACE.

In prayer the lips ne'er act the winning part
Without the sweet concurrence of the heart.
Hesperides : The Heart.   R. HERRICK.

As down in the sunless retreats of the ocean
    Sweet flowers are springing no mortal can see,
So deep in my soul the still prayer of devotion,
    Unheard by the world, rises silent to Thee.
As Down in the Sunless Retreats.   T. MOORE.

Her eyes are homes of silent prayer.
In Memoriam, XXXII.   A. TENNYSON.

Be not afraid to pray—to pray is right.
Pray, if thou canst, with hope ; but ever pray,
Though hope be weak or sick with long delay ;
Pray in the darkness, if there be no light.
Prayer.   H. COLERIDGE.

Pray to be perfect, though material leaven
Forbid the spirit so on earth to be ;
But if for any wish thou darest not pray,
Then pray to God to cast that wish away.
Prayer.   H. COLERIDGE.

And Satan trembles when he sees
    The weakest saint upon his knees.
Exhortation to Prayer.   W. COWPER.

Still raise for good the supplicating voice,
But leave to Heaven the measure and the choice.
The Vanity of Human Wishes.   DR. S. JOHNSON.

You few that loved me

.   .   .   .   .

Go with me, like good angels, to my end ;
And, as the long divorce of steel falls on me,
Make of your prayers one sweet sacrifice,
And lift my soul to heaven.
King Henry VIII., Act ii. Sc. 1.   SHAKESPEARE.

PREACHING.

I venerate the man whose heart is warm,
Whose hands are pure, whose doctrine and whose life,
Coincident, exhibit lucid proof
That he is honest in the sacred cause.
The Task, Bk. II. W. COWPER.

God preaches, a noted clergyman,
And the sermon is never long ;
So instead of getting to heaven at last,
I 'm going all along.
A Service of Song. E. DICKINSON.

Skilful alike with tongue and pen.
He preached to all men everywhere
The Gospel of the Golden Rule,
The new Commandment given to men,
Thinking the deed, and not the creed,
Would help us in our utmost need.
Tales of a Wayside Inn : Prelude. H. W. LONGFELLOW.

Seek to delight, that they may mend mankind.
And, while they captivate, inform the mind.
Hope. W. COWPER.

The gracious dew of pulpit eloquence,
And all the well-whipped cream of courtly sense.
Satires : Epilogues, Dialogue I. A. POPE.

The lilies say : Behold how we
Preach without words of purity.
Consider the Lilies of the Field. C. G. ROSSETTI.

Sow in the morn thy seed,
At eve hold not thy hand ;
To doubt and fear give thou no heed,
Broadcast it o'er the land.
The Field of the World. J. MONTGOMERY.

His preaching much, but more his practice wrought—
A living sermon of the truths he taught.
Character of a Good Parson. J. DRYDEN.

I preached as never sure to preach again,
And as a dying man to dying men.
Love breathing Thanks and Praise. R. BAXTER.

PRESENT, THE.

Lo ! on a narrow neck of land,
'Twixt two unbounded seas I stand.
Hymn. C. WESLEY.

This narrow isthmus 'twixt two boundless seas,
The past, the future, two eternities !
Lalla Rookh : The Veiled Prophet of Khorassan.
T. MOORE.

Heaven from all creatures hides the book of Fate,
All but the page prescribed, their present state.
Essay on Man, Epistle I.   A. POPE.

Happy the man, and happy he alone,
He who can call to-day his own :
He who, secure within, can say,
To-morrow, do thy worst, for I have lived to-day.
Imitation of Horace, Bk. I. Ode 29.   J. DRYDEN.

Defer not till to-morrow to be wise,
To-morrow's sun to thee may never rise.
Letter to Cobham.   W. CONGREVE.

Nothing is there to come, and nothing past,
But an eternal Now does always last.
Davideis, Vol. I. Bk. I.   A. COWLEY.

PRIDE.

Pride like an eagle builds amid the stars.
Night Thoughts, Night V.   DR. E. YOUNG.

Why, who cries out on pride,
That can therein tax any private party ?
Doth it not flow as hugely as the sea ?
As You Like It, Act ii. *Sc.* 7.   SHAKESPEARE.

'T is pride, rank pride, and haughtiness of soul ;
I think the Romans call it stoicism.
Cato, Act i. *Sc.* 4.   J. ADDISON.

Of all the causes which conspire to blind
Man's erring judgment, and misguide the mind,
What the weak head with strongest bias rules,
Is pride, the never failing vice of fools.
Essay on Criticism, Pt. II.   A. POPE.

Where wavering man, betrayed by venturous pride
To chase the dreary paths without a guide,
As treacherous phantoms in the mist delude,
Shuns fancied ills, or chases airy good.
The Vanity of Human Wishes.   DR. S. JOHNSON.

Pride (of all others the most dang'rous fault)
Proceeds from want of sense or want of thought.
Essay on Translated Verse.   W. DILLON.

Oft has it been my lot to mark
A proud, conceited, talking spark.
The Chameleon. J. MERRICK.

Prouder than rustling in unpaid-for silk.
Cymbeline, Act iii. *Sc.* 3. SHAKESPEARE.

Ask for whose use the heavenly bodies shine ;
Earth for whose use ? Pride answers,
'T is for mine !
Essay on Man, Pt. I. A. POPE.

PROGRESS.

From lower to the higher next,
Not to the top, is Nature's text ;
And embryo good, to reach full stature,
Absorbs the evil in its nature.
Festina Lente. J. R. LOWELL.

Finds progress, man's distinctive mark alone,
Not God's, and not the beast's ;
God is, they are,
Man partly is, and wholly hopes to be.
A Death in the Desert. R. BROWNING.

Progress is
The law of life, man is not
Man as yet.
Paracelsus, Pt. V. R. BROWNING.

The Lord let the house of a brute to the soul of a man,
And the man said, " Am I your debtor ? "
And the Lord—" Not yet : but make it as clean as you can,
And then I will let you a better."
By an Evolutionist. A. TENNYSON.

Eternal process moving on,
From state to state the spirit moves.
In Memoriam, LXXXIII. A. TENNYSON.

PROMISE.

Promise is most given when the least is said.
Musæus of Hero and Leander. G. CHAPMAN.

He was ever precise in promise-keeping.
Measure for Measure, Act i. *Sc.* 2. SHAKESPEARE.

And be these juggling fiends no more believed,
That palter with us in a double sense ;
That keep the word of promise to our ear,
And break it to our hope.
Macbeth, Act v. *Sc.* 7. SHAKESPEARE.

His promises were, as he then was, mighty ;
But his performance, as he is now, nothing.
King Henry VIII., Act iv. *Sc.* 2.　　SHAKESPEARE.

There buds the promise of celestial worth.
The Last Day, Bk. III.　　DR. E. YOUNG.

Thy promises are like Adonis' gardens
That one day bloomed and fruitful were the next.
King Henry VI., Pt. I. Act i. *Sc.* 6.　　SHAKESPEARE.

QUARREL.

O, shame to men ! devil with devil damned
Firm concord holds ; men only disagree
Of creatures rational.
Paradise Lost, Bk. II.　　MILTON.

O we fell out, I know not why,
And kissed again with tears.
The Princess.　　A. TENNYSON.

What dire offence from amorous causes springs,
What mighty contests rise from trivial things.
Rape of the Lock, Canto I.　　A. POPE.

　　　　　　　　　　Beware
Of entrance to a quarrel ; but, being in,
Bear 't that the opposèd may beware of thee.
Hamlet, Act i. *Sc.* 3.　　SHAKESPEARE.

Those who in quarrels interpose,
Must often wipe a bloody nose.
Fables : The Mastiffs.　　J. GAY.

But greatly to find quarrel in a straw
When honor 's at the stake.
Hamlet, Act iv. *Sc.* 4.　　SHAKESPEARE.

In a false quarrel there is no true valor.
Much Ado about Nothing, Act v. *Sc.* 1.　　SHAKESPEARE.

I 'm armed with more than complete steel,
The justice of my quarrel.
Lust's Dominion, Act iii. *Sc.* 4.　　C. MARLOWE.

RAIN.

The Clouds consign their treasures to the fields ;
And, softly shaking on the dimpled pool
Prelusive drops, let all their moisture flow,
In large effusion, o'er the freshened world.
The Seasons : Spring.　　J. THOMSON.

Drip, drip, the rain comes falling,
  Rain in the woods, rain on the sea ;
Even the little waves, beaten, come crawling
  As if to find shelter here with me.
Waiting in the Rain.   J. H. MORSE.

The rain-drops' showery dance and rhythmic beat,
  With tinkling of innumerable feet.
The Microcosm : Hearing.   A. COLES.

And the hooded clouds, like friars,
  Tell their beads in drops of rain.
Midnight Mass for the Dying Year.
                 H. W. LONGFELLOW.

See where it smokes along the sounding plain,
Blown all aslant, a driving, dashing rain ;
Peal upon peal, redoubling all around,
  Shakes it again and faster to the ground.
Truth.   W. COWPER.

The thirsty earth soaks up the rain,
  And drinks and gapes for drink again ;
The plants suck in the earth, and are
  With constant drinking fresh and fair.
Anacreontiques.   A. COWLEY.

When that I was and a little tiny boy,
  With hey, ho, the wind and the rain,
A foolish thing was but a toy,
  For the rain it raineth every day.
Twelfth Night, Act v. *Sc.* 1.   SHAKESPEARE.

RAINBOW.

Rain, rain, and sun ! a rainbow in the sky !
Idylls of the King : The Coming of Arthur.
                A. TENNYSON.

Mild arch of promise ! on the evening sky
Thou shinest fair with many a lovely ray,
  Each in the other melting.
The Evening Rainbow.   R. SOUTHEY.

Triumphal arch, that fill'st the sky,
  When storms prepare to part ;
I ask not proud Philosophy
  To teach me what thou art.
To the Rainbow.   T. CAMPBELL.

What skilful limner e'er would choose
To paint the rainbow's varying hues,
Unless to mortal it were given
To dip his brush in dyes of heaven?
Marmion, Canto VI.　　　　　SIR W. SCOTT.

Bright pledge of peace and sunshine! the sure tie
Of thy Lord's hand, the object of His eye!
When I behold thee, though my light be dim,
Distinct, and low, I can in thine see Him
Who looks upon thee from His glorious throne,
And minds the covenant between all and One.
The Rainbow.　　　　　H. VAUGHAN.

READING.

I had found the secret of a garret room
Piled high with cases in my father's name;
Piled high, packed large,—where, creeping in and out
Among the giant fossils of my past,
Like some small nimble mouse between the ribs
Of a mastodon, I nibbled here and there
At this or that box, pulling through the gap,
In heats of terror, haste, victorious joy,
The first book first.　And how I felt it beat
Under my pillow, in the morning's dark,
An hour before the sun would let me read!
Aurora Leigh, Bk. I.　　　　E. B. BROWNING.

Come, and take choice of all my library,
And so beguile thy sorrow.
Titus Andronicus, Act iv. Sc. 1.　　　SHAKESPEARE.

He furnished me
From mine own library with volumes that
I prize above my dukedom.
Tempest, Act i. Sc. 2.　　　　SHAKESPEARE.

There studious let me sit,
And hold high converse with the mighty dead;
Sages of ancient time, as gods revered,
As gods beneficent, who blest mankind
With arts, with arms, and humanized a world.
The Seasons: Winter.　　　　J. THOMSON.

POLONIUS.—What do you read, my lord?
HAMLET.—Words, words, words.
Hamlet, Act ii. Sc. 2.　　　　SHAKESPEARE.

O Reader! had you in your mind
  Such stores as silent thought may bring,
O gentle Reader! you would find
  A tale in everything.
Simon Lee.   W. WORDSWORTH.

And choose an author as you choose a friend.
Essay on Translated Verse.   EARL OF ROSCOMMON.

When the last reader reads no more.
The Last Reader.   O. W. HOLMES.

REASONS.

All was false and hollow; though his tongue
Dropped manna, and could make the worse appear
The better reason, to perplex and dash
Maturest counsels; for his thoughts were low;
To vice industrious, but to nobler deeds
Timorous and slothful: yet he pleased the ear,
And with persuasive accent thus began.
Paradise Lost, Bk. II.   MILTON.

Give you a reason on compulsion! if reasons were as
plentiful as blackberries, I would give no man a reason
upon compulsion. I.
King Henry IV., Pt. I. Act ii. Sc. 4.   SHAKESPEARE.

Good reasons must, of force, give place to better.
Julius Cæsar, Act iv. Sc. 3:   SHAKESPEARE.

Whatever sceptic could inquire for,
  For every why he had a wherefore.
Hudibras, Pt. I.   S. BUTLER.

I was promised on a time
To have reason for my rhyme;
From that time unto this season,
I received nor rhyme nor reason.
Lines on his Promised Pension.   E. SPENSER.

REGRET.

For who, alas! has lived,
Nor in the watches of the night recalled
Words he has wished unsaid and deeds undone?
Reflections.   S. ROGERS.

Thou wilt lament
Hereafter, when the evil shall be done
And shall admit no cure.
Iliad, Bk. IX.   HOMER. *Trans. of* BRYANT.

The man who seeks one thing in life, and but one,
May hope to achieve it before life be done ;
But he who seeks all things, wherever he goes,
Only reaps from the hopes which around him he sows
A harvest of barren regrets.
Lucile, Pt. I. Canto II. LORD LYTTON (*Owen Meredith*).

O lost days of delight, that are wasted in doubting and
waiting !
O lost hours and days in which we might have been happy!
Tales of a Wayside Inn : The Theologian's Tale.
H. W. LONGFELLOW.

Calmly he looked on either Life, and here
Saw nothing to regret, or there to fear :
From Nature's temp'rate feast rose satisfied,
Thanked Heaven that he had lived, and that he died.
Epitaph X. A. POPE.

RELIGION.

God is not dumb, that he should speak no more ;
If thou hast wanderings in the wilderness
And find'st not Sinai, 't is thy soul is poor.
Bibliotres. J. R. LOWELL.

Religion, if in heavenly truths attired,
Needs only to be seen to be admired.
Expostulation. W. COWPER.

In religion,
What damnèd error, but some sober brow
Will bless it and approve it with a text.
Merchant of Venice, Act iii. *Sc. 2.* SHAKESPEARE.

I think while zealots fast and frown,
And fight for two or seven,
That there are fifty roads to town,
And rather more to Heaven.
Chant of Brazen Head. W. M. PRAED.

Religion stands on tiptoe in our land,
Ready to pass to the American strand.
The Church Militant. G. HERBERT.

A Christian is the highest type of man.
Night Thoughts, Night IV. DR. E. YOUNG.

Remote from man, with God he passed the days,
Prayer all his business, all his pleasure praise.
The Hermit. T. PARNELL.

Religion 's all. Descending from the skies
To wretched man, the goddess in her left
Holds out this world, and, in her right, the next.
Night Thoughts, Night IV.   DR. E. YOUNG.

My God, my Father, and my Friend,
Do not forsake me at my end.
Translation of Dies Iræ.   EARL OF ROSCOMMON.

REMORSE.

What exile from himself can flee?
To zones though more and more remote
Still, still pursues, where'er I be,
The blight of life—the demon Thought.
Childe Harold, Canto I.   LORD BYRON.

Now conscience wakes despair
That slumbered, wakes the bitter memory
Of what he was, what is, and what must be.
Paradise Lost, Bk. IV.   MILTON.

Unnatural deeds
Do breed unnatural troubles : infected minds
To their deaf pillows will discharge their secrets.
Macbeth, Act v. Sc. 1.   SHAKESPEARE.

MACBETH.—Canst thou not minister to a mind diseased,
Pluck from the memory a rooted sorrow,
Raze out the written troubles of the brain,
And with some sweet oblivious antidote
Cleanse the stuffed bosom of that perilous stuff,
Which weighs upon the heart?
      DOCTOR.—   Therein the patient
Must minister to himself.
Macbeth, Act v. Sc. 3.   SHAKESPEARE.

O, my offence is rank, it smells to heaven ;
It hath the primal eldest curse upon 't,
A brother's murder.
Hamlet, Act iii. Sc. 3.   SHAKESPEARE.

How guilt once harbored in the conscious breast,
Intimidates the brave, degrades the great.
Irene, Act iv. Sc. 8.   DR. S. JOHNSON.

High minds, of native pride and force,
Most deeply feel thy pangs, Remorse !
Fear for their scourge, mean villains have,
Thou art the torturer of the brave !
Marmion, Canto III.   SIR W. SCOTT.
16

Amid the roses, fierce Repentance rears
Her snaky crest ; a quick-returning pang
Shoots through the conscious heart.
The Seasons : Spring.   J. THOMSON.

There is no future pang
Can deal that justice on the self-condemned
He deals on his own soul.
Manfred, Act iii. *Sc.* 1.   LORD BYRON.

REPUTATION.

Good name in man and woman, dear my lord,
Is the immediate jewel of their souls :
Who steals my purse, steals trash ; 't is something, nothing ;
'T was mine, 't is his, and has been slave to thousands ;
But he that filches from me my good name
Robs me of that which not enriches him,
And makes me poor indeed.
Othello, Act iii. *Sc.* 3.   SHAKESPEARE.

Fear not the anger of the wise to raise,
They best can bear reproof who merit praise.
Essay on Criticism.   A. POPE.

The purest treasure mortal times afford
Is spotless reputation ; that away,
Men are but gilded loam or painted clay.
King Richard II., Act ii. *Sc.* 1.   SHAKESPEARE.

Thy death-bed is no lesser than thy land
Wherein thou liest in reputation sick.
King Richard II., Act ii. *Sc.* 1.   SHAKESPEARE.

Convey a libel in a frown,
And wink a reputation down !
Journal of a Modern Lady.   J. SWIFT.

After my death I wish no other herald,
No other speaker of my living actions,
To keep mine honor from corruption,
But such an honest chronicler as Griffith.
King Henry VIII., Act v. *Sc.* 2.   SHAKESPEARE.

I pray you, in your letters,
When you shall these unlucky deeds relate,
Speak of me as I am ; nothing extenuate,
Nor set down aught in malice : then, must you speak
Of one that loved, not wisely, but too well :
Of one not easily jealous, but, being wrought,
Perplexed in the extreme ; of one, whose hand,

Like the base Indian. threw a pearl away,
Richer than all his tribe ; of one, whose subdued eyes,
Albeit unused to the melting mood,
Drop tears as fast as the Arabian trees
Their medicinal gum.   Set you down this.
Othello, Act v. *Sc.* 2.   SHAKESPEARE.

O God !—Horatio, what a wounded name,
Things standing thus unknown. shall live behind me !
If thou didst ever hold me in thy heart,
Absent thee from felicity awhile,
And in this harsh world draw thy breath in pain,
To tell my story.
Hamlet, Act v. *Sc.* 2.   SHAKESPEARE.

RESIGNATION.

Behold, how brightly breaks the morning,
   Though bleak our lot, our hearts are warm.
Behold how brightly breaks.   J. KENNEY.

God is much displeased
That you take with unthankfulness his doing :
In common worldly things, 't is called ungrateful,
With dull unwillingness to repay a debt
Which with a bounteous hand was kindly lent ;
Much more to be thus opposite with heaven,
For it requires the royal debt it lent you.
King Richard III., Act ii. *Sc.* 2.   SHAKESPEARE.

Thus ready for the way of life or death,
   I wait the sharpest blow.
Pericles, Act i. *Sc.* 1.   SHAKESPEARE.

What 's gone and what 's past help
   Should be past grief.
Winter's Tale, Act iii. *Sc.* 2.   SHAKESPEARE.

But hushed be every thought that springs
   From out the bitterness of things.
Addressed to Sir G. H. B.   W. WORDSWORTH.

Down, thou climbing sorrow,
   Thy element 's below !
King Lear, Act ii. *Sc.* 4.   SHAKESPEARE.

'T is impious in a good man to be sad.
Night Thoughts, Night IV.   DR. E. YOUNG.

The path of sorrow, and that path alone,
   Leads to the land where sorrow is unknown.
To an Afflicted Protestant Lady.   W. COWPER.

Adversity's sweet milk, philosophy.
Romeo and Juliet, Act iii. *Sc.* 2.　　SHAKESPEARE.

Now let us thank the Eternal Power : convinced
That Heaven but tries our virtue by affliction.—
That oft the cloud which wraps the present hour
Serves but to brighten all our future days.
Barbarossa, Act v. *Sc.* 3.　　J. BROWN.

RESOLUTION.

Be stirring as the time : be fire with fire ;
Threaten the threatener and outface the brow
Of bragging horror : so shall inferior eyes,
That borrow their behaviors from the great,
Grow great by your example and put on
The dauntless spirit of resolution.
King John, Act v. *Sc.* 1.　　SHAKESPEARE.

My resolution 's placed, and I have nothing
Of woman in me : now from head to foot
I am marble—constant.
Antony and Cleopatra, Act v. *Sc.* 2.　　SHAKESPEARE.

When two
Join in the same adventure, one perceives
Before the other how they ought to act ;
While one alone, however prompt, resolves
More tardily and with a weaker will.
Iliad, Bk. X.　　HOMER. *Trans. of* BRYANT.,

I pull in resolution, and begin
To doubt the equivocation of the fiend
That lies like truth : " Fear not, till Birnam wood
Do come to Dunsinane."
Macbeth, Act v. *Sc.* 5.　　SHAKESPEARE.

In life's small things be resolute and great
To keep thy muscle trained : know'st thou when Fate
Thy measure takes, or when she 'll say to thee,
" I find thee worthy ; do this deed for me " ?
Epigram.　　J. R. LOWELL.

REST.

Take thou of me, sweet pillowes, sweetest bed ;
A chamber deafe of noise, and blind of light,
A rosie garland and a weary hed.
Astrophel and Stella.　　SIR PH. SIDNEY.

And to tired limbs and over-busy thoughts,
Inviting sleep and soft forgetfulness.
The Excursion, Bk. IV.   W. WORDSWORTH.

The wind breathed soft as lover's sigh,
And, oft renewed, seemed oft to die,
  With breathless pause between,
O who, with speech of war and woes,
Would wish to break the soft repose
  Of such enchanting scene !
Lord of the Isles, Canto IV.   SIR W. SCOTT.

Our foster-nurse of Nature is repose,
The which he lacks ; that to provoke in him,
Are many simples operative, whose power
Will close the eye of anguish.
King Lear, Act iv. Sc. 4.   SHAKESPEARE.

These should be hours for necessities,
Not for delights ; times to repair our nature
With comforting repose, and not for us
To waste these times.
King Henry VIII., Act v. Sc. 1.   SHAKESPEARE.

Who pants for glory finds but short repose ;
A breath revives him, or a breath o'erthrows.
Epistles of Horace, Ep. I. Bk. I.   J. DRYDEN.

                    Where peace
And rest can never dwell, hope never comes
That comes to all.
Paradise Lost, Bk. I.   MILTON.

  Absence of occupation is not rest,
  A mind quite vacant is a mind distressed.
Retirement.   W. COWPER.

RETRIBUTION.

The thorns which I have reaped are of the tree
I planted—they have torn me, and I bleed ;
I should have known what fruit would spring from such a
    seed.
Childe Harold, Canto IV.   LORD BYRON.

                  We but teach
Bloody instructions, which, being taught, return
To plague the inventor. This even-handed justice
Commends the ingredients of our poisoned chalice
To our own lips.
Macbeth, Act i. Sc. 7.   SHAKESPEARE.

So the struck eagle, stretched upon the plain,
No more through rolling clouds to soar again,
Viewed his own feather on the fatal dart,
And winged the shaft that quivered in his heart.
English Bards and Scotch Reviewers.   LORD BYRON.

Remember Milo's end,
Wedged in that timber which he strove to rend.
Essays on Translated Verse.   W. DILLON.

REVENGE.

Souls made of fire and children of the sun,
With whom Revenge is virtue.
The Revenge, Act V.   DR. E. YOUNG.

And if we do but watch the hour,
There never yet was human power
Which could evade, if unforgiven,
The patient search and vigil long
Of him who treasures up a wrong.
Mazeppa.   LORD BYRON

Vengeance is in my heart, death in my hand,
Blood and revenge are hammering in my head.
Titus Andronicus, Act ii. Sc. 3.   SHAKESPEARE

If I can catch him once upon the hip,
I will feed fat the ancient grudge I bear him.
Merchant of Venice, Act i. Sc. 3.   SHAKESPEARE.

If it will feed nothing else, it will feed my revenge.
Merchant of Venice, Act iii. Sc. 1.   SHAKESPEARE.

Vengeance to God alone belongs ;
But when I think on all my wrongs,
My blood is liquid flame.
Marmion, Canto VI.   SIR W. SCOTT.

Revenge, at first though sweet,
Bitter ere long back on itself recoils.
Paradise Lost, Bk. IX.   MILTON.

ROD, THE.

I pray ye, flog them upon all occasions.
It mends their morals, never mind the pain.
Don Juan, Canto II.   LORD BYRON.

Love is a boy by poets styled ;
Then spare the rod and spoil the child.
Hudibras, Pt. II. Canto I.   S. BUTLER.

Whipping, that 's virtue's governess,
Tutoress of arts and sciences ;
That mends the gross mistakes of nature,
And puts new life into dull matter ;
That lays foundation for renown,
And all the honors of the gown.
Hudibras, Pt. II. Canto I.   S. BUTLER.

ROMANCE.

Parent of golden dreams, Romance !
Auspicious queen of childish joys,
Who lead'st along, in airy dance,
Thy votive train of girls and boys.
To Romance.   LORD BYRON.

He loved the twilight that surrounds
The border-land of old romance ;
Where glitter hauberk, helm, and lance,
And banner waves, and trumpet sounds,
And ladies ride with hawk on wrist,
And mighty warriors sweep along,
Magnified by the purple mist,
The dusk of centuries and of song.
Tales of a Wayside Inn : Prelude. H. W. LONGFELLOW.

Lady of the Mere,
Sole-sitting by the shores of old romance.
A Narrow Girdle of Rough Stones. W. WORDSWORTH.

Romances paint at full length people's wooings,
But only give a bust of marriages :
For no one cares for matrimonial cooings.
There 's nothing wrong in a connubial kiss.
Think you, if Laura had been Petrarch's wife,
He would have written sonnets all his life ?
Don Juan, Canto III.   LORD BYRON.

ROYALTY.

When beggars die there are no comets seen ;
The heavens themselves blaze forth the death of princes.
Julius Cæsar, Act ii. Sc. 2.   SHAKESPEARE.

What infinite heart's ease
Must kings neglect, that private men enjoy ?
And what have kings that privates have not too,
Save ceremony, save general ceremony ?
King Henry V., Act v. Sc. 1.   SHAKESPEARE.

Not all the water in the rough rude sea
Can wash the balm from an anointed king.
King Richard II., Act iii. *Sc.* 2.　　SHAKESPEARE.

There 's such divinity doth hedge a king,
That treason can but peep to what it would,
Acts little of his will.
Hamlet, Act iv. *Sc.* 5.　　SHAKESPEARE.

Besides, the king's name is a tower of strength.
King Richard III., Act v. *Sc.* 3.　　SHAKESPEARE.

RURAL LIFE.

Far from gay cities and the ways of men.
Odyssey, Bk. XIV.　　HOMER. *Trans. of* POPE.

But on and up, where Nature's heart
Beats strong amid the hills.
Tragedy of the Lac de Gaube.
　　R. M. MILNES, LORD HOUGHTON.

They love the country, and none else, who seek
For their own sake its silence and its shade.
Delights which who would leave, that has a heart
Susceptible of pity or a mind
Cultured and capable of sober thought?
The Task, Bk. III.　　W. COWPER.

God made the country, and man made the town ;
What wonder then, that health and virtue, gifts
That can alone make sweet the bitter draught
That life holds out to all, should most abound
And least be threatened in the fields and groves.
The Task, Bk. I.: The Sofa.　　W. COWPER.

Before green apples blush,
　Before green nuts embrown,
Why, one day in the country
　Is worth a month in town.
Summer.　　C. G. ROSSETTI.

Nor rural sights alone, but rural sounds
Exhilarate the spirit, and restore
The tone of languid Nature.
The Task, Bk. I.　　W. COWPER.

At eve the ploughman leaves the task of day
And, trudging homeward, whistles on the way :
And the big-uddered cows with patience stand,
And wait the strokings of the damsel's hand.
Rural Sport.　　J. GAY.

Rustic mirth goes round ;
The simple joke that takes the shepherd's heart,
Easily pleased ; the long loud laugh sincere ;
The kiss snatched hasty from the sidelong maid,
On purpose guardless, or pretending sleep :
The leap, the slap, the haul ; and, shook to notes
Of native music, the respondent dance.
Thus jocund fleets with them the winter night.
The Seasons : Winter.   J. THOMSON.

As in the eye of Nature he has lived,
So in the eye of Nature let him die !
The Old Cumberland Beggar.   W. WORDSWORTH.

O for a seat in some poetic nook,
Just hid with trees and sparkling with a brook.
Politics and Poetics.   L. HUNT.

I care not, Fortune, what you me deny :
You cannot rob me of free Nature's grace.
The Castle of Indolence, Canto II.   J. THOMSON.

And this our life, exempt from public haunt,
Finds tongues in trees, books in the running brooks,
Sermons in stones, and good in everything.
As You Like It, Act ii. *Sc.* 1.   SHAKESPEARE.

SABBATH.

The cheerful Sabbath bells, wherever heard,
Strike pleasant on the sense, most like the voice
Of one who from the far-off hills proclaims
Tidings of good to Zion.
The Sabbath Bells.   C. LAMB.

The clinkum-clank o' Sabbath bells
Noo to the hoastin' rookery swells,
Noo faintin' laigh in shady dells,
        Sounds far an' near,
An' through the simmer kintry tells
        Its tale o' cheer.

An' noo, to that melodious play,
A' deidly awn the quiet sway—
A' ken their solemn holiday,
        Bestial an' human,
The singin' lintie on the brae,
        The restin' plou'man.
A Lowden Sabbath Morn.   R. L. STEVENSON.

Bright shadows of true rest ! some shoots of bliss :
Heaven once a week :
The next world's gladness prepossest in this ;
A day to seek ;
Eternity in time.
Sundays.   H. VAUGHAN.

As palmers wont to hail the nichèd seat
At desert well, where they put off the shoon
And robe of travel, so I, a pilgrim as they,
Tired with my six-days' track, would turn aside
Out of the scorch and glare into the shade
Of Sunday-stillness.
The Resting Place.   M. J. PRESTON.

But chiefly man the day of rest enjoys.
Hail, Sabbath ! Thee I hail, the poor man's day.
The Sabbath.   J. GRAHAME.

Yes, child of suffering, thou may'st well be sure,
He who ordained the Sabbath loves the poor !
Urania.   O. W. HOLMES.

SATIRE.

Prepare for rhyme—I 'll publish, right or wrong :
Fools are my theme, let satire be my song.
English Bards and Scotch Reviewers.   LORD BYRON.

Satire should, like a polished razor keen,
Wound with a touch that 's scarcely felt or seen.
To the Imitator of the first Satire of Horace, Bk. II.
                                        LADY M. W. MONTAGU.

Satire 's my weapon, but I 'm too discreet
To run amuck and tilt at all I meet.
Second Book of Horace.   A. POPE.

Satire or sense, alas ! can Sporus feel,
Who breaks a butterfly upon a wheel ?
Satires : Prologue.   A. POPE.

SCANDAL.

Damn with faint praise, assent with civil leer,
And, without sneering, teach the rest to sneer ;
Willing to wound, and yet afraid to strike,
Just hint a fault, and hesitate dislike.
Satires : Prologue.   A. POPE.

And there's a lust in man no charm can tame
Of loudly publishing our neighbor's shame ;
On eagles' wings immortal scandals fly.
While virtuous actions are but born and die.
Satire IX. JUVENAL. *Trans. of* G. HARVEY.

There's nothing blackens like the ink of fools.
If true, a woful likeness ; and, if lies,
" Praise undeserved is scandal in disguise."
Imitations of Horace, Epistle I. Bk. II. A. POPE.

A third interprets motions, looks and eyes ;
At every word a reputation dies.
Snuff, or the fan, supply each pause of chat,
With singing, laughing, ogling, and all that.
Rape of the Lock, Canto III. A. POPE.

Cursed be the verse, how well soe'er it flow,
That tends to make one worthy man my foe.
The Satires : Prologue. A. POPE.

SCHOOL.

The school-boy, with his satchel in his hand,
Whistling aloud to bear his courage up.
The Grave. R. BLAIR.

I do present you with a man of mine.
Cunning in music and the mathematics,
To instruct her fully in those sciences.
Taming of the Shrew, Act ii. *Sc. 1.* SHAKESPEARE.

Schoolmasters will I keep within my house,
Fit to instruct her youth. . . .
. . . for, to cunning men
I will be very kind, and liberal
To mine own children in good bringing up.
Taming of The Shrew, Act i. *Sc. 1.* SHAKESPEARE.

Grave is the Master's look : his forehead wears
Thick rows of wrinkles, prints of worrying cares :
Uneasy lie the heads of all that rule,
His worst of all whose kingdom is a school.
Supreme he sits ; before the awful frown
That binds his brows the boldest eye goes down ;
Not more submissive Israel heard and saw
At Sinai's foot the Giver of the Law.
The School-Boy. O. W. HOLMES.

Besides they always smell of bread and butter.
Manfred. LORD BYRON.

You 'd scarce expect one of my age
To speak in public on the stage ;
And if I chance to fall below
Demosthenes or Cicero,
Don't view me with a critic's eye,
But pass my imperfections by.
Large streams from little fountains flow,
Tall oaks from little acorns grow.
Lines written for a School Declamation.   D. EVERETT.

Ah ! happy years ! once more who would not be a boy !
Childe Harold, Canto II.   LORD BYRON.

SCIENCE.

While bright-eyed Science watches round.
Ode for Music : Chorus.   T. GRAY.

There live, alas ! of heaven-directed mien,
Of cultured soul, and sapient eye serene,
Who hail thee, Man ! the pilgrim of a day,
Spouse of the worm, and brother of the clay,
.   .   .   .   .
O Star-eyed Science ! hast thou wandered there,
To waft us home the message of despair ?
Pleasures of Hope.   T. CAMPBELL.

One science only will one genius fit,
So vast is art, so narrow human wit.
Essay on Criticism, Pt. I.   A. POPE.

By the glare of false science betrayed,
That leads to bewilder, and dazzles to blind.
The Hermit.   J. BEATTIE.

I value science—none can prize it more,
It gives ten thousand motives to adore :
Be it religious, as it ought to be,
The heart it humbles, and it bows the knee.
The Microcosm : Christian Science.   A. COLES.

SCOLD.

Unpack my heart with words,
And fall a cursing, like a very drab.
A scullion !
Fie upon 't !   Foh !
Hamlet, Act ii. *Sc.* 2.   SHAKESPEARE.

Find all his having and his holding
Reduced to eternal noise and scolding,—
The conjugal petard that tears
Down all portcullises of ears.
Hudibras. S. BUTLER.

Abroad too kind, at home 't is steadfast hate,
And one eternal tempest of debate.
Love of Fame. DR. E. YOUNG.

SCULPTURE.

As when, O lady mine,
With chiselled touch
The stone unhewn and cold
Becomes a living mould,
The more the marble wastes
The more the statue grows.
Sonnet. M. ANGELO. *Trans. of* MRS. H. ROSCOE.

Sculpture is more than painting. It is greater
To raise the dead to life than to create
Phantoms that seem to live.
Michael Angelo. H. W. LONGFELLOW.

So stands the statue that enchants the world,
So bending tries to veil the matchless boast,
The mingled beauties of exulting Greece.
The Seasons: Summer. J. THOMSON.

And the cold marble leapt to life a god.
The Belvedere Apollo. H. H. MILMAN.

Or view the lord of the unerring bow,
The god of life, and poesy, and light.—
The sun in human limbs arrayed, and brow
All radiant from his triumph in the fight ;
The shaft hath just been shot,—the arrow bright
With an immortal's vengeance ; in his eye
And nostril beautiful disdain, and might
And majesty, flash their full lightnings by,
Developing in that one glance the Deity.

But in his delicate form—a dream of love,
Shaped by some solitary nymph, whose breast
Longed for a deathless lover from above,
And maddened in that vision—are exprest
All that ideal beauty ever blessed
The mind within its most unearthly mood,
When each conception was a heavenly guest,
A ray of immortality. and stood,
Starlike, around, until they gathered to a god !
Childe Harold, Canto IV. LORD BYRON.

SEA.

Ocean ! great image of eternity,
And yet of fleeting time, of change, unrest,
Thou vast and wondrous realm of mystery,
Of thy great teachings too is man possessed.
Type of God's boundless might, the here and there
Uniting, thou dost with a righteous fear
Man's heart ennoble, awe, and purify,
As in thy mighty, multitudinous tones echoes of God roll by.
        Nature and Man.   J. W. MILES.

        What are the wild waves saying,
            Sister, the whole day long,
        That ever amid our playing
            I hear but their low, lone song?
What are the Wild Waves Saying ? J. E. CARPENTER.

        The land is dearer for the sea,
        The ocean for the shore.
On the Beach.   L. LARCOM.

        Distinct as the billows, yet one as the sea.
The Ocean.   J. MONTGOMERY.

            There the sea I found
Calm as a cradled child in dreamless slumber bound.
The Revolt of Islam, Canto I.   P. B. SHELLEY.

        And there, where the smooth, wet pebbles be,
        The waters gurgle longingly,
        As if they fain would seek the shore,
        To be at rest from the ceaseless roar,
        To be at rest forevermore.
The Sirens.   J. R. LOWELL.

            I am as a weed,
Flung from the rock, on Ocean's foam, to sail
Where'er the surge may sweep, the tempest's breath prevail.
Don Juan, Canto III.   LORD BYRON.

Watching the waves with all their white crests dancing
Come, like thick-plumed squadrons, to the shore
Gallantly bounding.
        Julian.   SIR A. HUNT.

        Once more upon the waters! yet once more !
        And the waves bound beneath me as a steed
        That knows his rider.
Don Juan, Canto III.   LORD BYRON.

I saw him beat the surges under him,
And ride upon their backs ; he trod the water,
Whose enmity he flung aside, and breasted
The surge most swoln that met him.
The Tempest, Act ii. *Sc.* 1.   SHAKESPEARE.

The sea heaves up, hangs loaded o'er the land,
Breaks there, and buries its tumultuous strength.
Luria, Act i.   R. BROWNING.

Thus, I steer my bark, and sail
On even keel, with gentle gale.
The Spleen.   M. GREEN.

What though the sea be calm ? trust to the shore.
Ships have been drowned, where late they danced before.
Safety on the Shore.   R. HERRICK.

Through the black night and driving rain
A ship is struggling, all in vain,
To live upon the stormy main ;—
Miserere Domine !
The Storm.   A. A. PROCTER.

But chief at sea, whose every flexile wave
Obeys the blast, the aerial tumult swells.
In the dread Ocean undulating wide,
Beneath the radiant line that girts the globe.
The Seasons : Summer.   J. THOMSON.

She comes majestic with her swelling sails,
The gallant Ship : along her watery way,
Homeward she drives before the favoring gales ;
Now flirting at their length the streamers play,
And now they ripple with the ruffling breeze.
Sonnet XIX.   R. SOUTHEY.

Thou wert before the Continents, before
The hollow heavens. which like another sea
Encircles them and thee ; but whence thou wert,
And when thou wast created, is not known,
Antiquity was young when thou wast old.
Hymn to the Sea.   R. H. STODDARD.

Strongly it bears us along in swelling and limitless billows.
Nothing before and nothing behind but the sky and the
ocean.
The Homeric Hexameter.
          SCHILLER.   *Trans. of* COLERIDGE.

SEASONS.

SPRING.

So forth issewed the Seasons of the yeare :
First, lusty Spring, all dight in leaves of flowres
That freshly budded and new bloomes did beare,
In which a thousand birds had built their bowres
That sweetly sung to call forth paramours ;
And in his hand a javelin he did beare,
And on his head (as fit for warlike stoures)
A guilt, engraven morion he did weare :
That, as some did him love, so others did him feare.
Faërie Queen, Bk. VII.   E. SPENSER.

The stormy March has come at last,
  With winds and clouds and changing skies ;
I hear the rushing of the blast
  That through the snowy valley flies.
March.   W. C. BRYANT.

March ! A cloudy stream is flowing,
And a hard, steel blast is blowing ;
  Bitterer now than I remember
Ever to have felt or seen,
  In the depths of drear December,
When the white doth hide the green.
March, April, May. B. W. PROCTER (*Barry Cornwall*).

A gush of bird-song, a patter of dew,
  A cloud, and a rainbow's warning,
Suddenly sunshine and perfect blue—
  An April day in the morning.
April.   H. P. SPOFFORD.

O, how this spring of love resembleth
  The uncertain glory of an April day !
The Tempest, Act i. *Sc.* 3.   SHAKESPEARE.

When proud-pied April, dressed all in his trim,
Hath put a spirit of youth in everything.
Sonnet XCVIII.   SHAKESPEARE.

Come, gentle Spring ! ethereal Mildness ! come.
The Seasons : Spring.   J. THOMSON.

But yesterday all life in bud was hid ;
  But yesterday the grass was gray and sere ;
To-day the whole world decks itself anew
  In all the glorious beauty of the year.
Sudden Spring in New England.   C. WELSH.

When April winds
Grew soft, the maple burst into a flush
Of scarlet flowers.
The Fountains.   W. C. BRYANT.

Now Nature hangs her mantle green
On every blooming tree,
And spreads her sheets o' daisies white
Out o'er the grassy lea.
Lament of Mary, Queen of Scots.   R. BURNS.

Daughter of heaven and earth, coy Spring,
With sudden passion languishing,
Teaching barren moors to smile,
Painting pictures mile on mile,
Holds a cup of cowslip wreaths
Whence a smokeless incense breathes.
May Day.   R. W. EMERSON.

Spring's last-born darling, clear-eyed, sweet,
Pauses a moment, with white twinkling feet,
And golden locks in breezy play,
Half teasing and half tender, to repeat
Her song of " May."
May.   S. C. WOOLSEY (*Susan Coolidge*).

For May wol have no slogardie a-night.
The seson priketh every gentil herte,
And maketh him out of his slepe to sterte.
Canterbury Tales: The Knightes Tale.   CHAUCER.

When daisies pied, and violets blue,
And lady-smocks all silver-white,
And cuckoo-buds of yellow hue
Do paint the meadows with delight.
Love's Labor's Lost, Act v. *Sc.* 2.   SHAKESPEARE.

SUMMER.

Then came the jolly Sommer, being dight
In a thin silken cassock, coloured greene,
That was unlynèd all, to be more light,
And on his head a garlande well beseene.
Faërie Queene, Bk. VII.   E. SPENSER.

All green and fair the Summer lies,
Just budded from the bud of Spring,
With tender blue of wistful skies,
And winds which softly sing.
Menace.   S. C. WOOLSEY (*Susan Coolidge*).
17

From brightening fields of ether fair-disclosed,
Child of the Sun, refulgent Summer comes.
In pride of youth, and felt through Nature's depth ;
He comes, attended by the sultry Hours,
And ever-fanning breezes, on his way.
The Seasons : Summer.   J. THOMSON.

From all the misty morning air, there comes a summer
    sound,
A murmur as of waters from skies, and trees, and ground.
The birds they sing upon the wing, the pigeons bill and
    coo.
A Midsummer Song.   R. W. GILDER.

> His labor is a chant,
>   His idleness a tune ;
> Oh, for a bee's experience
>   Of clovers and of noon !
The Bee.   E. DICKINSON.

> Still as night
> Or summer's noontide air.
Paradise Lost, Bk. II.   MILTON.

> Joy rises in me, like a summer's morn.
A Christmas Carol.   S. T. COLERIDGE.

> The Summer looks out from her brazen tower,
>   Through the flashing bars of July.
A Corymbus for Autumn.   F. THOMPSON.

Dead is the air, and still ! the leaves of the locust and
    walnut
Lazily hang from the boughs, inlaying their intricate
    outlines
Rather on space than the sky,—on a tideless expansion of
    slumber.
Home Pastorals : August.   B. TAYLOR.

AUTUMN.

Then came the Autumne, all in yellow clad,
As though he joyèd in his plenteous store,
Laden with fruits that made him laugh, full glad
That he had banished hunger, which to-fore
Had by the belly oft him pinchèd sore :
Upon his head a wreath, that was enrold
With ears of corne of every sort, he bore,
And in his hand a sickle he did holde,
To reape the ripened fruit the which the earth had yold.
Faërie Queene, Bk. VII.   E. SPENSER.

And the ripe harvest of the new-mown hay
Gives it a sweet and wholesome odor.
Richard III. (Altered), Act v. *Sc.* 3.   C. CIBBER.

All-cheering Plenty, with her flowing horn,
Led yellow Autumn, wreathed with nodding corn.
Brigs of Ayr.   R. BURNS.

Yellow, mellow, ripened days,
    Sheltered in a golden coating
O'er the dreamy, listless haze,
    White and dainty cloudlets floating ;

.   .   .   .   .

Sweet and smiling are thy ways,
Beauteous, golden Autumn days.
Autumn Days.   W. CARLETON.

While Autumn, nodding o'er the yellow plain,
Comes jovial on.
The Seasons : Autumn.   J. THOMSON.

From gold to gray
    Our mild sweet day
Of Indian summer fades too soon ;
    But tenderly
    Above the sea
Hangs, white and calm, the hunter's moon.
The Eve of Election.   J. G. WHITTIER.

The brown leaves rustle down the forest glade,
Where naked branches make a fitful shade,
And the lost blooms of Autumn withered lie.
October.   G. ARNOLD.

The dead leaves their rich mosaics
    Of olive and gold and brown
Had laid on the rain-wet pavements,
    Through all the embowered town.
November.   S. LONGFELLOW.

When shrieked
The bleak November winds, and smote the woods,
And the brown fields were herbless, and the shades
That met above the merry rivulet
Were spoiled, I sought, I loved them still ; they seemed
Like old companions in adversity.
A Winter Piece.   W. C. BRYANT.

Dry leaves upon the wall,
    Which flap like rustling wings and seek escape,
    A single frosted cluster on the grape
Still hangs—and that is all.
November.   S. C. WOOLSEY (*Susan Coolidge*).

WINTER.

> Lastly came Winter, clothèd all in frize,
> Chattering his teeth for cold that did him chill ;
> Whilst on his hoary beard his breath did freeze,
> And the dull drops that from his purple bill
> As from a limbeck did adown distill ;
> In his right hand a tippèd staff he held
> With which his feeble steps he stayèd still,
> For he was faint with cold and weak with eld,
> That scarce his loosèd limbs he able was to weld.

Faërie Queene, Bk. VII.   E. SPENSER.

> Chaste as the icicle,
> That 's curded by the frost from purest snow,
> And hangs on Dian's temple : dear Valeria !

Coriolanus, Act v. Sc. 3.   SHAKESPEARE.

> Silently as a dream the fabric rose,
> No sound of hammer or of saw was there.
> Ice upon ice, the well-adjusted parts
> Were soon conjoined.

The Task : Winter Morning Walk.   W. COWPER.

> When we shall hear
> The rain and wind beat dark December, how,
> In this our pinching cave, shall we discourse
> The freezing hours away ?

Cymbeline, Act iii. Sc. 3.   SHAKESPEARE.

> See, Winter comes, to rule the varied year,
> Sullen and sad, with all his rising train ;
> Vapors, and Clouds, and Storms.

The Seasons : Winter.   J. THOMSON.

> From snow-topped hills the whirlwinds keenly blow,
> Howl through the woods, and pierce the vales below,
> Through the sharp air a flaky torrent flies,
> Mocks the slow sight, and hides the gloomy skies.

Inebriety.   G. CRABBE.

> Let Winter come ! let polar spirits sweep
> The darkening world, and tempest-troubled deep !
> Though boundless snows the withered heath deform,
> And the dim sun scarce wanders through the storm,
> Yet shall the smile of social love repay,
> With mental light, the melancholy day !
> And, when its short and sullen noon is o'er,
> The ice-chained waters slumbering on the shore,
> How bright the fagots in his little hall
> Blaze on the hearth, and warm the pictured wall !

The Pleasures of Hope.   T. CAMPBELL.

Look ! the massy trunks
Are cased in the pure crystal ; each light spray,
Nodding and tinkling in the breath of heaven,
Is studded with its trembling water-drops,
That glimmer with an amethystine light.
A Winter Piece.   W. C. BRYANT.

Come when the rains
Have glazed the snow and clothed the trees with ice,
While the slant sun of February pours
Into the bowers a flood of light. Approach !
The incrusted surface shall upbear thy steps.
A Winter Piece.   W. C. BRYANT.

O Winter, ruler of the inverted year.

. . . . .

I love thee, all unlovely as thou seem'st,
And dreaded as thou art !
I crown thee king of intimate delights,
Fireside enjoyments, home-born happiness,
And all the comforts that the lowly roof
Of undisturbed Retirement, and the hours
Of long uninterrupted evening, know.
The Task : Winter Evening.   W. COWPER.

SECRET.

Two may keep counsel, putting one away.
Romeo and Juliet, Act ii. *Sc.* 4.   SHAKESPEARE.

And whatsoever else shall hap to-night,
Give it an understanding, but no tongue.
Hamlet, Act i. *Sc.* 2.   SHAKESPEARE.

If you have hitherto concealed this sight,
Let it be tenable in your silence still.
Hamlet, Act i. *Sc.* 2.   SHAKESPEARE.

I have played the fool, the gross fool, to believe
The bosom of a friend will hold a secret
Mine own could not contain.
Unnatural Combat, Act v. *Sc.* 2.   P. MASSINGER.

SHAME.

O shame, where is thy blush ?
Hamlet, Act iii. *Sc.* 4.   SHAKESPEARE.

Here shame dissuades him, there his fear prevails,
And each by turns his aching heart assails.
Metamorphoses : Actœon, Bk. III.
                    OVID. *Trans. of* ADDISON.

All is confounded, all !
Reproach and everlasting shame
Sits mocking in our plumes.
King Henry V., Act iv. *Sc.* 5.   SHAKESPEARE.

He was not born to shame :
Upon his brow shame was ashamed to sit.
Romeo and Juliet, Act iii. *Sc.* 2.   SHAKESPEARE.

Himself sole author of his own disgrace.
Hope.   W. COWPER.

Men the most infamous are fond of fame :
And those who fear not guilt, yet start at shame.
The Author.   C. CHURCHILL.

Had it pleased Heaven
To try me with affliction ; had he rained
All kinds of sores and shames on my bare head,
Steeped me in poverty to the very lips,
Given to captivity me and my utmost hopes,—
I should have found in some part of my soul
A drop of patience : but, alas, to make me
A fixèd figure, for the time of scorn
To point his slow unmoving finger at !
Othello, Act iv. *Sc.* 2.   SHAKESPEARE.

SHIP.

Build me straight, O worthy Master !
Stanch and strong, a goodly vessel,
That shall laugh at all disaster
And with wave and whirlwind wrestle.
The Building of the Ship.   H. W. LONGFELLOW.

She walks the waters like a thing of life,
And seems to dare the elements to strife.
The Corsair, Canto I.   LORD BYRON.

Hearts of oak are our ships,
Hearts of oak are our men.
Hearts of Oak.   D. GARRICK.

Sailing
Like a stately ship
Of Tarsus, bound for the isles
Of Javan or Gadire,
With all her bravery on, and tackle trim,
Sails filled, and streamers waving,
Courted by all the winds that hold them play,
An amber scent of odorous perfume
Her harbinger.
Samson Agonistes.   MILTON.

Behold the threaden sails,
Borne with the invisible and creeping wind,
Draw the huge bottoms through the furrowed sea,
Breasting the lofty surge.
King Henry V., Act iii. *Chorus.*   SHAKESPEARE.

Heaven speed the canvas, gallantly unfurled,
To furnish and accommodate a world,
To give the pole the produce of the sun,
And knit th' unsocial climates into one.
Charity.   W. COWPER.

Dangerous rocks,
Which touching but my gentle vessel's side,
Would scatter all her spices on the stream,
Enrobe the roaring waters with my silks,
And, in a word, but even now worth this,
And now worth nothing.
Merchant of Venice, Act i. *Sc.* 1.   SHAKESPEARE.

As rich . . .
As is the ooze and bottom of the sea
With sunken wreck and sumless treasuries.
King Henry V., Act i. *Sc.* 2.   SHAKESPEARE.

Her deck is crowded with despairing souls,
And in the hollow pauses of the storm
We hear their piercing cries.
Bertram.   C. R. MATURIN.

A brave vessel,
Who had no doubt some noble creatures in her,
Dashed all to pieces. O, the cry did knock
Against my very heart! Poor souls! they perished.
The Tempest, Act i. *Sc.* 2.   SHAKESPEARE.

They lit the high sea-light, and the dark began to fall.
" All hands to loose topgallant sails," I heard the captain call.
" By the Lord, she 'll never stand it," our first mate, Jackson, cried.
. . . " It 's the one way or the other, Mr. Jackson," he replied.

She staggered to her bearings, but the sails were new and good,
And the ship smelt up to windward just as though she understood.
As the winter's day was ending, in the entry of the night,
We cleared the weary headland, and passed below the light.
Christmas at Sea.   R. L. STEVENSON.

SIGH.

To love,
It is to be all made of sighs and tears.
As You Like It, Act v. *Sc.* 2.   SHAKESPEARE.

The world was sad,—the garden was a wild ;
And Man, the hermit, sighed—till Woman smiled.
Pleasures of Hope, Pt. I.   T. CAMPBELL.

Sighed and looked unutterable things.
The Seasons : Summer.   J. THOMSON.

My soul has rest, sweet sigh ! alone in thee.
To Laura in Death.   PETRARCH.

Yet sighes, deare sighes, indeede true friends you are
That do not leave your left friend at the wurst,
But, as you with my breast I oft have nurst,
So, gratefull now, you waite upon my care.
Sighes.   SIR PH. SIDNEY.

Sighs
Which perfect Joy, perplexed for utterance,
Stole from her sister Sorrow.
The Gardener's Daughter.   A. TENNYSON.

SILENCE.

Three Silences there are : the first of speech,
The second of desire, the third of thought.
The Three Silences of Molinos.   H. W. LONGFELLOW.

Stillborn silence ! thou that art
Flood-gate of the deeper heart !
Silence.   R. FLECKNOE

And silence, like a poultice, comes
To heal the blows of sound.
The Music Grinder.   O. W. HOLMES.

Silence in love bewrays more woe
Than words, though ne'er so witty ;
A beggar that is dumb, you know,
May challenge double pity.
The Silent Lover.   SIR W. RALEIGH.

Shallow brooks murmur moste,
deepe silent slide away.
The Arcadia, Thirsis and Dorus.   SIR PH. SIDNEY.

What, gone without a word ?
Aye, so true love should do : it cannot speak ;
For truth hath better deeds than words to grace it.
Two Gentlemen of Verona, Act ii. *Sc.* 3. SHAKESPEARE.

The rest is silence.
Hamlet, Act v. *Sc.* 2. SHAKESPEARE.

SIN.

Ay me, how many perils doe enfold
The righteous man, to make him daily fall.
Faërie Queene, Bk. I. E. SPENSER.

There is a method in man's wickedness,
It grows up by degrees.
A King and no King, Act v. *Sc.* 4.
BEAUMONT AND FLETCHER.

Where is the man who has not tried
How mirth can into folly glide,
And folly into sin !
The Bridal of Triermain, Canto I. SIR W. SCOTT.

I see the right, and I approve it too,
Condemn the wrong, and yet the wrong pursue.
Metamorphoses, VII. 20.
OVID. *Trans. of* TATE AND STONESTREET.

I am a man
More sinned against than sinning.
King Lear, Act iii. *Sc.* 2. SHAKESPEARE.

The good he scorned
Stalked off reluctant, like an ill-used ghost,
Not to return ; or, if it did, in visits
Like those of angels, short and far between.
The Grave, Pt. II. R. BLAIR.

Man-like is it to fall into sin,
Fiend-like is it to dwell therein,
Christ-like is it for sin to grieve,
God-like is it all sin to leave.
Sin. F. VON LOGAU. *Trans. of* LONGFELLOW.

O, what authority and show of truth
Can cunning sin cover itself withal !
Much Ado about Nothing, Act iv. *Sc.* 1. SHAKESPEARE.

Though every prospect pleases,
And only man is vile.
Missionary Hymn. BISHOP R. HEBER.

And he that does one fault at first,
And lies to hide it, makes it two.
Divine Songs.   DR. I. WATTS.

Commit
The oldest sins the newest kind of ways.
Henry IV., Pt. II. Act iv. *Sc.* 4.   SHAKESPEARE.

And out of good still to find means of evil.
Paradise Lost, Bk. I.   MILTON.

But evil is wrought by want of thought,
As well as want of heart !
The Lady's Dream.   T. HOOD.

Timely advised, the coming evil shun :
Better not do the deed, than weep it done.
Henry and Emma.   M. PRIOR.

SINCERITY.

Men should be what they seem ;
Or those that be not, would they might seem none !
Othello, Act iii. *Sc.* 3.   SHAKESPEARE.

O, how much more doth beauty beauteous seem
By that sweet ornament which truth doth give !
Sonnet LIV.   SHAKESPEARE.

O, while you live, tell truth, and shame the devil.
King Henry IV. Pt. I. Act iii. *Sc.* 1.   SHAKESPEARE.

His words are bonds, his oaths are oracles,
His love sincere, his thoughts immaculate,
His tears pure messengers sent from his heart,
His heart as far from fraud as heaven from earth.
Two Gentlemen of Verona, Act ii. *Sc.* 7. SHAKESPEARE.

An honest tale speeds best being plainly told.
King Richard III., Act iv. *Sc.* 4.   SHAKESPEARE.

Were there no heaven nor hell
I should be honest.
Duchess of Malfi, Act i. *Sc.* 1.   J. WEBSTER.

SKY.

One of those heavenly days that cannot die.
Nutting.   W. WORDSWORTH.

Green calm below, blue quietness above.
The Pennsylvania Pilgrim.   J. G. WHITTIER.

The soft blue sky did never melt
Into his heart ; he never felt
The witchery of the soft blue sky !
Peter Bell.   W. WORDSWORTH.

But now the fair traveller's come to the west.
His rays are all gold, and his beauties are best ;
He paints the skies gay as he sinks to his rest,
  And foretells a bright rising again.
A Summer Evening.   DR. I. WATTS.

How bravely Autumn paints upon the sky
  The gorgeous fame of Summer which is fled !
Written in a Volume of Shakespeare.   T. HOOD.

                         Of evening tinct,
  The purple-streaming Amethyst is thine.
Seasons : Summer.   J. THOMSON.

                  Heaven's ebon vault,
Studded with stars unutterably bright,
Through which the moon's unclouded grandeur rolls,
Seems like a canopy which love has spread
To curtain her sleeping world.
Queen Mab, Pt. IV.   P. B. SHELLEY.

    This majestical roof fretted with golden fire.
Hamlet, Act ii. *Sc.* 2.   SHAKESPEARE.

SLEEP.

Tired nature's sweet restorer, balmy Sleep !
He, like the world, his ready visit pays
Where fortune smiles ; the wretched he forsakes :
Swift on his downy pinions flies from woe,
  And lights on lids unsullied with a tear.
Night Thoughts, Night I.   DR. E. YOUNG.

Thou hast been called, O sleep ! the friend of woe ;
  But 't is the happy that have called thee so.
Curse of Kehama, Canto XV.   R. SOUTHEY.

    Sleep seldom visits sorrow ; when it doth,
      It is a comforter.
The Tempest, Act ii. *Sc.* 1.   SHAKESPEARE.

                       Weariness
  Can snore upon the flint, when restive sloth
  Finds the down pillow hard.
Cymbeline, Act iii. *Sc.* 6.   SHAKESPEARE.

O magic sleep ! O comfortable bird,
That broodest o'er the troubled sea of the mind
Till it is hushed and smooth !
Endymion, Bk. I.   J. KEATS.

Sleep, that sometimes shuts up sorrow's eye,
Steal me awhile from mine own company.
Midsummer Night's Dream, Act iii. *Sc.* 2.
                                        SHAKESPEARE.

Then Sleep and Death, two twins of wingèd race,
Of matchless swiftness, but of silent pace.
Iliad, Bk. XVI.   HOMER.   *Trans. of* POPE.

Care-charming sleep, thou easer of all woes,
Brother to Death, sweetly thyself dispose
On this afflicted prince ; fall like a cloud
In gentle showers ; . . . sing his pain
Like hollow murmuring wind or silver rain.
Valentinian.   BEAUMONT AND FLETCHER.

SMILE.

Smiles from reason flow,
To brute denied, and are of love the food.
Paradise Lost, Bk. IX.   MILTON.

Why should we faint and fear to live alone,
Since all alone, so Heaven has willed, we die,
Nor even the tenderest heart, and next our own,
Knows half the reasons why we smile and sigh ?
The Christian Year, 24th Sunday after Trinity.
                                        J. KEBLE.

And the tear that is wiped with a little address,
May be followed perhaps by a smile.
The Rose.   W. COWPER.

The social smile, the sympathetic tear.
Education and Government.   T. GRAY.

Eternal smiles his emptiness betray,
As shallow streams run dimpling all the way.
Satires : Prologue.   A. POPE.

So comes a reckoning when the banquet 's o'er,
The dreadful reckoning, and men smile no more.
The What d' ye Call 't.   J. GAY.

SOCIETY.

Heav'n forming each on other to depend,
A master, or a servant, or a friend,
Bids each on other for assistance call,
Till one man's weakness grows the strength of all.
Essay on Man, Epistle II.   A. POPE.

Love all, trust a few,
Do wrong to none : be able for thine enemy
Rather in power than use, and keep thy friend
Under thy own life's key : be checked for silence,
But never taxed for speech.
All's Well That Ends Well, Act i. *Sc.* 1.   SHAKESPEARE.

A people is but the attempt of many
To rise to the completer life of one—
And those who live as models for the mass
Are singly of more value than they all.
Luria, Act v.   R. BROWNING.

There my retreat the best companions grace,
Chiefs out of war, and statesmen out of place ;
There St. John mingles with my friendly bowl,
The feast of reason and the flow of soul.
Imitations of Horace, Satire I. Bk. II.   A. POPE.

Here thou, great Anna ! whom three realms obey,
Dost sometimes counsel take—and sometimes tea.
Rape of the Lock, Canto III.   A. POPE.

Among unequals what society
Can sort, what harmony, or true delight ?
Paradise Lost, Bk. VIII.   MILTON.

The company is " mixed " (the phrase I quote is
As much as saying, they 're below your notice).
Beppo.   LORD BYRON.

Society is now one polished horde,
Formed of two mighty tribes, the *Bores* and *Bored.*
Don Juan, Canto XI.   LORD BYRON.

SOLDIER.

He stands erect : his slouch becomes a walk ;
He steps right onward, martial in his air,
His form and movement.
The Task, Bk. IV.   W. COWPER.

A braver soldier never couchèd lance,
A gentler heart did never sway in court.
King Henry VI., Pt. I. Act iii. *Sc.* 2.   SHAKESPEARE.

Unbounded courage and compassion joined,
Tempering each other in the victor's mind,
Alternately proclaim him good and great,
And make the hero and the man complete.

.   .   .   .   .

And, pleased the Almighty's orders to perform,
Rides in the whirlwind and directs the storm.
The Campaign.   J. ADDISON.

So restless Cromwell could not cease
In the inglorious arts of peace.
But through adventurous war
Urgèd his active star.
A Horatian Ode : Upon Cromwell's Return from Ireland.
      A. MARVELL.

'T is the soldier's life
To have their balmy slumbers waked with strife.
Othello, Act ii. *Sc.* 3.   SHAKESPEARE.

Some for hard masters, broken under arms,
In battle lopt away, with half their limbs,
Beg bitter bread thro' realms their valor saved.
Night Thoughts, Night I.   DR. E. YOUNG.

His breast with wounds unnumbered riven,
His back to earth, his face to heaven.
The Giaour.   LORD BYRON.

Wut 's words to them whose faith an' truth
On War's red techstone rang true metal,
Who ventured life an' love an' youth
For the gret prize o' death in battle ?
The Biglow Papers, Second Series, No. X.
      J. R. LOWELL.

God's soldier he be !
Had I as many sons as I have hairs.
I would not wish them to a fairer death :
And so his knell is knolled.
Macbeth, Act v. *Sc.* 8.   SHAKESPEARE.

O, now, forever
Farewell the tranquil mind ! farewell content !
Farewell the plumèd troop, and the big wars,
That make ambition virtue ! O, farewell !
Farewell the neighing steed, and the shrill trump,

The spirit-stirring drum, the ear-piercing fife,
The royal banner, and all quality,
Pride, pomp, and circumstance of glorious war !
And, O you mortal engines, whose rude throats
The immortal Jove's dread clamors counterfeit,
Farewell ! Othello's occupation 's gone !
Othello, Act iii. *Sc.* 3.   SHAKESPEARE.

SOLITUDE.

All heaven and earth are still,—though not in sleep,
But breathless, as we grow when feeling most ;
And silent, as we stand in thoughts too deep ;—
All heaven and earth are still ;

.   .   .   .   .

Then stirs the feeling infinite, so felt
In solitude, where we are *least* alone.
Childe Harold, Canto III.   LORD BYRON.

When, musing on companions gone,
We doubly feel ourselves alone.
Marmion, Canto II. Introduction.   SIR W. SCOTT.

Alone !—that worn-out word,
So idly spoken, and so coldly heard ;
Yet all that poets sing, and grief hath known,
Of hopes laid waste, knells in that word—*Alone!*
The New Timon, Pt. II.   E. BULWER-LYTTON.

O ! lost to virtue, lost to manly thought,
Lost to the noble sallies of the soul !
Who think it solitude to be alone.
Night Thoughts, Night IV.   DR. E. YOUNG.

Converse with men makes sharp the glittering wit,
But God to man doth speak in solitude.
Highland Solitude.   J. S. BLACKIE.

But, if much converse perhaps
Thee satiate, to short absence I could yield ;
For solitude sometimes is best society,
And short retirement urges sweet return.
Paradise Lost, Bk. IX.   MILTON.

Few are the faults we flatter when alone.
Night Thoughts, Night V.   DR. E. YOUNG.

'T is solitude should teach us how to die ;
It hath no flatterers ; vanity can give
No hollow aid ; alone—man with his God must strive.
Childe Harold, Canto II.   LORD BYRON.

How sweet, how passing sweet is solitude?
But grant me still a friend in my retreat,
Whom I may whisper—solitude is sweet.
Retirement.   W. COWPER.

SORROW.

When sorrows come, they come not single spies,
But in battalions.
Hamlet, Act iv. Sc. 5.   SHAKESPEARE.

One woe doth tread upon another's heel,
So fast they follow.
Hamlet, Act iv. Sc. 7.   SHAKESPEARE.

Woes cluster ; rare are solitary woes ;
They love a train, they tread each other's heel.
Night Thoughts, Night III.   DR. E. YOUNG.

Who ne'er his bread in sorrow ate,
    Who ne'er the mournful midnight hours
Weeping upon his bed has sate,
    He knows you not, ye Heavenly Powers.
Hyperion, Bk. I. Motto : from Goethe's Wilhelm Meister.
                              H. W. LONGFELLOW.

One fire burns out another's burning ;
One pain is lessened by another's anguish ;
Turn giddy, and be helped by backward turning ;
One desp'rate grief cures with another's languish ;
Take thou some new infection to the eye,
And the rank poison of the old will die.
Romeo and Juliet, Act i. Sc. 2.   SHAKESPEARE.

All that 's bright must fade,—
    The brightest still the fleetest ;
All that 's sweet was made
    But to be lost when sweetest !
National Airs : All that's bright must fade.
                                     T. MOORE.

O God ! O God !
How weary, stale, flat, and unprofitable
Seem to me all the uses of this world !
Hamlet, Act i. Sc. 2.   SHAKESPEARE.

Weep no more, nor sigh, nor groan,
Sorrow calls no time that 's gone :
Violets plucked, the sweetest rain
Makes not fresh nor grow again.
The Queen of Corinth, Act iii. Sc. 2.   J. FLETCHER.

Sorrows remembered sweeten present joy.
The Course of Time, Bk. I.   R. POLLOK.

Wreaths that endure affliction's heaviest showers,
And do not shrink from sorrow's keenest winds.
Misc. Sonnets, Pt. I. XXXIII.   W. WORDSWORTH.

Affliction is the good man's shining scene ;
Prosperity conceals his brightest ray ;
As night to stars. woe lustre gives to man.
Night Thoughts, Night IX.   DR. E. YOUNG.

Like a ball that bounds
According to the force with which 't was thrown
So in affliction's violence, he that 's wise
The more he 's cast down will the higher rise.
Microcosmos.   T. NABBES.

O, fear not in a world like this,
    And thou shalt know erelong,—
Know how sublime a thing it is
    To suffer and be strong.
The Light of Stars.   H. W. LONGFELLOW.

SOUL.

Summe up at night what thou hast done by day ;
And in the morning what thou hast to do.
Dresse and undresse thy soul ; mark the decay
And growth of it : if, with thy watch, that too
    Be down, then winde up both ; since we shall be
    Most surely judged, make thy accounts agree.
The Temple : The Church Porch.   G. HERBERT.

Go to your bosom ;
Knock there, and ask your heart what it doth know.
Measure for Measure, Act ii. Sc. 2.   SHAKESPEARE.

O ignorant, poor man ! what dost thou bear
    Locked up within the casket of thy breast ?
What jewels and what riches hast thou there ?
    What heavenly treasure in so weak a chest ?
Worth of the Soul.   SIR J. DAVIES.

Let Fortune empty all her quiver on me ;
I have a soul that, like an ample shield,
Can take in all. and verge enough for more.
Sebastian, Act i. Sc. 1.   J. DRYDEN.

And keeps that palace of the soul serene.
Of Tea.   E. WALLER.
18

A happy soul, that all the way
To heaven hath a summer's day.
In Praise of Lessius' Rule of Health.   R. CRASHAW.

And rest at last where souls unbodied dwell,
In ever-flowing meads of Asphodel.
Odyssey, Bk. XXIV.   HOMER. *Trans. of* POPE.

SPEECH.

Persuasive speech, and more persuasive sighs,
Silence that spoke, and eloquence of eyes.
Iliad, Bk. XIV.   HOMER. *Trans. of* POPE.

Discourse may want an animated "No"
To brush the surface, and to make it flow ;
But still remember, if you mean to please,
To press your point with modesty and ease.
Conversation.   W. COWPER.

One whom the music of his own vain tongue
Doth ravish like enchanting harmony.
Love's Labor's Lost, Act i. *Sc.* 1.   SHAKESPEARE.

Turn him to any cause of policy,
The Gordian knot of it he will unloose,
Familiar as his garter : that, when he speaks,
The air, a chartered libertine, is still.
King Henry V., Act i. *Sc.* 1.   SHAKESPEARE.

Persuasion tips his tongue whene'er he talks.
Parody on Pope.   C. CIBBER.

Yet hold it more humane, more heavenly, first,
By winning words to conquer willing hearts,
And make persuasion do the work of fear.
Paradise Regained, Bk. I.   MILTON.

Give every man thine ear, but few thy voice :
Take each man's censure, but reserve thy judgment.
Hamlet, Act i. *Sc.* 3.   SHAKESPEARE.

" Careful with fire," is good advice, we know,
" Careful with words," is ten times doubly so.
Thoughts unexpressed may sometimes fall back dead ;
But God Himself can't kill them when they 're said.
First Settler's Story.   W. CARLETON.

SPIRITS.

GLENDOWER.—I can call spirits from the vasty deep.
HOTSPUR.—Why, so can I, or so can any man ;
But will they come when you do call for them ?
King Henry IV., Pt. I. Act iii. *Sc.* 1.   SHAKESPEARE.

Millions of spiritual creatures walk the earth
Unseen, both when we wake, and when we sleep.
Paradise Lost, Bk. IV. MILTON.

Spirits when they please
Can either sex assume, or both,

. . . .

Can execute their airy purposes,
And works of love or enmity fulfil.
Paradise Lost, Bk. I. MILTON.

But shapes that come not at an earthly call
Will not depart when mortal voices bid ;
Lords of the visionary eye, whose lid,
Once raised, remains aghast, and will not fall !
Dion. W. WORDSWORTH.

I shall not see thee. Dare I say
No spirit ever brake the band
That stays him from the native land,
Where first he walked when clasped in clay ?

No visual shade of some one lost,
But he, the spirit himself, may come
Where all the nerve of sense is numb ;
Spirit to spirit, ghost to ghost.
In Memoriam, XCII. A. TENNYSON.

STAGE, THE.

Where is our usual manager of mirth ?
What revels are in hand ? Is there no play,
To ease the anguish of a torturing hour ?
Midsummer Night's Dream, Act v. Sc. 1. SHAKESPEARE.

Prologues, like compliments, are loss of time :
'T is penning bows and making legs in rhyme.
Prologue to Crisp's Tragedy of Virginia. D. GARRICK.

Prologues precede the piece in mournful verse,
As undertakers walk before the hearse.
Prologue to Apprentice. D. GARRICK.

On the stage he was natural, simple, affecting,
'T was only that when he was off, he was acting.
Retaliation. O. GOLDSMITH.

The drama's laws, the drama's patrons give.
For we that live to please, must please to live.
*Prologue. Spoken by Mr. Garrick on Opening Drury
Lane Theatre, 1747.* DR. S. JOHNSON.

To wake the soul by tender strokes of art,
To raise the genius, and to mend the heart ;
To make mankind, in conscious virtue bold,
Live o'er each scene, and be what they behold—
For this the tragic Muse first trod the stage.
Prologue to Addison's Cato.   A. POPE.

As in a theatre, the eyes of men,
After a well-graced actor leaves the stage,
Are idly bent on him that enters next,
Thinking his prattle to be tedious.
Richard II., Act v. Sc. 2.   SHAKESPEARE.

Is it not monstrous that this player here,
But in a fiction, in a dream of passion,
Could force his soul so to his own conceit
That from her working all his visage wanned ?
Hamlet, Act ii. Sc. 2.   SHAKESPEARE.

What 's Hecuba to him, or he to Hecuba,
That he should weep for her? What would he do,
Had he the motive and the cue for passion
That I have? He would drown the stage with tears.
Hamlet, Act ii. Sc. 2.   SHAKESPEARE.

I hold the world but as the world, Gratiano ;
A stage, where every man must play a part,
And mine a sad one.
Merchant of Venice, Act i. Sc. 1.   SHAKESPEARE.

I have heard
That guilty creatures, sitting at a play,
Have by the very cunning of the scene
Been struck so to the soul, that presently
They have proclaimed their malefactions.

.   .   .   .   .

The play 's the thing
Wherein I 'll catch the conscience of the King.
Hamlet, Act ii. Sc. 2.   SHAKESPEARE.

Lo, where the stage, the poor, degraded stage,
Holds its warped mirror to a gaping age.
Curiosity.   C. SPRAGUE.

A veteran see ! whose last act on the stage
Entreats your smiles for sickness and for age ;
Their cause I plead,—plead it in heart and mind ;
A fellow-feeling makes one wondrous kind.
Prologue on Quitting the Stage in 1776.   D. GARRICK.

Who teach the mind its proper face to scan,
And hold the faithful mirror up to man.
The Actor. R. LLOYD.

STAR.

That full star that ushers in the even.
Sonnet CXXXII. SHAKESPEARE.

Her blue eyes sought the west afar,
For lovers love the western star.
Lay of the Last Minstrel, Canto III. SIR W. SCOTT.

And fast by, hanging in a golden chain
This pendent world, in bigness as a star
Of smallest magnitude close by the moon.
Paradise Lost, Bk. II. MILTON.

Devotion ! daughter of astronomy !
An undevout astronomer is mad.
Night Thoughts, Night IX. DR. E. YOUNG.

There does a sable cloud
Turn forth her silver lining on the night,
And cast a gleam over this tufted grove.
Comus. MILTON.

Blossomed the lovely stars, the forget-me-nots of the
angels.
Evangeline, Pt. I. H. W. LONGFELLOW.

'T is the witching hour of night,
Orbed is the moon and bright,
And the stars they glisten, glisten,
Seeming with bright eyes to listen—
For what listen they ?
A Prophecy. J. KEATS.

There is no light in earth or heaven
But the cold light of stars ;
And the first watch of night is given
To the red planet Mars.
The Light of Stars. H. W. LONGFELLOW.

Sweet Phosphor, bring the day ;
Light will repay
The wrongs of night ;
Sweet Phosphor, bring the day !
Emblems, Bk. I. F. QUARLES.

At whose sight all the stars
Hide their diminished heads.
Paradise Lost, Bk. IV. MILTON.

Nor sink those stars in empty night,—
They hide themselves in heaven's own light.
Issues of Life and Death.   J. MONTGOMERY.

STATECRAFT.

A thousand years scarce serve to form a state :
An hour may lay it in the dust.
Childe Harold, Canto II.   LORD BYRON.

Who 's in or out, who moves this grand machine,
Nor stirs my curiosity nor spleen :
Secrets of state no more I wish to know
Than secret movements of a puppet show :
Let but the puppets move, I 've my desire,
Unseen the hand which guides the master wire.
Night.   C. CHURCHILL.

Resolved to ruin or to rule the state.
Absalom and Achitophel, Pt. II.   J. DRYDEN.

And lives to clutch the golden keys,
To mould a mighty state's decrees,
And shape the whisper of the throne.
In Memoriam, LXIII.   A. TENNYSON.

And statesmen at her council met
Who knew the seasons when to take
Occasion by the hand, and make
The bounds of freedom wider yet.
To the Queen.   A. TENNYSON.

What should it be, that thus their faith can bind ?
The power of Thought—the magic of the Mind !
Linked with success, assumed and kept with skill,
That moulds another's weakness to its will.
The Corsair.   LORD BYRON.

'T is thus the spirit of a single mind
Makes that of multitudes take one direction.
Don Juan.   LORD BYRON.

For just experience tells, in every soil,
That those that think must govern those that toil.
The Traveller.   O. GOLDSMITH.

A cutpurse of the empire and the rule,
That from a shelf the precious diadem stole,
And put it in his pocket !
Hamlet, Act iii. Sc. 4.   SHAKESPEARE.

Some of their chiefs were princes of the land ;
In the first rank of these did Zimri * stand ;
A man so various, that he seemed to be
Not one, but all mankind's epitome :
Stiff in opinions, always in the wrong ;
Was everything by starts, and nothing long;
But, in the course of one revolving moon.
Was chymist, fiddler, statesman, and buffoon ;
Then all for women, painting, rhyming, drinking,
Besides ten thousand freaks that died in thinking.
Absalom and Achitophel, Pt. I.   J. DRYDEN.

For close designs and crooked councils fit ;
Sagacious, bold, and turbulent of wit ;
Restless, unfixed in principles and place ;
In power unpleased, impatient of disgrace :
A fiery soul. which, working out its way,
Fretted the pygmy-body to decay,
And o'er informed the tenement of clay.
A daring pilot in extremity ;
Pleased with the danger, when the waves went high
He sought the storms ; but for a calm unfit,
Would steer too nigh the sands to boast his wit.
Great wits are sure to madness near allied,
And thin partitions do their bounds divide.
Absalom and Achitophel, Pt. I. (Earl of Shaftesbury.)
          J. DRYDEN.

STEALING.

I'll example you with thievery :
The sun's a thief, and with his great attraction
Robs the vast sea : the moon's an arrant thief,
And her pale fire she snatches from the sun :
The sea's a thief, whose liquid surge resolves
The moon into salt tears : the earth's a thief,
That feeds and breeds by composture stolen
From general excrement : each thing's a thief.
Timon of Athens, Act iv. Sc. 3.   SHAKESPEARE.

Kill a man's family and he may brook it,
But keep your hands out of his breeches' pocket.
Don Juan, Canto X.   LORD BYRON.

Stolen sweets are always sweeter :
Stolen kisses much completer ;
Stolen looks are nice in chapels :
Stolen, stolen be your apples.
Song of Fairies.   T. RANDOLPH.

* George Villiers, Duke of Buckingham.

A tailor, though a man of upright dealing,—
True but for lying,—honest but for stealing.
Of a Precise Tailor.   SIR J. HARRINGTON.

Thieves for their robbery have authority
When judges steal themselves.
Measure for Measure, Act ii. *Sc.* 2.   SHAKESPEARE.

Thou hast stolen both mine office and my name ;
The one ne'er got me credit, the other mickle blame.
Comedy of Errors, Act iii. *Sc.* 1.   SHAKESPEARE.

In vain we call old notions fudge
And bend our conscience to our dealing,
The Ten Commandments will not budge
And stealing will continue stealing.
Motto of American Copyright League, 1885.

STORM.

The lowering element
Scowls o'er the darkened landscape.
Paradise Lost, Bk. II.   MILTON.

At first, heard solemn o'er the verge of Heaven,
The tempest growls ; but as it nearer comes,
And rolls its awful burden on the wind,
The lightnings flash a larger curve, and more
The noise astounds ; till overhead a sheet
Of livid flame discloses wide, then shuts,
And opens wider ; shuts and opens still
Expansive, wrapping ether in a blaze.
Follows the loosened aggravated roar,
Enlarging, deepening, mingling, peal on peal,
Crushed, horrible, convulsing Heaven and Earth.
The Seasons : Summer.   J. THOMSON.

From cloud to cloud the rending lightnings rage,
Till, in the furious elemental war
Dissolved, the whole precipitated mass
Unbroken floods and solid torrents pour.
The Seasons : Summer.   J. THOMSON.

Poor naked wretches, wheresoe'er you are,
That bide the pelting of this pitiless storm,
How shall your houseless heads and unfed sides,
Your looped and windowed raggedness, defend you
From seasons such as these ?
King Lear, Act iii. *Sc.* 4.   SHAKESPEARE.

Blow wind, swell billow, and swim bark !
The storm is up, and all is on the hazard.
Julius Cæsar, Act v. *Sc.* 1.   SHAKESPEARE.

I have seen tempests. when the scolding winds
Have rived the knotty oaks, and I have seen
The ambitious ocean swell and rage and foam,
To be exalted with the threat'ning clouds.
Julius Cæsar, Act i. *Sc.* 3.   SHAKESPEARE.

                    Seas
    Rough with black winds, and storms
    Unwonted.
Book I. Ode V.   HORACE. *Trans. of* MILTON.

Lightnings, that show the vast and foamy deep,
The rending thunders, as they onward roll,
The loud, loud winds, that o'er the billows sweep—
Shake the firm nerve, appal the bravest soul!
Mysteries of Udolpho : The Mariner.

                    MRS. ANN RADCLIFFE.

SUCCESS.

In the lexicon of youth, which fate reserves
For a bright manhood, there is no such word
As—*fail.*
Richelieu, Act ii. *Sc.* 2.   E. BULWER-LYTTON.

    The star of the unconquered will.
The Light of Stars.   H. W. LONGFELLOW.

'T is not in mortals to command success,
But we 'll do more, Sempronius ; we 'll deserve it.
Cato, Act i. *Sc.* 2.   J. ADDISON.

And many strokes, though with a little axe,
Hew down and fell the hardest-timbered oak.
King Henry VI., Pt. III. Act ii. *Sc.* 1.   SHAKESPEARE.

                    Such a nature.
Tickled with good success, disdains the shadow
Which he treads on at noon.
Coriolanus, Act i. *Sc.* 1.   SHAKESPEARE.

In my school-days. when I had lost one shaft,
I shot his fellow of the self-same flight
The self-same way, with more advisèd watch.
To find the other forth ; and by adventuring both,
I oft found both.
Merchant of Venice, Act i. *Sc.* 1.   SHAKESPEARE.

        Success is counted sweetest
        By those who ne'er succeed.
Success.   EMILY DICKINSON.

SUICIDE.

He

That kills himself t' avoid misery, fears it,
And at the best shows but a bastard valor :
This life 's a fort committed to my trust,
Which I must not yield up, till it be forced ;
Nor will I : he 's not valiant that dares die,
But he that boldly bears calamity.
The Maid of Honor.   P. MASSINGER.

All mankind
Is one of these two cowards ;
Either to wish to die
When he should live, or live when he should die.
The Blind Lady.   SIR R. HOWARD.

Against self-slaughter
There is a prohibition so divine
That cravens my weak hand.

Cymbeline, Act iii. *Sc.* 4.   SHAKESPEARE.

SUN.

That orbèd continent the fire
That severs day from night.

Twelfth Night, Act v. *Sc.* 1.   SHAKESPEARE.

O thou that, with surpassing glory crowned,
Look'st from thy sole dominion like the God
Of this new world, . . .
O Sun !
Paradise Lost, Bk. IV.   MILTON.

Fires the proud tops of the eastern pines.
King Richard II., Act iii. *Sc.* 2.   SHAKESPEARE.

The lessening cloud,

The kindling azure, and the mountain's brow,
Illumed with fluid gold, his near approach
Betoken glad.   Lo ! now, apparent all
Aslant the dew-bright earth, and colored air,
He looks in boundless majesty abroad ;
And sheds the shining day, that burnished plays
On rocks, and hills, and towers, and wand'ring streams.
High gleaming from afar.
The Seasons : Summer.   J. THOMSON.

The sun had long since in the lap
Of Thetis taken out his nap,
And, like a lobster boiled, the morn
From black to red began to turn.
Hudibras, Pt. II. Canto II.   DR. S. BUTLER.

" But," quoth his neighbor, " when the sun
From East to West his course has run,
How comes it that he shows his face
Next morning in his former place ? "
" Ho ! there 's a pretty question, truly ! "
Replied our wight, with an unruly
Burst of laughter and delight,
So much his triumph seemed to please him :
" Why, blockhead ! he goes back at night,
And that 's the reason no one sees him ! "
The Astronomical Alderman.   H. SMITH.

Behold him setting in his western skies,
The shadows lengthening as the vapors rise.
Absalom and Achitophel, Pt. I.   J. DRYDEN.

Now sunk the sun : the closing hour of day
Came onward, mantled o'er with sober gray ;
Nature in silence bid the world repose.
The Hermit.   T. PARNELL.

                              Parting day
Dies like the dolphin, whom each pang imbues
With a new color as it gasps away,
The last still loveliest, till—'t is gone—and all is gray.
Childe Harold, Canto IV.   LORD BYRON.

Come watch with me the shaft of fire that glows
In yonder West : the fair, frail palaces,
The fading Alps and archipelagoes,
And great cloud-continents of sunset-seas.
Miracles.   T. B. ALDRICH.

The setting sun, and music at the close,
As the last taste of sweets, is sweetest last.
King Richard II., Act ii. Sc. 1.   SHAKESPEARE.

SUSPICION.

Yet, where an equal poise of hope and fear
Does arbitrate the event, my nature is
That I incline to hope rather than fear,
And gladly banish squint suspicion.
Comus.   MILTON.

All seems infected that the infected spy,
As all looks yellow to the jaundiced eye.
Essay on Criticism.   A. POPE.

Suspicion, poisoning his brother's cup.
Catiline.   G. CROLY.

SYMPATHY.

He jests at scars, that never felt a wound.
Romeo and Juliet, Act ii. *Sc.* 1.　　SHAKESPEARE.

No one is so accursed by fate,
No one so utterly desolate,
　　But some heart, though unknown,
　　Responds unto his own.
Endymion.　　　H. W. LONGFELLOW.

There is in souls a sympathy with sounds,
And as the mind is pitched the ear is pleased
With melting airs of martial, brisk, or grave ;
Some chord in unison with what we hear
Is touched within us, and the heart replies.
The Task : Winter Walk at Noon.　　W. COWPER.

Oh ! who the exquisite delights can tell,
The joy which mutual confidence imparts ?
Or who can paint the charm unspeakable,
Which links in tender bands two faithful hearts?
Psyche.　　　MRS. M. TIGHE.

O ! ask not, hope thou not too much
　　Of sympathy below :
Few are the hearts whence one same touch
　　Bids the same fountain flow.
Kindred Hearts.　　　MRS. F. D. HEMANS.

Yet, taught by time, my heart has learned to glow
For other's good, and melt at other's woe.
Odyssey, Bk. XVIII.　　HOMER. *Trans. of* POPE.

TABLE, THE.

Some hae meat and canna eat,
And some wad eat that want it ;
But we hae meat, and we can eat ;
Sae let the Lord be thankit.
Grace before Meat.　　　R. BURNS.

And do as adversaries do in law,
Strive mightily, but eat and drink as friends.
Taming of the Shrew, Act i. *Sc.* 2.　　SHAKESPEARE.

They are as sick that surfeit with too much, as they that
　　starve with nothing.
Merchant of Venice, Act i. *Sc.* 2.　　SHAKESPEARE.

He hath eaten me out of house and home.
King Henry IV., Pt. II. Act ii. *Sc.* 1.　　SHAKESPEARE.

My cake is dough : but I'll in among the rest,
Out of hope of all but my share of the feast.
Taming of the Shrew, Act v. *Sc.* 1.   SHAKESPEARE.

And gazed around them to the left and right
With the prophetic eye of appetite.
Don Juan, Canto V.   LORD BYRON.

Blest be those feasts, with simple plenty crowned,
Where all the ruddy family around
Laugh at the jests or pranks that never fail
Or sigh with pity at some mournful tale.
The Traveller.   O. GOLDSMITH.

They eat, they drink, and in communion sweet
Quaff immortality and joy.
Paradise Lost, Bk. V.   MILTON.

Bone and Skin, two millers thin,
Would starve us all, or near it ;
But be it known to Skin and Bone
That Flesh and Blood can't bear it.
On Two Monopolists.   J. BYROM.

Nothing's more sure at moments to take hold
Of the best feelings of mankind, which grow
More tender, as we every day behold,
Than that all-softening, overpowering knell,
The tocsin of the soul—the dinner bell !
Don Juan, Canto V.   LORD BYRON.

Their various cares in one great point combine
The business of their lives, that is—to dine.
Love of Fame.   DR. E. YOUNG.

Across the walnuts and the wine.
The Miller's Daughter.   A. TENNYSON.

No, pray thee, let it serve for table-talk ;
Then, howsoe'er thou speak'st, 'mong other things
I shall digest it.
Merchant of Venice, Act iii. *Sc.* 5.   SHAKESPEARE.

TASTE.

Some say, compared to Bononcini,
That Mynheer Handel's but a ninny ;
Others aver,—that he to Handel
Is scarcely fit to hold a candle :
Strange all this difference should be,
'Twixt tweedle-dum and tweedle-dee !
On the Feuds between Handel and Bononcini.   J. BYROM.

What 's one man's poison, signor,
Is another's meat or drink.
Love's Cure, Act iii. *Sc. 2.*   BEAUMONT AND FLETCHER.

Different minds
Incline to different objects : one pursues
The vast alone, the wonderful, the wild ;
Another sighs for harmony, and grace,
And gentlest beauty.

.   .   .   .   .

Such and so various are the tastes of men.
Pleasures of the Imagination, Bk. III.   M. AKENSIDE.

TEAR.

The rose is fairest when 't is budding new,
And hope is brightest when it dawns from fears.
The rose is sweetest washed with morning dew,
And love is loveliest when embalmed in tears.
Lady of the Lake, Canto IV.   SIR W. SCOTT.

O father, what a hell of witchcraft lies
In the small orb of one particular tear !
A Lover's Complaint, Stanza XLII.   SHAKESPEARE.

Sunshine and rain at once.
King Lear, Act iv. *Sc. 3.*   SHAKESPEARE.

The drying up a single tear has more
Of honest fame, than shedding seas of gore.
Don Juan, Canto VIII.   LORD BYRON.

And weep the more, because I weep in vain.
On the Death of Mr. West.   T. GRAY.

Oh ! would I were dead now,
Or up in my bed now,
To cover my head now
And have a good cry !
A Table of Errata.   T. HOOD.

So bright the tear in Beauty's eye,
Love half regrets to kiss it dry.
Bride of Abydos.   LORD BYRON.

I cannot speak. tears so obstruct my words,
And choke me with unutterable joy.
Caius Marius.   T. OTWAY.

Sorrow preys upon
Its solitude and nothing more diverts it
From its sad visions of the other world
Than calling it at moments back to this.
The busy have no time for tears.

The Two Foscari, Act iv.   LORD BYRON.

TEMPER.

Oh ! blessed with temper, whose unclouded ray
Can make to-morrow cheerful as to-day.

Moral Essays, Epistle II.   A. POPE.

From loveless youth to unrespected age,
No passion gratified, except her rage,
So much the fury still outran the wit,
That pleasure missed her, and the scandal hit.

Moral Essays, Epistle II.   A. POPE.

Good-humor only teaches charms to last,
Still makes new conquests and maintains the past.

Epistle to Mrs. Blount.   A. POPE.

What then remains. but well our power to use,
And keep good-humor still whate'er we lose ?
And trust me, dear, good-humor can prevail,
When airs, and flights. and screams, and scolding fail.

Rape of the Lock, Canto V.   A. POPE.

TEMPTATION.

How oft the sight of means to do ill deeds
Makes ill deeds done !

King John, Act iv. *Sc.* 2.   SHAKESPEARE.

O opportunity, thy guilt is great !
'T is thou that executest the traitor's treason ;
Thou sett'st the wolf where he the lamb may get ;
Whoever plots the sin, thou 'point'st the season ;
'T is thou that spurn'st at right, at law, at reason.

The Rape of Lucrece.   SHAKESPEARE.

Sometimes we are devils to ourselves,
When we will tempt the frailty of our powers,
Presuming on their changeful potency.

Troilus and Cressida, Act iv. *Sc.* 4.   SHAKESPEARE.

In part to blame is she.
Which hath *without consent* bin only tride ;
He comes *too neere,* that comes to be *denide.*

A Wife.   SIR T. OVERBURY.

Vice is a monster of so frightful mien,
As to be hated needs but to be seen ;
Yet seen too oft, familiar with her face,
We first endure. then pity, then embrace.
Essay on Man, Epistle II.   A. POPE.

Temptations hurt not, though they have accesse ;
Satan o'ercomes none but by willingnesse.
Hesperides' Temptations.   R. HERRICK.

THEOLOGY.

In Adam's fall
We sinnèd all.
                              New England Primer.

Hold thou the good : define it well :
   For fear divine Philosophy
   Should push beyond her mark, and be
Procuress to the Lords of Hell.
In Memoriam.   A. TENNYSON.

For forms of government let fools contest ;
Whate'er is best administered is best :
For modes of faith let graceless zealots fight ;
His can't be wrong whose life is in the right.
Essay on Man, Epistle III.   A. POPE.

His *faith*, perhaps, in some nice tenets might
Be wrong ; his *life*. I 'm sure, was in the right.
On the Death of Crashaw.   A. COWLEY.

Slave to no sect, who takes no private road,
But looks through nature up to nature's God.
          .   .   .
And knows where faith. law, morals. all began,
All end, in love of God and love of man.
Essay on Man, Epistle IV.   A. POPE.

THOUGHT.

Thought can wing its way
Swifter than lightning-flashes or the beam
That hastens on the pinions of the morn.
Sonnet.   J. G. PERCIVAL.

I and my bosom must debate awhile,
And then I would no other company.
King Henry V., Act iv. *Sc.* 1.   SHAKESPEARE.

He that has light within his own clear breast,
May sit i' th' centre and enjoy bright day :
But he that hides a dark soul, and foul thoughts,
Benighted walks under the midday sun.
Comus.   MILTON.

So Thought flung forward is the prophecy
Of Truth's majestic march, and shows the way
Where future time shall lead the proud array
Of peace, of power, and love of liberty.
                                 SIR J. BOWRING.

There is nothing either good or bad, but thinking makes
it so.
Hamlet, Act ii. *Sc.* 2.   SHAKESPEARE.

TIME.

O Time ! the beautifier of the dead,
Adorner of the ruin, comforter
And only healer when the heart hath bled—
Time ! the corrector where our judgments err,
The test of truth, love,—soul philosopher,
For all besides are sophists, from thy thrift
Which never loses though it doth defer—
Time, the avenger ! unto thee I lift
My hands, and eyes, and heart, and crave of thee a gift.
Childe Harold, Canto IV.   LORD BYRON.

The more we live, more brief appear
   Our life's succeeding stages :
A day to childhood seems a year,
   And years like passing ages.

.   .   .   .   .

Heaven gives our years of fading strength
   Indemnifying fleetness ;
And those of youth, a seeming length,
   Proportioned to their sweetness.
The River of Life.   T. CAMPBELL.

Yet Time, who changes all, had altered him
In soul and aspect as in age ; years steal
Fire from the mind as vigor from the limb :
And life's enchanted cup but sparkles near the brim.
Childe Harold, Canto III.   LORD BYRON.

Catch ! then, O catch, the transient hour ;
Improve each moment as it flies ;
Life 's a short summer—man a flower.
Winter: An Ode.   DR. S. JOHNSON.
19

Come what come may,
Time and the hour runs through the roughest day.
Macbeth, Act i. *Sc.* 3.   SHAKESPEARE.

And then he drew a dial from his poke,
And, looking on it with lack-lustre eye,
Says very wisely, " It is ten o'clock :
Thus may we see," quoth he, " how the world wags :
'T is but an hour ago since it was nine ;
And after one hour more 't will be eleven ;
And so, from hour to hour, we ripe and ripe,
And then, from hour to hour, we rot and rot ;
And thereby hangs a tale."
As You Like It, Act ii. *Sc.* 7.   SHAKESPEARE.

Seven hours to law, to soothing slumber seven,
Ten to the world allot, and all to heaven.
Ode in Imitation of Alcæus.   SIR W. JONES.

Nought treads so silent as the foot of Time ;
Hence we mistake our autumn for our prime.
Love of Fame, Satire IV.   DR. E. YOUNG.

Not one word more of the consumèd time.
Let 's take the instant by the forward top ;
For we are old, and on our quick'st decrees
The inaudible and noiseless foot of Time
Steals ere we can effect them.
All's Well that End's Well, Act v. *Sc.* 3. SHAKESPEARE.

TOBACCO.

Sublime tobacco ! which from east to west,
Cheers the tar's labor or the Turkman's rest,

.   .   .   .   .

Divine in hookahs, glorious in a pipe,
When tipped with amber, mellow, rich and ripe ;
Like other charmers, wooing the caress
More dazzlingly when daring in full dress ;
Yet thy true lovers more admire by far
Thy naked beauties—Give me a cigar !
The Island, Canto II.   LORD BYRON.

Yes, social friend, I love thee well,
In learnèd doctors' spite ;
Thy clouds all other clouds dispel,
And lap me in delight.
To my Cigar.   C. SPRAGUE.

Such often, like the tube they so admire,
Important triflers ! have more smoke than fire.
Pernicious weed ! whose scent the fair annoys,
Unfriendly to society's chief joys,
Thy worst effect is banishing for hours
The sex whose presence civilizes ours.
Conversation.   W. COWPER.

Tobacco 's a musician,
    And in a pipe delighteth ;
It descends in a close
Through the organ of the nose,
    With a relish that inviteth.
Song : Play of Technogamia.   B. HOLIDAY.

Some sigh for this and that ;
    My wishes don't go far ;
The world may wag at will,
    So I have my cigar.
The Cigar.   T. HOOD.

The pipe, with solemn interposing puff,
Makes half a sentence at a time enough ;
The dozing sages drop the drowsy strain,
Then pause, and puff—and speak, and pause again.
Conversation.   W. COWPER.

To him 't was meat and drink and physic,
To see the friendly vapor
Curl round his midnight taper.
And the black fume
Clothe all the room,
In clouds as dark as science metaphysic.
Points of Misery.   C. M. WESTMACOTT.

Just where the breath of life his nostrils drew,
A charge of snuff the wily virgin threw ;
The gnomes direct, to every atom just,
The pungent grains of titillating dust ;
Sudden, with starting tears each eye o'erflows,
And the high dome re-echoes to his nose.
Rape of the Lock, Canto V.   A. POPE.

TO-MORROW.

To-morrow yet would reap to-day,
    As we bear blossoms of the dead ;
    Earn well the thrifty months, nor wed
Raw Haste, half-sister to Delay.
Love Thou the Land.   A. TENNYSON.

In human hearts what bolder thoughts can rise,
Than man's presumption on to-morrow's dawn !
Where is to-morrow ?
Night Thoughts, Night I.   DR. E. YOUNG.

To-morrow is a satire on to-day,
And shows its weakness.
The Old Man's Relapse.   DR. E. YOUNG.

Nothing that is can pause or stay ;
The moon will wax, the moon will wane,
The mist and cloud will turn to rain,
The rain to mist and cloud again,
To-morrow be to-day.
Kéramos.   H. W. LONGFELLOW.

To-morrow is, ah, whose ?
Between Two Worlds.   D. M. MULOCK CRAIK.

TREASON.

Smooth runs the water where the brook is deep,
And in his simple show he harbors treason.
The fox barks not, when he would steal the lamb.
King Henry VI., Pt. II. Act iii. *Sc.* 1.   SHAKESPEARE.

Treason is not owned when 't is descried ;
Successful crimes alone are justified.
Medals.   J. DRYDEN.

Treason doth never prosper : what 's the reason?
For if it prosper, none dare call it treason.
Epigrams.   SIR J. HARRINGTON.

Hast thou betrayed my credulous innocence
With vizored falsehood and base forgery ?
Comus.   MILTON.

Oh, for a tongue to curse the slave
Whose treason, like a deadly blight,
Comes o'er the councils of the brave,
And blasts them in their hour of might !
Lalla Rookh : The Fire Worshippers.   T. MOORE.

To say the truth, so Judas kissed his master,
And cried " All hail ! " whereas he meant all harm.
King Henry VI., Pt. III. Act v. *Sc.* 7.   SHAKESPEARE.

Tellest thou me of " ifs " ?   Thou art a traitor :
Off with his head ! so much for Buckingham !
King Richard III. Altered, Act iv. *Sc.* 3.   C. CIBBER.

TREE.

Welcome, ye shades ! ye bowery thickets hail !
Ye lofty pines ! ye venerable oaks !
Ye ashes wild, resounding o'er the steep !
Delicious is your shelter to the soul.
Seasons: Summer.　　　　　　　　　J. THOMSON.

Now all the tree-tops lay asleep,
　　Like green waves on the sea,
As still as in the silent deep
　　The ocean woods may be.
The Recollection.　　　　　　　　P. B. SHELLEY.

Like two cathedral towers these stately pines
　　Uplift their fretted summits tipped with cones ;
　　The arch beneath them is not built with stones,
Not Art but Nature traced these lovely lines,
And carved this graceful arabesque of vines ;
　　No organ but the wind here sighs and moans,
　　No sepulchre conceals a martyr's bones,
No marble bishop on his tomb reclines.
Enter ! the pavement, carpeted with leaves,
　　Gives back a softened echo to thy tread !
Listen ! the choir is singing ; all the birds,
In leafy galleries beneath the eaves,
　　Are singing ! listen, ere the sound be fled,
And learn there may be worship without words.
My Cathedral.　　　　　　　H. W. LONGFELLOW.

Those green-robed senators of mighty woods,
Tall oaks, branch-charmèd by the earnest stars,
Dream, and so dream all night without a stir.
Hyperion, Bk. I.　　　　　　　　J. KEATS.

A brotherhood of venerable Trees.
Sonnet composed at —— Castle.　　W. WORDSWORTH.

Cedar, and pine, and fir, and branching palm,
A sylvan scene, and as the ranks ascend
Shade above shade, a woody theatre
Of stateliest view.
Paradise Lost, Bk. IV.　　　　　　MILTON.

Of vast circumference and gloom profound,
This solitary Tree ! A living thing
Produced too slowly ever to decay ;
Of form and aspect too magnificent
To be destroyed.
Yew-Trees.　　　　　　　W. WORDSWORTH.

TRIFLE.

A little fire is quickly trodden out,
Which, being suffered. rivers cannot quench.
King Henry VI., Pt. III. Act iv. *Sc.* 8.   SHAKESPEARE.

Pretty ! in amber to observe the forms
Of hair, or straws, or dirt, or grubs, or worms !
The things, we know, are neither rich nor rare,
But wonder how the devil they got there !
Epistle to Dr. Arbuthnot : Prologue to Satires. A. POPE.

At every trifle scorn to take offence ;
That always shows great pride or little sense.
Essay on Criticism.   A. POPE.

Think naught a trifle, though it small appear ;
Small sands the mountain, moments make the year,
And trifles life.
Love of Fame, Satire VI.   DR. E. YOUNG.

TRUTH.

Truth is the highest thing that man may keep.
The Frankeleines Tale.   CHAUCER.

But truths on which depends our main concern,
That 't is our shame and misery not to learn,
Shine by the side of every path we tread
With such a lustre he that runs may read.
Tirocinium.   W. COWPER.

For truth has such a face and such a mien,
As to be loved needs only to be seen.
The Hind and Panther.   J. DRYDEN.

And simple truth miscalled simplicity,
And captive good attending captain ill.
Sonnet LXVI.   SHAKESPEARE.

The firste vertue, sone, if thou wilt lere,
Is to restreine, and kepen wel thy tonge.
The Manciples Tale.   CHAUCER.

'T is strange—but true ; for truth is always strange ;
Stranger than fiction.
Don Juan, Canto XIV.   LORD BYRON.

But what is truth ? 'T was Pilate's question put
To Truth itself. that deigned him no reply.
The Task, Bk. III.   W. COWPER.

The sages say, Dame Truth delights to dwell
(Strange mansion !) in the bottom of a well :
Questions are then the windlass and the rope
That pull the grave old Gentlewoman up.
Birthday Ode.　　　　　J. WOLCOTT (*Peter Pindar*).

Get but the truth once uttered, and 't is like
A star new-born that drops into its place
And which, once circling in its placid round,
Not all the tumult of the earth can shake.
Glance Behind the Curtain.　　　　　J. R. LOWELL.

TYRANNY.

So spake the Fiend, and with necessity,
The tyrant's plea, excused his devilish deeds.
Paradise Lost, Bk. IV.　　　　　MILTON.

　　　　　　　　Tyranny
Absolves all faith ; and who invades our rights,
Howe'er his own commence, can never be
But an usurper.
Gustavus Vasa, Act iv. Sc. 1.　　　　　H. BROOKE.

　　　　　　　　Tyranny
Is far the worst of treasons.　Dost thou deem
None rebels except subjects ?　The prince who
Neglects or violates his trust is more
A brigand than the robber-chief.
The Two Foscari, Act ii. Sc. 1.　　　　　LORD BYRON.

Slaves would be tyrants if the chance were theirs.
The Vanished City.　　　　　V. HUGO.

'Twixt kings and tyrants there 's this difference known :
Kings seek their subjects' good, tyrants their owne.
Kings and Tyrants.　　　　　R. HERRICK.

　　　　　　　　Oh ! it is excellent
To have a giant's strength ; but it is tyrannous
To use it like a giant.
　　．　　　．　　　．　　　．　　　．　　　．
Could great men thunder
As Jove himself does, Jove would ne'er be quiet ;
For every pelting, petty officer
Would use his heaven for thunder,—
Nothing but thunder.　Merciful Heaven !
Thou rather, with thy sharp and sulphurous bolt,
Split'st the unwedgeable and gnarlèd oak,
Than the soft myrtle: but man, proud man !
Drest in a little brief authority,—

Most ignorant of what he 's most assured,
His glassy essence,—like an angry ape,
Plays such fantastic tricks before high heaven,
As make the angels weep ; who, with our spleens,
Would all themselves laugh mortal.
Measure for Measure, Act ii. *Sc.* 2.　　SHAKESPEARE.

VANITY.

As eddies draw things frivolous and light,
How is man's heart by vanity drawn in !
Night Thoughts, Night VIII.　　DR. E. YOUNG.

One prospect lost, another still we gain ;
And not a vanity is giv'n in vain :
Even mean Self-love becomes, by force divine,
The scale to measure others' wants by thine.
Essay on Man, Epistle II.　　A. POPE.

Sir Plume (of amber snuff-box justly vain,
And the nice conduct of a clouded cane),
With earnest eyes, and round unthinking face,
He first the snuff-box opened, then the case.
Rape of the Lock.　　A. POPE.

Light vanity, insatiate cormorant,
Consuming means, soon preys upon itself.
King Richard II., Act ii. *Sc.* 1.　　SHAKESPEARE.

VARIETY.

The earth was made so various, that the mind
Of desultory man, studious of change,
And pleased with novelty, might be indulged.
The Task, Bk. I.　　W. COWPER.

Variety 's the very spice of life,
That gives it all its flavor.
The Timepiece : The Task, Bk. II.　　W. COWPER.

Not chaos-like together crushed and bruised,
But, as the world, harmoniously confused,
Where order in variety we see,
And where, though all things differ, all agree.
Windsor Forest.　　A. POPE.

How various his employments whom the world
Calls idle, and who justly in return
Esteems that busy world an idler too !
The Task : The Timepiece.　　W. COWPER.

VIRTUE.

The world in all doth but two nations bear,
The good, the bad, and these mixed everywhere.
The Loyal Scot.   A. MARVELL.

What nothing earthly gives or can destroy,—
The soul's calm sunshine, and the heartfelt joy,
Is Virtue's prize.
Essay an Man, Epistle IV.   A. POPE.

Virtue. not rolling suns, the mind matures,
That life is long, which answers life's great end.
The time that bears no fruit, deserves no name.
Night Thoughts, Night V.   DR. E. YOUNG.

Good, the more
Communicated, more abundant grows.
Paradise Lost, Bk. V.   MILTON.

Her virtue and the conscience of her worth,
That would be wooed. and not unsought be won.
Paradise Lost, Bk. VIII.   MILTON.

Know then this truth (enough for man to know),
" Virtue alone is happiness below."
Essay on Man, Epistle IV.   A. POPE.

For blessings ever wait on virtuous deeds,
And though a late. a sure reward succeeds.
The Mourning Bride, Act v. Sc. 12.   W. CONGREVE.

That virtue only makes our bliss below,
And all our knowledge is, ourselves to know.
Essay on Man, Epistle IV.   A. POPE.

Pygmies are pygmies still, though perched on Alps ;
And pyramids are pyramids in vales.
Each man makes his own stature, builds himself :
Virtue alone outbuilds the Pyramids ;
Her monuments shall last when Egypt's fall.
Night Thoughts, Night VI.   DR. E. YOUNG.

Abashed the devil stood.
And felt how awful goodness is, and saw
Virtue in her shape how lovely.
Paradise Lost, Bk. IV.   MILTON.

So dear to heaven is saintly chastity,
That, when a soul is found sincerely so,
A thousand liveried angels lacky her,
Driving far off each thing of sin and guilt.
Comus.   MILTON.

Adieu, dear, amiable youth !
Your heart can ne'er be wanting !
May prudence, fortitude, and truth
Erect your brow undaunting !

In ploughman phrase, " God send you speed,"
Still daily to grow wiser ;
And may you better reck the rede,
Than ever did the adviser !
Epistle to a Young Friend.   R. BURNS.

Though lone the way as that already trod,
Cling to thine own integrity and God !
To One Deceived.   H. T. TUCKERMAN.

Virtue she finds too painful to endeavor,
Content to dwell in decencies forever.
Moral Essays, Epistle II.   A. POPE.

Keep virtue's simple path before your eyes,
Nor think from evil good can ever rise.
Tancred, Act v. *Sc.* 8.   J. THOMSON.

Count that day lost whose low descending sun
Views from thy hand no worthy action done.
Staniford's Art of Reading.   ANONYMOUS.

This above all,—to thine own self be true ;
And it must follow, as the night the day,
Thou canst not then be false to any man.
Hamlet, Act i. *Sc.* 3.   SHAKESPEARE.

VISIONS.

My thoughts by night are often filled
With visions false as fair :
For in the past alone I build
My castles in the air.
Castles in the Air.   T. L. PEACOCK.

It is a dream, sweet child ! a waking dream,
A blissful certainty, a vision bright,
Of that rare happiness, which even on earth
Heaven gives to those it loves.
The Spanish Student, Act iii. *Sc.* 5.
            H. W. LONGFELLOW.

Hence the fool's paradise, the statesman's scheme,
The air-built castle, and the golden dream,
The maid's romantic wish, the chemist's flame,
And poet's vision of eternal fame.
Dunciad, Bk. III.   A. POPE.

And still they dream, that they shall still succeed ;
And still are disappointed. Rings the world
With the vain stir. I sum up half mankind,
And add two-thirds of the remaining half,
And find the total of their hopes and fears
Dreams, empty dreams.
The Task, Bk. VI.   W. COWPER.

                       [*Witches vanish.*
BANQUO.—The earth hath bubbles as the water has,
And these are of them. Whither are they vanished?
   MACBETH.—Into the air ; and what seemed corporal melted
As breath into the wind.
Macbeth, Act i. *Sc.* 3.   SHAKESPEARE.

Fierce fiery warriors fought upon the clouds.
In ranks and squadrons, and right form of war,
Which drizzled blood upon the Capitol.
O Cæsar ! these things are beyond all use,
And I do fear them.
Julius Cæsar, Act ii. *Sc.* 2.   SHAKESPEARE.

Lochiel, Lochiel ! beware of the day ;
For, dark and despairing, my sight I may seal,
But man cannot cover what God would reveal ;
'T is the sunset of life gives me mystical lore,
And coming events cast their shadows before.
Lochiel's Warning.   T. CAMPBELL.

WAR.

My sentence is for open war ; of wiles
More unexpert I boast not : then let those
Contrive who need, or when they need, not now.
Paradise Lost, Bk. II.   MILTON.

And Cæsar's spirit, ranging for revenge,

     .   .   .   .   .

Cry " Havock ! " and let slip the dogs of war.
Julius Cæsar, Act iii. *Sc.* 1.   SHAKESPEARE.

                   In every heart
Are sown the sparks that kindle fiery war ;
Occasion needs but fan them, and they blaze.
The Task : Winter Morning Walk.   W. COWPER.

               Long peace, I find,
But nurses dangerous humors up to strength,
License and wanton rage, which war alone
Can purge away.
Mustapha.   D. MALLET.

The fire-eyed maid of smoky war
All hot and bleeding will we offer them.
King Henry IV., Pt. I. Act iv. *Sc.* 1.   SHAKESPEARE.

Lochiel, Lochiel! beware of the day
When the Lowlands shall meet thee in battle array!
For a field of the dead rushes red on my sight,
And the clans of Culloden are scattered in fight.
They rally, they bleed, for their kingdom and crown;
Woe, woe to the riders that trample them down!
Proud Cumberland prances, insulting the slain,
And their hoof-beaten bosoms are trod to the plain.
Lochiel's Warning.   T. CAMPBELL.

He is come to ope
The purple testament of bleeding war;
But ere the crown he looks for live in peace,
Ten thousand bloody crowns of mothers' sons
Shall ill become the flower of England's face,
Change the complexion of her maid-pale peace
To scarlet indignation, and bedew
Her pastures' grass with faithful English blood.
King Richard II., Act iii. *Sc.* 3.   SHAKESPEARE.

War, my lord,
Is of eternal use to human kind;
For ever and anon when you have passed
A few dull years in peace and propagation,
The world is overstocked with fools, and wants
A pestilence at least, if not a hero.
Edwin.   G. JEFFERYS.

O War! thou hast thy fierce delight,
Thy gleams of joy intensely bright!
Such gleams as from thy polished shield
Fly dazzling o'er the battle-field!
Lord of the Isles.   SIR W. SCOTT.

The tyrant custom, most grave senators,
Hath made the flinty and steel couch of war
My thrice-driven bed of down.
Othello, Act i. *Sc.* 3.   SHAKESPEARE.

Hang out our banners on the outward walls;
The cry is still, *They come.* Our castle's strength
Will laugh a siege to scorn: here let them lie
Till famine and the ague eat them up.
Macbeth, Act v. *Sc.* 5.   SHAKESPEARE.

War, war is still the cry,—" war even to the knife!"
Childe Harold, Canto I.   LORD BYRON.

O, the sight entrancing,
When morning's beam is glancing
    O'er files arrayed
    With helm and blade,
And plumes, in the gay wind dancing!
When hearts are all high beating,
And the trumpet's voice repeating
    That song, whose breath
    May lead to death,
But never to retreating.
O, the sight entrancing,
When morning's beam is glancing
    O'er files arrayed
    With helm and blade,
And plumes, in the gay wind dancing.
O, the sight entrancing.   T. MOORE.

              From the tents.
The armorers, accomplishing the knights,
With busy hammers closing rivets up,
Give dreadful note of preparation.
King Henry V., Act iv. *Chorus.*   SHAKESPEARE.

Father, I call on thee !
Clouds from the thunder-voiced cannon enveil me,
Lightnings are flashing, death's thick darts assail me :
Ruler of battles, I call on thee !
    Father, oh lead thou me !
Prayer During the Battle.   *German of* K. T. KÖRNER.
                         Trans. of J. S. BLACKIE.

Lochiel, untainted by flight or by chains,
While the kindling of life in his bosom remains,
Shall victor exult, or in death be laid low,
With his back to the field, and his feet to the foe ;
And leaving in battle no blot on his name,
Look proudly to Heaven from the death-bed of fame !
Lochiel's Warning.   T. CAMPBELL.

  Not hate, but glory, made these chiefs contend ;
    And each brave foe was in his soul a friend.
The Iliad, Bk. VII.   HOMER. *Trans. of* POPE.

      Ay me ! what perils do environ
      The man that meddles with cold iron.
Hudibras, Pt. I. Canto III.   S. BUTLER.

Now swells the intermingling din ; the jar
Frequent and frightful of the bursting bomb ;
The falling beam, the shriek, the groan, the shout,
The ceaseless clangor, and the rush of men
Inebriate with rage ;—loud, and more loud
The discord grows ; till pale Death shuts the scene,
And o'er the conqueror and the conquered draws
His cold and bloody shroud.

.   .   .   .   .   .

War is the statesman's game, the priest's delight,
The lawyer's jest, the hired assassin's trade,
And to those royal murderers whose mean thrones
Are bought by crimes of treachery and gore,
The bread they eat, the staff on which they lean.
War.   P. B. SHELLEY.

One to destroy is murder by the law ;
And gibbets keep the lifted hand in awe ;
To murder thousands takes a specious name,
War's glorious art, and gives immortal fame.
Love of Fame, Satire VII.   DR. E. YOUNG.

Great princes have great playthings.

.   .   .   .   .   .

But war's a game which, were their subjects wise,
Kings would not play at.
The Task : Winter Morning Walk.   W. COWPER.

One murder made a villain,
Millions a hero.   Princes were privileged
To kill, and numbers sanctified the crime.
Death.   B. PORTEUS.

Mark where his carnage and his conquest cease !
He makes a solitude, and calls it—peace !
The Bride of Abydos, Canto II.   LORD BYRON.

Some undone widow sits upon mine arm,
And takes away the use of it ; and my sword,
Glued to my scabbard with wronged orphans' tears,
Will not be drawn.
A New Way to Pay Old Debts, Act v. Sc. 1.
                                         P. MASSINGER.

Ez fer war, I call it murder,—
There you hev it plain an' flat ;
I don't want to go no furder
Than my Testyment fer that.
The Biglow Papers, First Series, No. I.   J. R. LOWELL.

WATERS.

Water is the mother of the vine,
The nurse and fountain of fecundity.
The adorner and refresher of the world.
The Dionysia.   C. MACKAY.

Till taught by pain,
Men really know not what good water 's worth ;
If you had been in Turkey or in Spain,
Or with a famished boat's-crew had your berth,
Or in the desert heard the camel's bell,
You 'd wish yourself where Truth is—in a well.
Don Juan, Canto II.   LORD BYRON.

Water its living strength first shows,
When obstacles its course oppose.
God, Soul, and World.   J. W. GOETHE.

The current, that with gentle murmur glides,
Thou know'st, being stopped, impatiently doth rage ;
But, when his fair course is not hindered,
He makes sweet music with the enamelled stones,
Giving a gentle kiss to every sedge
He overtaketh in his pilgrimage.
Two Gentlemen of Verona, Act ii. *Sc.* 7. SHAKESPEARE.

Mine be the breezy hill that skirts the down ;
Where a green grassy turf is all I crave,
With here and there a violet bestrewn,
Fast by a brook or fountain's murmuring wave :
And many an evening sun shine sweetly on my grave.
The Minstrel, Book II.   J. BEATTIE.

Along thy wild and willowed shore ;
Where'er thou wind'st, by dale or hill,
All, all is peaceful, all is still.
Lay of the Last Minstrel, Canto IV.   SIR W. SCOTT.

With spots of sunny openings, and with nooks
To lie and read in, sloping into brooks.
The Story of Rimini.   L. HUNT.

The torrent's smoothness, ere it dash below !
Gertrude, Pt. III.   T. CAMPBELL.

Thou hastenest down between the hills to meet me at the
road,
The secret scarcely lisping of thy beautiful abode
Among the pines and mosses of yonder shadowy height,
Where thou dost sparkle into song, and fill the woods with
light.
Friend Brook.   LUCY LARCOM.

Brook ! whose society the poet seeks,
Intent his wasted spirits to renew ;
And whom the curious painter doth pursue
Through rocky passes, among flowery creeks,
And tracks thee dancing down thy waterbreaks.
Brook! Whose Society the Poet Seeks.
W. WORDSWORTH.

The roar of waters !—from the headlong height
Velino cleaves the wave-worn precipice ;
The fall of waters ! rapid as the light
The flashing mass foams shaking the abyss :
The hell of waters ! where they howl and hiss,
And boil in endless torture.
Childe Harold, Canto IV.   LORD BYRON.

Let beeves and home-bred kine partake
The sweets of Burn-mill meadow ;
The swan on still St. Mary's Lake
Float double, swan and shadow !
Yarrow Unvisited.   W. WORDSWORTH.

Under the cooling shadow of a stately elm,
Close sat I by a goodly river's side,
Where gliding streams the rocks did overwhelm ;
A lonely place, with pleasures dignified.
I, that once loved the shady woods so well,
Now thought the rivers did the trees excel,
And if the sun would ever shine, there would I dwell.
Contemplations.   ANNE BRADSTREET.

Two ways the rivers
Leap down to different seas, and as they roll
Grow deep and still, and their majestic presence
Becomes a benefaction to the towns
They visit, wandering silently among them,
Like patriarchs old among their shining tents.
Christus : The Golden Legend, Pt. V.
H. W. LONGFELLOW.

Sweet Teviot ! on thy silver tide
The glaring bale-fires blaze no more ;
No longer steel-clad warriors ride
Along thy wild and willowed shore.
Lay of the Last Minstrel, Canto IV.   SIR W. SCOTT.

Is it not better, then, to be alone,
And love Earth only for its earthly sake ?
By the blue rushing of the arrowy Rhone
Or the pure bosom of its nursing lake . . . ?
Childe Harold, Canto III.   LORD BYRON.

You leave us; you will see the Rhine,
And those fair hills I sailed below,
When I was there with him ; and go
By summer belts of wheat and vine.
In Memoriam, XCVII.   A. TENNYSON.

There is a hill beside the silver Thames,
Shady with birch and beech and odorous pine ;
And brilliant underfoot with thousand gems,
Steeply the thickets to his floods decline.
There is a Hill beside the Silver Thames.

R. S. BRIDGES.

The torrent roared ; and we did buffet it
With lusty sinews, throwing it aside,
And stemming it with hearts of controversy.
Julius Cæsar, Act i. Sc. 2.   SHAKESPEARE.

That was the River. It looked cool and deep,
And as I watched, I felt it slipping past
As if it smoothly swept along in sleep,
Gleaning and gliding fast.
A London Idyl.   R. BUCHANAN.

It flows through old hushed Egypt and its sands,
Like some grave mighty thought threading a dream.
The Nile.   L. HUNT.

WEALTH.

Here Wisdom calls, "Seek virtue first, be bold ;
As gold to silver, virtue is to gold."
There London's voice, "Get money, money still,
And then let Virtue follow if she will."
Imitations of Horace, Epistle I. Bk. I.   A. POPE.

The devil was piqued such saintship to behold,
And longed to tempt him, like good Job of old ;
For Satan now is wiser than of yore,
And tempts by making rich, not making poor.
Moral Essays, Epistle III.   A. POPE.

Mammon, the least erected spirit that fell
From heaven ; for even in heaven his looks and thoughts
Were always downward bent, admiring more
The riches of heaven's pavement, trodden gold,
Than ought divine or holy else enjoyed
In vision beatific.
Paradise Lost, Bk. I.   MILTON.
20

Religious, punctual, frugal, and so forth ;
His word would pass for more than he was worth.
One solid dish his week-day meal affords,
An added pudding solemnized the Lord's.
Constant at church and change, his gains were sure,
His giving rare, save farthings to the poor.
Moral Essays, Epistle III.   A. POPE.

Gold begets in brethren hate ;
Gold in families debate ;
Gold does friendship separate ;
Gold does civil wars create.
Anacreontics : Gold.   A. COWLEY.

Trade it may help, society extend,
But lures the Pirate, and corrupts the friend :
It raises armies in a nation's aid,
But bribes a senate, and the land 's betrayed.
Moral Essays, Epistle II.   A. POPE

The lust of gold succeeds the rage of conquest ;
The lust of gold, unfeeling and remorseless !
The last corruption of degenerate man.
Irene, Act i. Sc. 1.   DR. S. JOHNSON.

But in the temple of their hireling hearts
Gold is a living god, and rules in scorn
All earthly things but virtue.
Queen Mab, Pt. V.   P. B. SHELLEY.

Gold ! gold ! gold ! gold !
Bright and yellow, hard and cold,
Molten, graven, hammered and rolled ;
Heavy to get, and light to hold ;
Hoarded, bartered, bought, and sold,
Stolen, borrowed, squandered, doled :
Spurned by the young, but hugged by the old
To the very verge of the churchyard mold ;
Price of many a crime untold :
Gold ! gold ! gold ! gold !
Good or bad a thousand-fold !
  How widely its agencies vary,—
To save, to ruin, to curse, to bless,—
As even its minted coins express.
Now stamped with the image of good Queen Bess,
  And now of a Bloody Mary.
Miss Kilmansegg.   T. HOOD.

But all thing, which that shineth as the gold,
Ne is no gold, as I have herd it told.
Canterbury Tales. Chanones Yemannes Tale.
          CHAUCER.

Shame and woe to us, if we our wealth obey ;
    The horse doth with the horseman run away.
Imitations of Horace, Bk. I.   A. COWLEY.

You have too much respect upon the world :
    They lose it, that do buy it with much care.
Merchant of Venice, Act i. *Sc.* 1.   SHAKESPEARE.

WIFE.

The world well tried—the sweetest thing in life
    Is the unclouded welcome of a wife.
Lady Jane, Canto II.   N. P. WILLIS.

Look through mine eyes with thine. True wife,
    Round my true heart thine arms entwine ;
My other dearer life in life,
    Look through my very soul with thine !
The Miller's Daughter.   A. TENNYSON.

        She gave me eyes, she gave me ears ;
        And humble cares, and delicate fears,
        A heart, the fountain of sweet tears ;
        And love, and thought, and joy.
The Sparrow's Nest.   W. WORDSWORTH.

                    My latest found,
    Heaven's last best gift, my ever new delight.
Paradise Lost, Bk. V.   MILTON.

                    She is mine own !
    And I as rich in having such a jewel
    As twenty seas, if all their sand were pearl,
    The water nectar, and the rocks pure gold.
Two Gentlemen of Verona, Act ii. *Sc.* 4. SHAKESPEARE.

        A wife, domestic, good, and pure,
        Like snail, should keep within her door ;
        But not, like snail, with silver track,
        Place all her wealth upon her back.
Good Wives.   W. W. HOW.

How much the wife is dearer than the bride.
An Irregular Ode.   LORD LYTTELTON.

But earthlier happy is the rose distilled,
    Than that which, withering on the virgin thorn,
    Grows, lives, and dies, in single blessedness.
Midsummer Night's Dream, Act i. *Sc.* 1. SHAKESPEARE.

To cheer thy sickness, watch thy health,
Partake, but never waste thy wealth,
Or stand with smile unmurmuring by,
And lighten half thy poverty.
Bride of Abydos, Canto I.   LORD BYRON.

This flour of wifely patience.
The Clerkes Tale, Pt. V.   CHAUCER.

And mistress of herself, though china fall.
Moral Essays, Epistle II.   A. POPE.

Time still, as he flies, brings increase to her truth,
And gives to her mind what he steals from her youth.
The Happy Marriage.   E. MOORE.

Of earthly goods, the best is a good wife ;
A bad, the bitterest curse of human life.
        SIMONIDES.

WIND.

Yet true it is, as cow chews cud,
And trees, at spring, do yield forth bud,
Except wind stands as never it stood,
It is an ill wind turns none to good.
The Properties of Winds.   T. TUSSER.

Ill blows the wind that profits nobody.
King Henry VI., Pt. III. Act ii. *Sc.* 5.   SHAKESPEARE.

Pure was the temperate air, an even calm
Perpetual reigned, save what the zephyrs bland
Breathed o'er the blue expanse.
Seasons : Spring.   J. THOMSON.

Under the yaller-pines I house,
When sunshine makes 'em all sweet-scented,
An' hear among their furry boughs
The baskin' west-wind purr contented.
Biglow Papers, Second Series, No. X.   J. R. LOWELL.

A breeze came wandering from the sky,
Light as the whispers of a dream ;
He put the o'erhanging grasses by,
And softly stooped to kiss the stream,
The pretty stream, the flattered stream,
The shy, yet unreluctant stream.
The Wind and the Stream.   W. C. BRYANT.

As winds come whispering lightly from the West,
Kissing, not ruffling, the blue deep's serene.
Childe Harold, Canto II.   LORD BYRON.

The moaning winds of autumn sang their song.
A Sicilian Story. B. W. PROCTER (*Barry Cornwall*).

Loud wind, strong wind, sweeping o'er the mountains,
Fresh wind, free wind, blowing from the sea,
Pour forth thy vials like streams from airy mountains,
Draughts of life to me.
The North Wind. D. M. MULOCK CRAIK.

I hear the wind among the trees
Playing celestial symphonies ;
I see the branches downward bent,
Like keys of some great instrument.
A Day of Sunshine. H. W. LONGFELLOW.

In winter when the dismal rain
Came down in slanting lines,
And wind, that grand old harper, smote
His thunder-harp of pines.
A Life Drama. A. SMITH.

'T was when the sea was roaring
With hollow blasts of wind.
The What d' ye Call 't. J. GAY.

Blow, winds, and crack your cheeks ! rage ! blow !
King Lear, Act iii. Sc. 2. SHAKESPEARE.

The Lord descended from above
And bowed the heavens high ;
And underneath his feet he cast
The darkness of the sky.

On cherubs and on cherubims
Full royally he rode ;
And on the wings of all the winds
Came flying all abroad.
Hymns : Psalm CIV. T. STERNHOLD.

WINE.

Bacchus, that first from out the purple grape
Crushed the sweet poison of misusèd wine.
Comus. MILTON.

In courts and palaces he also reigns,
And in luxurious cities, where the noise
Of riot ascends above their loftiest towers,
And injury, and outrage : and when night
Darkens the streets, then wander forth the sons
Of Belial, flown with insolence and wine.
Paradise Lost, Bk. I. MILTON.

From wine what sudden friendship springs !
The Squire and his Cur.   J. GAY.

And wine can of their wits the wise beguile,
Make the sage frolic, and the serious smile.
Odyssey, Bk. XIV.   HOMER.   *Trans. of* POPE.

O, when we swallow down
Intoxicating wine, we drink damnation ;
Naked we stand, the sport of mocking fiends,
Who grin to see our nobler nature vanquished,
Subdued to beasts.
Wife's Reick.   C. JOHNSON.

WISDOM.

By wisdom wealth is won ;
But riches purchased wisdom yet for none.
The Wisdom of Ali.   B. TAYLOR.

On every thorn, delightful wisdom grows,
In every rill a sweet instruction flows.
Love of Fame : Satire I.   DR. E. YOUNG.

In idle wishes fools supinely stay ;
Be there a will, and wisdom finds a way.
The Birth of Flattery.   G. CRABBE.

Wealth may seek us, but wisdom must be sought.
Night Thoughts, Night VIII.   DR. E. YOUNG.

And Wisdom's self
Oft seeks to sweet retired solitude,
Where, with her best nurse, Contemplation,
She plumes her feathers, and lets grow her wings,
That in the various bustle of resort
Were all-to ruffled, and sometimes impaired.
Comus.   MILTON.

The weak have remedies, the wise have joys,
Superior wisdom is superior bliss.
Night Thoughts, Night VIII.   DR. E. YOUNG.

Fears of the brave, and follies of the wise !
Vanity of Human Wishes.   DR. S. JOHNSON.

Wisdom is ofttimes nearer when we stoop
Than when we soar.
The Excursion, Bk. III.   W. WORDSWORTH.

To know
That which before us lies in daily life
Is the prime wisdom.
Paradise Lost, Bk. VIII.   MILTON.

Good sense, which only is the gift of Heaven,
And though no science, fairly worth the seven.
Moral Essays, Epistle IV.   A. POPE.

WOMAN.

What a strange thing is man! and what a stranger
Is woman! What a whirlwind is her head,
And what a whirlpool full of depth and danger
Is all the rest about her.
Don Juan, Canto IX.   LORD BYRON.

O woman! lovely woman! nature made thee
To temper man; we had been brutes without you.
Angels are painted fair, to look like you:
There is in you all that we believe of heaven;
Amazing brightness, purity, and truth,
Eternal joy, and everlasting love.
Venice Preserved, Act i. Sc. 1.   T. OTWAY.

Without the smile from partial beauty won,
O, what were man?—a world without a sun.
Pleasures of Hope, Pt. II.   T. CAMPBELL.

If the heart of a man is depressed with cares,
The mist is dispelled when a woman appears.
The Beggar's Opera, Act ii. Sc. 1.   J. GAY.

In her first passion, woman loves her lover:
In all the others, all she loves is love.
Don Juan, Canto III.   LORD BYRON.

Man's love is of man's life a thing apart;
'T is woman's whole existence. Man may range
The court, camp, church, the vessel, and the mart,
Sword, gown, gain, glory. offer in exchange
Pride, fame, ambition, to fill up his heart,
And few there are whom these cannot estrange:
Men have all these resources, we but one,—
To love again, and be again undone.
Don Juan, Canto I.   LORD BYRON.

She's beautiful, and therefore to be wooed;
She is a woman, therefore to be won.
King Henry VI., Part I. Act v. Sc. 3.   SHAKESPEARE.

Alas, the love of women ! it is known
To be a lovely and a fearful thing ;
For all of theirs upon that die is thrown,
And if 't is lost, life hath no more to bring
To them but mockeries of the past alone,
And their revenge is as the tiger's spring,
Deadly and quick and crushing ; yet as real
Torture is theirs—what they inflict they feel.
Don Juan, Canto II.   LORD BYRON.

We call it only pretty Fanny's way.
An Elegy to an Old Beauty.   T. PARNELL.

The fair, the chaste, and unexpressive she.
As You Like It, Act iii. Sc. 2.   SHAKESPEARE.

With prudes for proctors, dowagers for deans,
And sweet girl-graduates in their golden hair.
The Princess : Prologue.   A. TENNYSON.

If ladies be but young and fair,
They have the gift to know it.
As You Like It, Act ii. Sc. 7.   SHAKESPEARE.

Ladies like variegated tulips show,
'T is to their changes half their charms we owe.
Fine by defect, and delicately weak,
Their happy spots the nice admirer take.
Moral Essays, Pt. II.   A. POPE.

And when a lady 's in the case,
You know all other things give place.
The Hare and Many Friends.   J. GAY.

A woman moved is like a fountain troubled,
Muddy, ill-seeming, thick, bereft of beauty.
Taming of the Shrew, Act v. Sc. 2. SHAKESPEARE.

For several virtues
Have I liked several women ; never any
With so full soul but some defect in her
Did quarrel with the noblest grace she owed,
And put it to the foil.
Tempest, Act iii. Sc. 1.   SHAKESPEARE.

IAGO.—Come on, come on ; you are pictures out of doors,
Bells in your parlors, wild-cats in your kitchens,
Saints in your injuries, devils being offended.
         .   .   .   .   .

For I am nothing if not critical.
Othello, Act ii. Sc. 1.   SHAKESPEARE.

Had she been true,
If heaven would make me such another world
Of one entire and perfect chrysolite,
I'd not have sold her for it.

Othello, Act v. Sc. 2.　　　SHAKESPEARE.

Lightly thou say'st that woman's love is false,
The thought is falser far.

Bertram.　　　C. R. MATURIN.

But woman's grief is like a summer storm,
Short as it violent is.

Basil, Act v. Sc. 3.　　　JOANNA BAILLIE.

When greater perils men environ,
Then women show a front of iron;
And, gentle in their manner, they
Do bold things in a quiet way.

Betty Zane.　　　T. D. ENGLISH.

First, then, a woman will, or won't, depend on 't;
If she will do 't, she will, and there's an end on 't.
But if she won't, since safe and sound your trust is,
Fear is affront, and jealousy injustice.

Epilogue to Zara.　　　A. HILL.

I have no other but a woman's reason;
I think him so because I think him so.

Two Gentlemen of Verona, Act i. Sc. 2.　SHAKESPEARE.

She hugged the offender, and forgave the offence.
Sex to the last.

Cymon and Iphigenia.　　　J. DRYDEN.

Woman may err, woman may give her mind
To evil thoughts, and lose her pure estate;
But, for one woman who affronts her kind
By wicked passions and remorseless hate,
A thousand make amends in age and youth,
By heavenly pity, by sweet sympathy,
By patient kindness, by enduring truth,
By love, supremest in adversity.

Praise of Women.　　　C. MACKAY.

Not she with traitorous kiss her Saviour stung,
Not she denied him with unholy tongue;
She, while apostles shrank, could danger brave,
Last at his cross and earliest at his grave.

Woman, her Character and Influence.　E. S. BARRETT.

Earth's noblest thing, a woman perfected.

Irenè.　　　J. R. LOWELL.

Shalt show us how divine a thing
A woman may be made.
To a Young Lady.   W. WORDSWORTH.

Her voice was ever soft,
Gentle, and low,—an excellent thing in woman.
King Lear, Act v. *Sc.* 3.   SHAKESPEARE.

Not stepping o'er the bounds of modesty.
Romeo and Juliet, Act iv. *Sc.* 2.   SHAKESPEARE.

And yet believe me, good as well as ill,
Woman 's at best a contradiction still.
Moral Essays, Epistle II.   A. POPE.

For woman is not undeveloped man
But diverse ; could we make her as the man
Sweet love were slain ; his dearest bond is this:
Not like to like but like in difference.
The Princess, XII.   A. TENNYSON.

Through all the drama—whether damned or not—
Love gilds the scene, and women guide the plot.
The Rivals: Epilogue.   R. B. SHERIDAN.

YOUTH.

Bliss was it in that dawn to be alive,
But to be young was very Heaven !
The Prelude, Bk. XI.   W. WORDSWORTH.

O Life ! how pleasant in thy morning,
Young Fancy's rays the hills adorning !
Cold-pausing Caution's lesson scorning,
        We frisk away,
Like school-boys at th' expected warning,
        To joy and play.
Epistle to James Smith.   R. BURNS.

O, would I were a boy again,
    When life seemed formed of sunny years,
And all the heart then knew of pain
    Was wept away in transient tears !
O, would I were a boy again.   M. LEMON.

This morning, like the spirit of a youth
That means to be of note, begins betimes.
Antony and Cleopatra, Act iv. *Sc.* 4.   SHAKESPEARE.

Long as the year's dull circle seems to run
When the brisk minor pants for twenty-one.
Imitations of Horace, Epistle I. Bk. I.   A. POPE.

A lovely being, scarcely formed or moulded,
A rose with all its sweetest leaves yet folded.
Don Juan, Canto XV.   LORD BYRON.

" Young, gay, and fortunate ! " Each yields a theme.
And, first, thy youth : what says it to gray hairs?
Narcissa, I 'm become thy pupil now ;—
Early, bright, transient, chaste as morning dew,
She sparkled, was exhaled, and went to heaven.
Night Thoughts, Night V.   DR. E. YOUNG.

This bud of lovely Summer's ripening breath,
May prove a beauteous flower when next we meet.
Romeo and Juliet, Act ii. *Sc.* 2.   SHAKESPEARE.

The nimble-footed mad-cap Prince of Wales,
And his comrades, that daffed the world aside,
And bid it pass.
King Henry IV., Pt. I. Act iv. *Sc.* 1.   SHAKESPEARE.

Is in the very May-morn of his youth,
Ripe for exploits and mighty enterprises.
King Henry V., Act i. *Sc.* 2.   SHAKESPEARE.

We think our fathers fools, so wise we grow ;
Our wiser sons, no doubt, will think us so.
Essay on Criticism.   A. POPE.

My salad days :
When I was green in judgment.
Antony and Cleopatra, Act iv. *Sc.* 5.   SHAKESPEARE.

The spirit of a youth
That means to be of note, begins betimes.
Antony and Cleopatra, Act iv. *Sc.* 4.   SHAKESPEARE.

Returning, he proclaims by many a grace,
By shrugs and strange contortions of his face,
How much a dunce that has been sent to roam,
Excels a dunce that has been kept at home.
The Progress of Error.   W. COWPER.

Young fellows will be young fellows.
Love in a Village, Act ii. *Sc.* 2.   I. BICKERSTAFF.

Young men soon give and soon forget affronts ;
Old age is slow in both.
Canto, Act ii.   J. ADDISON.

Ah who, when fading of itself away,
Would cloud the sunshine of his little day !
Now is the May of life.   Careering round,
Joy wings his feet, joy lifts him from the ground !
Human Life.   S. ROGERS.

Our youth we can have but to-day ;
    We may always find time to grow old.
Can Love be Controlled by Advice ? BISHOP G. BERKELEY.

Flowers are lovely ; Love is flower-like ;
Friendship is a sheltering tree :
O ! the joys, that came down shower-like,
Of Friendship, Love, and Liberty,
        Ere I was old !
Ere I was old ! Ah woful Ere,
Which tells me, Youth 's no longer here !
Youth and Age.   S. T. COLERIDGE.

ZEAL.

Zeal and duty are not slow ;
But on occasion's forelock watchful wait.
Paradise Regained, Bk. III.   MILTON.

For virtue's self may too much zeal be had ;
The worst of madmen is a saint run mad.
Satires of Horace, Sat. I Bk. II.   A. POPE.

No seared conscience is so fell
As that, which has been burned with zeal ;
For Christian charity 's as well
A great impediment to zeal,
As zeal 's a pestilent disease
To Christian charity and peace.
Miscellaneous Thoughts.   S. BUTLER.

Easy still it proves, in factious times,
With public zeal to cancel private crimes.
Absalom and Achitophel.   J. DRYDEN.

Awake, my soul ; stretch every nerve,
And press with vigor on :
A heavenly race demands thy zeal,
And an immortal crown.
Zeal and Vigor in the Christian Race. PH. DODDRIDGE.

THE END.

GENERAL INDEX OF AUTHORS
AND TITLES.

317

GENERAL INDEX OF AUTHORS
AND TITLES.

GENERAL INDEX OF TITLES AND FIRST LINES.

385

GENERAL INDEX OF TITLES AND FIRST LINES.

N. B.— Titles are in bold-faced type; where title and first line are identical they are in bold-face inclosed in quotation marks.

A.

F.

I.

O.

S.

W.

018284